Everyman, I will go with thee,
and be thy guide

THE EVERYMAN
LIBRARY

*The Everyman Library was founded by J. M. Dent
in 1906. He chose the name Everyman because he wanted
to make available the best books ever written in every
field to the greatest number of people at the cheapest possible
price. He began with Boswell's 'Life of Johnson';
his one-thousandth title was Aristotle's 'Metaphysics',
by which time sales exceeded forty million.*

*Today Everyman paperbacks remain true to
J. M. Dent's aims and high standards, with a wide range
of titles at affordable prices in editions which address
the needs of today's readers. Each new text is reset to give
a clear, elegant page and to incorporate the latest thinking
and scholarship. Each book carries the pilgrim logo,
the character in 'Everyman', a medieval morality play,
a proud link between Everyman
past and present.*

ELIZABETHAN SONNETS

Edited by
MAURICE EVANS
Revised by
ROY J. BOOTH
University of London

EVERYMAN
J. M. DENT · LONDON
CHARLES E. TUTTLE
VERMONT

Introduction © David Campbell Publishers Ltd, 1977
Selection and other critical apparatus © J. M. Dent 1994

This edition first published in Everyman in 1977
New edition 1994
Reprinted 1996

J.M.Dent
Orion Publishing Group
Orion House, 5 Upper St Martin's Lane, London WC2H 9EA
and
Charles E. Tuttle Co. Inc.
28 South Main Street,
Rutland, Vermont, 05701, USA

Typeset by The Spartan Press Ltd,
Lymington, Hants
Printed in Great Britain by
The Guernsey Press Co. Ltd, Guernsey, C.I.

British Library Cataloguing-in-Publication Data
for this title is available on request.

ISBN 0 460 87363 6

CONTENTS

NOTE ON THE EDITORS

MAURICE EVANS was Emeritus Professor of English, University of Exeter. His works include *English Poetry in the Sixteenth Century* (1955); *Spenser's Anatomy of Heroism* (1970); and an edition of Sidney's *Arcadia* (1977).

ROY J. BOOTH is a lecturer within the English department at Royal Holloway, University of London.

CHRONOLOGY OF THE SONNET

Year	Key events
13th century	Giacomo da Lentini (fl. 1233–40) develops the sonnet as a form: 'sonnetto = little sound'
	Dante (1265–1321) is the first major practitioner
1290	Death of Beatrice, aged 24
1292–4	Dante *Vita nuova*
1327	Petrarch (1304–74) sees Laura, 6 April, Avignon
1348	6 April: death of Laura (plague)
c. 1385	Chaucer adapts Petrarch's Rime 132 as the Canticus Troili, *Troilus and Criseyde* Book 1 400–420
early–mid 15th century	Marquis de Santillana (1398–1458) writing first sonnets in Spanish
1498	Publication of poems by Tebaldeo (1463–1539)
1502	Publication of poems by Serafino Aquilano (1466–1500); with Tebaldeo, the 'extravagant' phase of Italian Petrarchism
late 1520s	Wyatt (1503–42) writes first sonnets in English
1530	Publication of *Rime* by Pietro Bembo (1470–1547), renewing Italian Petrarchism

CHRONOLOGY OF CULTURAL/HISTORICAL EVENTS

_____

Year	Cultural/Historical Events
1476	Caxton establishes his printing press
1478	Spanish Inquisition established
1485	Battle of Bosworth Field, Henry Tudor ascends throne as Henry VII
1492	Conquest of Granada, expulsion of Jews from Spain, Columbus sails
1503–6	'Mona Lisa' painted
1509	Accession of Henry VIII; Torrigiano's tomb for Henry VII shows first use of Italian Renaissance motifs in England
1512	Michaelangelo completes Sistine Chapel frescoes
1517	Luther's Wittenberg Theses
1525	Tyndale's *New Testament* (in English)
1528	Castiglione's *Il Libro del Cortegiano*

Year	Key events
1530s	Henry Howard, Earl of Surrey (1517?–47) writes further English sonnets
	Juan Boscán y Almogáver (c. 1490–1542), Garcilaso de la Vega (1503–36) write sonnets in Spanish
	Clement Marot (1496–1544) writing first sonnets in French
1536–46	Lord Morley, in the Preface to his translation, *Tryumphs of Fraunces Petrarke*, uses the word 'sonnet' in English: 'triumphs all to the laude of hys Ladye Laura, by whome he made many a swete sonnet'
1549	Joachim du Bellay (1522–60) publishes first French (and first non-Italian) sonnet sequence, *L'Olive*
1552–4	Pierre de Ronsard (c. 1524–85), *Amours* (sonnets to Cassandre de Salviati)
1557	Tottel's Miscellany (*Songes and Sonnettes*)
1582	Sidney writing *Astrophel and Stella*; Thomas Watson (c. 1557–92) *Hecatompathia* (100 18-line sonnets)
1584	John Soowthern, *Pandora*
1590	Mark Alexander Boyd (1563–1601), 'Sonet'
1591	Newman's pirated edition of *Astrophel and Stella*
1592	Daniel, *Delia*; Constable, *Diana*; Sir William Alexander (1567?–1640), *Aurora* written before this date
1593	Barnes (1569?–1609), *Parthenophil and Parthenope*; Lodge, *Phillis*; Giles Fletcher, *Licia*
1594	Anon, *Zepheria*

Year	Cultural/Historical Events
1597	John Dowland *The First Booke of Songes*
1600	Thomas Morley *The First Booke of Ayres*: including setting for *Astrophel and Stella* Song xi
1603	Death of Elizabeth I
1607	Monteverdi *La Favola d'Orfeo* (first opera)
1610	Robert Dowland (ed.) *A Musicall Banquet*: including settings for *Astrophel and Stella* Songs viii, ix, x
1611	Aemilia Lanyer (1569–1639) *Salve Deux Rex Judaeorum*
1613	Elizabeth Cary (1586–1639) *The Tragedie of Mariam* (first full-scale tragedy written by Englishwoman); John Ward *The First Set of English Madrigals*: including setting of a stanza for *Astrophel and Stella* Song x
1616	Inigo Jones, The Queen's House, Greenwich
1620	Mayflower lands in America
1621	May: death of Barbara Sidney (mother of Lady Wroth); September: death (smallpox) of Mary Sidney (b. 1561); publication of Lady Mary Wroth's *Urania* (entered for publication 13 July)

INTRODUCTION

The fulfilment and the frustration of passion have been the two great subjects of love poetry since time began, and whether, in Yeats's words, the imagination dwells most upon a woman won or a woman lost is a question not easily answered. The Petrarchan sonneteer, however, would have no doubts about the matter: the love sonnet is the most committed form of that poetry of frustration which, taking its origin from Ovid, came down the centuries picking up refinements and elaborations on its way. From the Provençal love song and medieval Amour Courtois it gained romantic colouring and something approaching religious fervour on the one hand, and formal structure and a set of conventions on the other. From Petrarch, after Ovid the most influential love poet of the western world, it absorbed a new personal and lyrical intensity and became especially associated with the sonnet form. Petrarch is the bridge between medieval and Renaissance, converting what had been predominantly narrative into lyric, but handing on, nevertheless, essentially traditional attitudes in a form which remained relatively unchanged for the next two hundred years. There were minor accretions with the High Renaissance − a touch of Neo-Platonism from fifteenth-century Italy; and more important, a new image of Cupid to temper that of the fierce and merciless deity of the Middle Ages. This is the sportive child, blind Cupid with his little bow and arrows, who derives from Anacreon and the *Greek Anthology*, among the classical Greek texts rediscovered by the Renaissance humanists. The mixture, handed on by the post-Petrarchan Italian sonneteers to the French Pléiade in the middle of the sixteenth century, reached England effectively only by the 1580s. The Elizabethan love sonnet is at the end of an unbroken tradition of love poetry which reaches back through the *Roman de la Rose* to classical antiquity.

The Elizabethan sonneteer inherited, therefore, not only the basic Petrarchan situation of the adoring lover and the unresponsive mistress but also a large number of traditional *topoi* inseparable from it, which offer elaborations upon the central theme and time-honoured modes for their expression. The sonnet lady, for example, the longed-for but unreachable Stella or Idea or Diana, is likely at some point in her story to fall ill, or be misled by 'venomous tongues', or tear up her lover's poems or treat him less kindly than her lap dog or pet sparrow. The lover in his turn will suffer the tempestuous and warring passions of love: he will lie awake all night, or if he sleeps, have erotic dreams of his mistress: he will hear her singing or watch her as she plies her needle or steal a kiss while she sleeps: he will itemise all her beauties and he will protest the power of his verse to keep that beauty alive in spite of the ravages of time. These and similar stereotypes make up the body of most sonnet sequences and are expressed through conventional images as essential to the sonnet tradition as the situations themselves: the unsuccessful siege of the fortress of love and the innumerable variations on the metaphor of love's war, for example: the lover as the ship in the storm; the hot ice and freezing fire which afflict him; the lady's eyes like the sun to burn, her eyelashes like nets to catch him; her eyebrows the bows for Cupid's arrows; her face the cherry tree on which her lips are cherries. One has only to read a few of the cycles to recognise the underlying framework of event and style which they have in common, and to see that these form the poetic medium of the genre. The Petrarchan sonnet is the most 'conventional' of forms, and a large part of its appeal to the Renaissance writer lay in the challenge it offered to emulate what others had done before.

For all but the greatest of Renaissance sonneteers, the sonnet is less concerned with the exploration of love itself than with the processes by which a moment of passion is transformed into a polished artefact. In discussing the sonnet in his *Defence of Ryme*,[1] Daniel praises its capacity to shape the 'unformed Chaos without fashion' of our imagination into 'an Orbe of order and forme' (p. 138); and this is something encouraged by the very shape of the sonnet, with its elaborate organisation of rhymes and its fourteen lines giving just enough scope to erect a verbal structure which is complete and easily perceived. The term most commonly associated with the sonnet is the 'conceit', which is the basic conception of the organisation within the poem, the rhetorical figure upon which the framework of an individual

[1] *Poems and A Defence of Ryme* ed. A. C. Sprague, 1950.

sonnet depends: and a good sonnet in Renaissance terms is one in which the conceit is worked out perfectly in fourteen lines so that form and content fit each other like hand and glove. To quote Daniel again,

> Besides, is it not most delightfull to see much excellently ordred in a small roome, or little gallantly disposed and made to fill up a space of like capacitie, in such sort, that the one would not appeare so beautifull in a larger circuite, nor the other do well in a lesse. (p. 138)

The conceit takes innumerable forms. Among the commonest are the single metaphor extended through the whole sonnet and reaching its natural climax in the last line (*Amoretti*, 14: *A and S*, 49: *Zepheria*, 37, for example); the classical myth applied as an allegory of the lover's state (*Delia*, 5: *Amoretti*, 23); the debate (*Idea*, 38: *A and S*, 34); the paradox (*A and S*, 61, 62); the pattern of anaphora worked out with perfect symmetry through the three quatrains and the couplet (*Amoretti*, 1: *Diana*, 9), to name only a few obvious types. None of these are mutually exclusive, and any of them can be worked out in conjunction with any other or with a central argument, often in the form of a dilemma which is resolved in the final couplet. Spenser is particularly fond of this kind of conceit, as in *Amoretti*, 30, for example, which, beginning with the traditional comparison that 'My love is lyke to yse, and I to fyre', asks how two such opposites can co-exist, and answers that it is love's unique power to perform miracles. Giles Fletcher plays some amusing variations upon the same theme in *Licia*, 41 and 42. Again, in *Amoretti*, 43, Spenser asks, 'Shall I then silent be or shall I speake?', for if he speaks he is overwhelmed by his mistress's wrath, and if he stays silent his heart will break. The answer is to teach his heart and eyes the language of silent communication which her wit will soon learn to construe. The final couplet, which is a feature of so many English sonnets even when in other respects they are Petrarchan in form, lends itself to the summing up or the solution of paradox or dilemma and gives to the sonnet, in consequence, the quality of epigram.

The conceit is probably the most important dimension of the sonnet, and something which the Elizabethan poet and his reader, trained alike in rhetoric, were more aware of than we are. If this were not so, I do not think that Spenser would have left his *Amoretti*, 64 in the form in which we have it. It is a conventional icon of the mistress's parts but framed in terms of the scents of garden flowers:

> Comming to kisse her lyps, (such grace I found)
> me seemd I smelt a gardin of sweet flowres,

Thus her lips smell like gillyflowers, her bosom like a strawberry bed, her breast like lilies and so on very pleasantly, as long as the reader keeps his mind fixed upon the idea of scent, to the exclusion of all other considerations. But if one forgets the terms of the conceit and allows the attention to stray into the world of vision and colour, for example, the consequences are unfortunate: 'her ruddy cheekes lyke unto Roses red' is passable in terms both of scent and of colour, but 'her lovely eyes lyke Pincks but newly spred' (i.e. opened) is certainly not. Either the Elizabethans had the capacity to exclude from their consciousness everything which is outside the terms of the central conceit, or else Spenser has fallen down through using images too strongly loaded with traditional visual associations.

That poets composed their sonnets with these elaborate schemes consciously in mind is demonstrated most explicitly in the works of one of the earliest and dullest of the tribe, Thomas Watson, whose *Passionate Centurie of Love*[2] came out in 1582. His poems are not strict sonnets, being all of eighteen lines, and he calls them 'Passions', although he clearly makes no distinction between them and the strict quatorzain. Watson prefaces each Passion with a little précis in prose which outlines the conceit and sometimes analyses the specific method. Thus, number 41 is based on 'that figure in Rhetorique . . . called . . . of the Latines *Reduplicatio*'; number 3 'is all framed in manner of a dialogue, wherein the Author talketh with his owne heart . . .'; in number 4, 'The chiefe grounde and matter of this Sonnet standeth upon the rehearsall of such thinges as by reporte of the Poets, are dedicated unto Venus.' Watson is one of the most minor and academic of Elizabethan sonneteers but he nevertheless defines, however crudely, the general practice. We shall see that even Astrophel sets about writing his sonnets in the same deliberate way, and that Sidney's objection is not to the method itself but to the material it uses.

Because of its preoccupation with the conceit, the Elizabethan sonnet cycle is not primarily a narrative form but rather the by-

[2] Arber English Reprints, 1870.

product of narrative. Occasionally, as in the songs which Sidney weaves throughout *Astrophel and Stella*, the story is told explicitly; but normally it is too traditional to need telling, and the various episodes can be deduced from the emotional and intellectual responses to them which the individual sonnets record. The sonnet is an introspective, witty, cerebral form of verse in which the momentary response is analysed or played with in terms of a conceit, and for this reason the individual sonnet is complete in itself and can stand alone, independent of the rest of the cycle. The difference, indeed, between a genuine sonnet cycle and a mere sequence of sonnets depends upon the ability of the poet to impose a common structure or tone upon a collection of individual units, and there are very few genuine cycles among the Elizabethans. Sidney and Shakespeare impose a dramatic unity upon their sequences, Spenser a common mood, Drayton a common quality of immediacy, but the rest are mostly memorable for good sonnets rather than for significant groupings. Spenser and Sidney never forget that the purpose of the sonnet is to woo and win the lady, and everything is related to the processes and pains of this central function. In *Amoretti* 68, for example, Spenser celebrates the Christian significance of Easter day as the expression of God's love, which he then uses in the last couplet as an argument to forward his own:

> So let us love, deare love, lyke as we ought:
>   love is the lesson which the Lord us taught.

The most elaborate conceits of Sidney's sonnets often spring out of the frustrations of Astrophel which can find no satisfaction except in words. In sonnet 61, the lover laments that he has besieged Stella with sighs and tears, with words and even silences, but her reply is always that if he truly loves her, he will respect her chaste desires and withdraw his attentions. In this dilemma, Astrophel can only appeal hopelessly to Cupid for help, for what possible solution can there be to the paradox that he can only prove his love by ceasing to love, 'That I love not, without I leave to love'? There is at least a bitter-sweet satisfaction in the formulation of the paradox, as Astrophel gets some of his sufferings off his chest by means of wit. In this way the conceit takes on a dramatic function and the individual sonnet, while complete in itself, can yet form part of the larger unit. For this reason, too, in spite of its basically unhappy subject matter, the sonnet is one of the lightest and most scintillating forms of verse.

One further general point needs to be made, namely, that the sonnet is the 'personal kind' in the Elizabethan poetic hierarchy, the type of verse in which the poet is expected to speak *in propria persona*. This, however, must not be taken too literally. Petrarch had written in the first person as of his own love, but it is far from certain that the Laura of his poems corresponded to any Laura in real life; and the association of the laurel with the poetic 'bays' led to all kinds of allegorical interpretations which Sidney, for example, shows himself aware of in sonnet 90. In his preface to *Licia*, Giles Fletcher warns his reader:

> If thou muse what my Licia is, take her to be some Diana, at the least chaste, or some Minerva, no Venus, fairer farre: it may be shee is Learnings image, or some heavenlie woonder . . . perhaps under that name I have shadowed Discipline . . . it may bee some Colledge; it may bee my conceit, and portends nothing . . .[3]

This, I think, is nearer to the Elizabethan conception of the sonnet mistress than much of the modern biographical research into the private lives of Stella or the dark lady. Many of the sonnet personae resemble their poet creators, and many of the sonnet ladies were explicitly identified with contemporary figures; yet the fact that all the sonnet sequences with the exception of Shakespeare's tell substantially the same story and fill it out with the same detail should put us on our guard against a simple biographical approach. Astrophel has much in common with Sidney, and Stella was known by everyone to be Penelope Devereux, yet there is no historical evidence to suggest that Sidney's life followed the pattern of his hero's or that he ever fell in love with Penelope, to whom incidentally, Constable also dedicated Petrarchan sonnets. The 'personal' mode of poetry represents for the Elizabethans a dramatic exercise in first-person writing rather than the exposure of the poet's own bleeding heart, and unlike romantic poetry, the object of the sonnet is ritual and ceremonial rather than autobiographical. A sonnet sequence may be anything from a humanist exercise in the fashionable mode of love poetry to a public compliment paid to a patroness or a friend or even, in the case of Spenser, to his own wife.

Sidney bases his defence of poetry on the argument that it is by

[3]ed. Lloyd E. Berry. University of Wisconsin, 1964.

definition a form of fiction, and discusses the use of proper names in this connection. He compares them to the generic names such as John a Stile and John a Noakes in hypothetical legal cases and adds, 'Their naming of men is but to make their picture the more lively, and not to build any history: painting men, they cannot leave men nameless' (*Defence*, p. 124).[4] *Astrophel and Stella* was written as a poetic fiction, a tragedy in three acts, and it is possible that Sidney was making his fictional characters more lively (and, incidentally, following the example of Petrarch) by giving them real identities. He is alluding to the ambiguous relationship between fact and fiction in poetry in sonnet 45 when Astrophel argues that since Stella is more moved by a story of lovers which she is reading than by the reality of his love, let her remember that poetry is fiction and respond to his sonnets accordingly:

> Then thinke, my deare, that you in me do reed
> Of Lover's ruine some sad Tragedie:
> I am not I, pitie the tale of me.

II

I pass now from the sonnet in general to those sonnets which make up this anthology. The term 'sonnet' was used very loosely in the period to describe almost any short love poem, as can be seen in Donne's *Songs and Sonets* for example: there are sonnets of fifteen lines, as in Barnes, or of eighteen, in Watson, and the type goes under a variety of names – Canzoni in *Zepheria*, Passions in Watson's *Passionate Centurie*, Amours in Drayton's *Idea*. In this anthology, with the exception of two fifteen-line sonnets by Barnes, I restrict myself to the strict quatorzain which was always the dominant form. Wyatt and Surrey had made brilliant translations and adaptations of Petrarch in sonnet form as far back as the reign of Henry VIII, and these had been widely circulated through the many editions of *Tottel's Miscellany* throughout the second half of the sixteenth century. The great burst of sonneteering in the 1590s, however, was sparked off by the work of Sidney, a pioneer in this as in so many other fields. His *Astrophel and Stella*, written about 1582 and circulated in manuscript until the pirated editions of 1591, created the taste

[4]ed. Geoffrey Shepperd. Nelson, 1965.

and set the fashion going. Between 1591 and the end of the decade there were sonnet cycles by Daniel, Constable, Barnes, Drayton, Lodge, Percy, the anonymous author of *Zepheria*, Griffin, Smith, Tofte, Lynche, to mention only those reprinted by Sidney Lee in the two volumes of his *Elizabethan Sonnets* (1904). He does not include those of Shakespeare and Spenser and a host of very minor writers. The sonnet was the bow of Ulysses which every established or would-be poet, every young man of the Inns of Court with a literary taste, felt it his duty to bend.

This anthology prints the four major sequences of the period, excluding that of Shakespeare, with a brief selection from the minor sonneteers to give some idea of the normal level which the form achieved and the extravagances of which it was capable. Shakespeare is not included because he is easily accessible elsewhere, but he should nevertheless be considered in the context of the Elizabethan sonnet. His cycle is revolutionary in that it stands the conventional Petrarchan situation on its head, turning the sonnet-lady into a whore and attaching all the idealised emotion to a young man. It offers a more complex analysis of the relationship between love and passion than that of any other writer, but also a more fragmented vision in that it turns its back on the attempts of most serious sonneteers to achieve some reconciliation between the two. Shakespeare's sonnet drama is most profitably approached, I think, through the orthodox Petrarchism against which it is a reaction, and in terms of the contemporary sonnet conceit which it exploits to the full. To read Shakespeare's sonnets as though they were an isolated phenomenon is to ignore one of their major dimensions.

Of the sonnets in this collection, *Astrophel and Stella* is the only sequence to follow Petrarch in systematically interweaving songs with its sonnets and to form a complete organic whole. Sidney was a theorist of poetry as well as a poet, and his sonnets are as much a part of his humanist programme for the rehabilitation of English poetry as are his pastorals or his revised *Arcadia*. The sonnets themselves are full of references to literary theory and insist throughout that we read them from this perspective. In his survey of English poetry in his *Defence*, Sidney is especially scathing about the love poetry of the period:

But truly many of such writings as come under the banner of unresistible love, if I were a mistress, would never persuade me they were in love; so coldly they apply fiery speeches, as men that had rather read lovers' writings . . . than that in truth they feel those passions. (pp. 137–8).

He could be describing Watson's *Passionate Centurie of Love*; and in contrasting love poetry based on other love poetry with that derived from the direct human experience, he raises a fundamental literary problem of Renaissance humanism — how to copy the best models from the past, and yet remain true to life. It is, in the final analysis, the conflict between Nature and Art, but more specifically, one between the two common conceptions of 'Imitation' as defined by Aristotle and Horace. Aristotle's *Poetics*, newly discovered in the sixteenth century and used by Sidney for his *Defence*, defines poetry as 'Mimesis', the imitation of human action through the medium of words. In this process, the irrelevances and imperfections are stripped off, and the representation of life which emerges is more intense, more universal, but in no way a falsification of reality. Horace's definition of Imitation in his so-called 'Art of poetry', however, and that to be found in all the rhetorical textbooks from Cicero and Quintilian onwards, is the imitation of the best models as a method of extending one's literary or oratorical techniques. It is the standard method in Renaissance schools of teaching children to write and speak well, as can be seen from the very full account in Ascham's *Scholemaster*, to name only one of many examples. It is by this kind of Imitation that Spenser and Sidney hoped to extend the bounds of English literature by introducing the classical modes which it lacked.

Ideally, of course, the two modes of Imitation are not in conflict: the writer imitates the form of the best literary model and puts into it the appropriate human experience. The classical forms were created as vehicles to express human behaviour and can still be made to perform their task. Where, however, a convention is highly mannered, it is inevitable that the hack writers will imitate the surface mannerisms and ignore the underlying content; and this is the cause of Sidney's criticism of contemporary love poetry. Generations of love poets following Petrarch have mechanically reproduced his 'long-deceased woes' and made hackneyed imitations of his time-worn conceits of ice and fire, while in the process the love out of which all originally sprang has leaked away. Sidney is not therefore attacking the Petrarchan conventions but trying to put some blood back into them, to restore love to love poetry and heal the breach between Horace and Aristotle.

Astrophel and Stella is written explicitly with this object in view. The opening sonnets in particular are so packed with reference to critical theory that they form a manifesto of Sidney's intention, and are worth analysing in some detail for what they tell us about the way we ought to approach the sequence. We must remember that Sidney's poem is about a poet writing poems to his mistress, which provides him with the ideal cover for his own theories of poetry. In his first sonnet, Astrophel, 'Loving in truth' and not merely going through the fashionable poses, sits down with pen in hand to write a poem to Stella, since he knows, from his *Poetics*, that tragedy gives pleasure and so presumably may the account of his pains, and from his Horace, that pleasure may move her to read, to know, to pity and by this route to show grace. He seeks fit words, therefore, in which to present his grief in the pure and absolute form – 'the blackest face of woe' – which, according to Aristotle, Imitation alone makes possible; but he has been thinking along Horatian lines so that his first impulse is to follow Horace's precepts and turn to other men's inventions for his models. 'Invention' is a complex word and one in process of transition at this period. It already has its modern meaning of things invented, things found out or made up by other people's wits, but it also carries for the Renaissance a traditional technical meaning which it has since lost. Invention is the first part of classic rhetoric, the process of finding out whatever materials are appropriate for a given task, whether one is making up an oration or writing a poem. Once the relevant materials have been chosen, the poet or orator proceeds to the second part of rhetoric, Disposition, the choice of the appropriate mode of presenting the material for the task in hand, and thence to Elocution, the third part, which is the selection of 'fit words'. It is interesting – and a point which an educated reader of Sidney's time would immediately recognise – that Astrophel approaches his composition in entirely the wrong order: he seeks fit words before he has chosen his basic materials or considered their presentation; he jumps straight to Elocution, leaving out Invention and Disposition, and this is why he finds it so hard to write. When he turns belatedly to Invention it is the wrong kind for this moment, Horatian: he seeks his materials in 'others' leaves' which can provide him with the proper form but not the proper materials for a love poem. He is, in fact, confusing Invention with Disposition. The true source of knowledge about love is not to be found in books but in the human heart, and it is to this source which his Muse therefore bids him turn. She is not telling him to write his own autobiography, but to look for the materials for a love poem in the proper place.

Astrophel immediately follows her advice in the very revolutionary second sonnet which presents love as it is in fact rather than as it has been represented in literature. In the medieval tradition of which Petrarch himself was only a late inheritor, literary lovers had always fallen in love at first sight – 'Whoever loved that loved not at first sight' – but Astrophel, when he looks into his own heart, finds that this does not tally with experience: he fell in love only gradually, without knowing what was happening, and when he discovered it, he resisted with all his might. Now he has reached the stage when he knows there is no escape and is trying to persuade himself that all is for the best, although he knows in his heart of hearts that it is not so. This sonnet challenges the centuries-old tradition of Courtly Love; and Astrophel, speaking with the voice of Sidney, draws attention to this in the next sonnet when he contrasts his own verse based on the reality of love – 'then all my deed/But Copying is what in her Nature writes' – with that of love poets who merely copy what has been written before. It is a theme to which Sidney returns continually – in sonnets 6, 15 and 55, for example, and a central point about the nature of love poetry which he uses his sonnet cycle to demonstrate.

The ape referred to in sonnet 3, with its capacity for mimicry, was a common Renaissance symbol for art; but Sidney is not anticipating Wordsworth's plea for a poetry of nature which shall reject all art. The philosophy of the period, which pictured even Nature herself as manifesting the art of God, involved too deep a reverence for good art for it ever to be repudiated. Stella's beauty in the third sonnet is, after all, 'what in her Nature *writes*'; and the poet is the most god-like among men because by means of his art he can re-create what God, the supreme artist, has already created. The art of true poetry is divine because it is based on Nature.

Yet when we look at the mass of sonnet conceits and patterns which make up *Astrophel and Stella*, our first impression is of a triumphant and self-sufficient art, though Astrophel denies that this is so throughout the sequence; and Sidney for once would have agreed with Watson in his notes to his Passion 40 which handles the time-honoured theme of the contradictory passions of love, 'I feare, and hope, I burne, yet freeze withall.' These paradoxes, says Watson, are in fact true to life:

> The sense contained in this Sonnet will seeme straunge to such as never have acquainted themselves with Love and his Lawes, because of the contrarieties mentioned therein. But to such, as Love at any time hath had under his banner, all and every part of it will appeare to be a familiar truth.

Throughout all love poetry from Ovid to Yeats, lovers have gazed at the moon or tossed on their beds as Astrophel does in sonnets 31 and 39, and the great clichés of poetry correspond to the permanent patterns of human behaviour. More specifically, a witty man will be witty in his love, especially if he is a poet, and Astrophel's wit turns every occasion into a means of wooing Stella. He twists the double negative of her 'No, No' into a grammatical affirmative (63), or turns her coat-of-arms into a compliment to her beauty (13), or his own into proof of a relationship with her (65). In the same way Donne turns his casual encounter with a flea into an argument for seduction. Even the traditional conceits about Cupid's bow and arrows (17, 20) become miniature pieces of Spenserean-type allegory and inner histories of his own soul wounded by the shafts of passion. Moreover, for the first part of the sequence at least, Astrophel is busily using the remnant of wit which love has left him 'To make my selfe beleeve that all is well'; and in his efforts to justify himself to himself and to the traditional rational 'friend' of love poetry, he drags in every argument, every support, every rag of philosophy that he can. Reason can be made to prove that love is better than reason (10); the fashionable Platonism of the time can be evoked in the defence of passion (5); even the astrological belief in the power of the stars can be brought in – not with entire flippancy in this period – to explain the irresistible power of Stella's eyes over him (26).

Sidney is in fact giving his sonnet conceits a dramatic justification. The whole witty structure of the poem is a dramatic projection of the character of Astrophel the poet, just as the characters of Richard II or Hamlet produce their own kinds of wit. These witty and conceited sonnets are natural from a lover such as Astrophel who, dramatically, is nearly twenty years ahead of the times. A Hamlet with only love to plague him would behave as he does. There is nothing comparable to his wry, half-humorous self-awareness until we come to Shakespeare's plays. In the first sixty-three sonnets, he is torn between the claims of this highly inconvenient love and those of the active life for which he is trained; but his capacity for action is undermined even more by his consciousness of the slightly ridiculous figure he cuts as an unwilling lover, 'prauncing' in Mars's livery when he is really Cupid's man (53), or posing as the symbol of authority on his great horse when he himself is being ridden by Cupid (49). For a brief period his passion becomes strong enough to drive out all hesitation, and the insistent rhythms of the first song express a whole-heartedness in his approach which at once evokes a response from Stella: 'And do I see some cause a hope to feede . . .' (66). But Stella's love for him is coupled to an invincible chastity; and after a brief period of euphoric rapture, when continence seems a small price to pay for the joys of such platonic love, passion again cries for food (71) and the old conflicts are there once more in a new and more acute form. The poem moves to its predictable end as Stella sticks to her principles and Astrophel respects them, suffering in consequence moods of despair or taking refuge in erotic wishful thinking in the tenth song – itself a thoroughly conventional erotic vision. It ends bleakly with the hint of a more willing mistress in the offing, and a request from Astrophel to be released so that he may get on with his duties for the state (107).

Sidney has written a new dramatic version of the old Petrarchan situation, with the central role filled by a modern lover whose particular character breathes new life into the old conventions. Sidney's dramatic power in this cannot be overstated, and the character he has created must never be confused with himself. There is the clearest distinction in the first sonnet between the confused and pedantic Astrophel fumbling over his poem, and Sidney, the literary theorist, showing him how to do it; and throughout the cycle we are conscious of Sidney looking over Astrophel's shoulder with an amused detachment and doing things within the sonnet which undercut what Astrophel claims to be doing. In this way sonnet 34 presents a very unconfused description of a mind claiming itself to be in a state of utter confusion, while sonnet 35, professing the complete inadequacy of words to express the paradoxes of Stella's perfection, yet succeeds in expressing them through paradox itself. Sidney's control of his character, even when the character contains so much of himself, is much surer than, say, that of Byron with Childe Harold, and is capable of very subtle nuances. In sonnet 90, for example, in a supremely neat poem, Sidney makes Astrophel deny that he wishes to be thought a poet – which offers the same kind of complex perspective as we find in Shakespeare's plays, with boy actors playing the part of girls dressed up as boys.

The range and originality of Sidney's art is extraordinary, and he takes the English sonnet form at a bound virtually from birth to maturity. His favourite form is a Petrarchan one modified by a final couplet, but he experiments with a great variety of rhyme schemes and with lines of varying lengths, and achieves remarkably different effects from the same basic patterns. His final couplet sometimes rounds off and neatly closes up the sonnet statement, sometimes explodes and stands the sonnet on its head (71, 72), sometimes introduces a note of ambiguity which leaves the mind wondering: is Stella or is she not the country to which our souls should move? (5). Is virtue ungratefulness or ungratefulness virtue on the moon? (31). Within the formal structure he can include with equal ease a process of argument (7), a comment on the contemporary scene (30), a vividly dramatic episode (47, 53) or a piece of animated dialogue (34, 54, 92). With Shakespeare the freer sonnet form can on occasion disappear altogether under the pressure of its content. The great sonnet on Lust (sonnet 129), for example, becomes an undivided unit of fourteen lines rather than a pattern of quatrains and couplets. This is never the case with Sidney. However colloquial and conversational the statement he is making or however compressed the thought, he always leaves us conscious of the sonnet form and aware of the individual tension between form and content. In this strait-jacket of the sonnet Sidney can move about with the ease of a Houdini.

The sonnets of Samuel Daniel, in contrast, are less dramatic in content and gentler in their appeal. In his *Elegie* to Henry Reynolds, Drayton says of Daniel that some consider him 'To be too much *Historian* in verse', and continues:

> His rimes were smooth, his meeters well did close,
> But yet his maner better fitted prose.[5]

[5]*Works of Michael Drayton*, ed. Hebel, vol. iii, p. 229.

Such a comment would be quite inapplicable to Sidney with his artistic flamboyance, or to Drayton himself with his mastery of the decorum of so many different styles; but for Daniel it is not wholly inappropriate. He might even have taken it as a compliment, for he says, with reference to his own longer historical poems, 'I versify the truth not poetise'. He is here alluding to the common conception, held, as we have seen, by Sidney, that poetry is 'imitation', fiction, 'feigning', and he believes that truth is more important than poetry. The Renaissance literary theorists did not share the modern assumption that the form and the content of poetry are inseparable, but usually conceived of style and form as the clothes in which content is dressed up for a given occasion. In Daniel, this dichotomy is extreme. For him, the poetry *is* the content, it is the intensity and truth of the vision which makes the poetry. The style, though it may sometimes help to move and persuade, is more commonly something which distorts and gets in the way. Although his affection for rhyme makes him defend it as appropriate to English poetry against the claims of classical metres, he makes it clear that he considers both to be merely superficial matters of local fashion, and that only the truth within is important:

> Eloquence and gay wordes are not of the Substance of wit, it is but the garnish of a nice time, the Ornaments that doe but decke the house of a State . . . Hunger is as well satisfied with meat served in pewter as silver. Discretion is the best measure, the rightest foote in what habit soever it runne. (*Defence of Ryme*, p. 145)

The pretty puns on foot and measure in the last line of this quotation suggest that as a poet Daniel was not quite so indifferent to the pleasure of verbal effects as he pretends, yet he is very conscious that they may get in the way. His own style shows the influence of this way of thought. At its best in his later poetry it has a transparency which forces us to ignore the outer cover and come to grips at once with the naked thought inside, as if we were reading very packed prose, although paradoxically it is the poetic technique itself which creates this illusion.

Daniel's belief in the pre-eminence of content in poetry makes him more dependent on his subject matter than is the case with most of his contemporaries. Unlike Sidney and most of the sonneteers, he cannot make poetry out of the sheer excitement and pleasure of rhetorical or metrical virtuosity, nor can he trifle elegantly in the fashions of the day: his writing achieves greatness only when he has a subject about which he cares and has thought deeply. For this reason he is not wholly at home in the sonnet convention, although as a young and budding poet he felt the need to try his hand at the genre, and as a result, *Delia* is very uneven in its quality. A large number of the sonnets are what the anti-Petrarchan satirists at the end of the century called 'whining sonnets' – numbers 2, 4, 20, 21, 29 exemplify the 'wayling' and 'plaintive' modes to which they took exception – and they are often obscure, clumsy or even flabby in their diction, suggesting that Daniel had no great taste for what he was doing. The conceits have not the audacity of Sidney's, though Sidney's influence is apparent in the elaborate patterning of 11 and 14, for example. The control of the sonnet form and the matching of it to the sonnet argument are at times inadequate. The most successful are perhaps those like 13 or 31 which are organised around a central metaphor taken from a classical myth; and in this respect Daniel goes beyond Sidney in moving outside the range of Cupid-Venus conceits on which Sidney mainly relied. In subsequent editions Daniel revised his sonnets extensively and attempted to eliminate their weaknesses – he has, as he says in the 1607 preface, 'Repaird some parts defective here and there' – but this mainly took the form of cutting feminine endings and omitting the more plaintive of the sonnets. He often tinkers without improving or making less obscure, as in 21 line 4, where the relative immediacy of 1592 'Whilst my best blood my younge desiers sealeth' is replaced in 1594 by the cliché 'Whilst age upon my wasted body steales'; or in 40, where the difficult line 12 of 1592, 'Which shall instarre the needle and the trayle' is altered to the no less obscure 'Which must instarre the needle and the Raile' of 1594. Unlike Drayton, Daniel's sonnets changed but did not improve with his age, and the greater poetic maturity of his other poetry does not show itself here.

This, however, is only true when Daniel is handling the conventional sonnet situation. Whenever he finds an important theme to deal with within the sonnet, his verse rises magnificently to the challenge, and the sequence of sonnets, 32–8 and 45, all dealing with the decay of beauty, are among the greatest in the language. Mortality and change haunted Daniel's consciousness, and the great commonplaces, the passing from spring to winter, the flowers of beauty born only to wither and die, ring out in his poetry with an authority equal to that of Shakespeare, though with less than Shakespeare's certainty that his sonnets are strong enough to keep that beauty ever young. There is nothing in Daniel quite so triumphant as Shakespeare's 'Not marble nor the guilded monuments' (55). The nearest he ever gets to it is in sonnets 40 and 50, but number 38 is more typical, where he laments that 'thou a Laura hast no Petrarch found'. Daniel's faith in the divinity not merely of his own but of all poetry was harder won than that of Shakespeare or Sidney, and his need to justify poetry in the modern world more anxious and acute. He was only too conscious that the Philistines can get on very well without the help of poetry:

> How many thousands never heard the name
> Of Sydney, or of Spenser, or their bookes?
> And yet brave fellowes, and presume of fame . . .
> (*Musophilus*, 440–2)[6]

Daniel's wrestling with the problem and his eventual justification to himself of the fact that he is a poet is finely worked out in his great poem of philosophical self-revelation, *Musophilus*; and in the end, it is by an act of faith that he finds comfort, rather than by the argument that poetry can confer immortality or persuade to virtue:

> This is the thing that I was borne to do,
> This is my Scene, this part I must fulfill.
> (*Musophilus*, 577–8)

Like Daniel, Michael Drayton was very conscious that he was born to be a poet. As he writes in his *Elegie* to Henry Reynolds:

> From my cradle (you must know) that I
> Was still inclin'd to noble Poesie
> (Hebel, vol. iii, p. 226)

but he never doubted his calling. Drayton, after Spenser, is the arch-poet of his period, the true professional who systematically covers the whole range of literary 'kinds' from pastoral through to heroic and satiric, taking in the sonnet on the way in his *Ideas Mirrour* of 1594 which, like Daniel, he revised continually until its final appearance as *Idea* in 1619. His revisions in part consist in the rejection of the more extravagantly conceited of the earlier sonnets, but there is little real consistency in his method. He

[6] *Poems and a Defence of Ryme*, ed. Sprague.

retains number 40, based on the old heart/anvil image, from 1594, but he rejects the wittier Amour 11 dealing with the alphabet of love. The 1619 version, indeed, has a new line of conceits of its own, more knotty and cerebral than those of the earlier version, but not essentially different. The play on 'I' and 'Aye' in sonnet 5, or the sophisticated logic of sonnet 26 are cases in point. As in Daniel, so Drayton's later versions include fewer of the 'whining' sonnets, a point to which the poet alludes in his sonnet 'To the Reader of these Sonnets' prefacing the 1619 edition:

> No farre-fetch'd Sigh shall ever wound my Brest,
> Love from mine Eye a Teare shall never wring,
> Nor in Ah-mees my whyning Sonnets drest,

In this vein, and following Sidney, Drayton compliments himself in sonnet 24 on his ability to conceal his feelings under a show of wit. Indeed, his debt to Sidney is very great, increasing with each revision; and it is paradoxical that the claim to originality with which he concludes his dedicatory sonnet to the edition of 1594 should explicitly echo Sidney's own claim to originality in sonnet 74 of *Astrophel and Stella*:

> Divine Syr Phillip, I avouch thy writ,
> I am no Pickpurse of anothers wit.
>   (Hebel, vol. i, *Ideas Mirrour*)

There is a superficial similarity between Drayton's sonnet 24 and Sidney's 54; between his 38 and Sidney's 10; his 39 and 15; his 51 and 30, and many others. But the debt is deeper than this: the two poets have the same range of conversational tones, the same involvement in contemporary affairs and critical debates. Like the sonnets of Sidney but unlike those of Daniel and Spenser, Drayton's sonnets do not exist in a world of which love is the only dimension and where the function of the sonnet is to look inward into the private and traditional sufferings of the heart. Drayton's sonnets look outwards and in their imagery acknowledge the existence of a social situation and of other activities going on outside. Sonnets 2, 7, 10, 21, 28, 50, to name only a few, share this extrovert quality with *Astrophel and Stella*, and their conceits draw on the world of everyday experience, on the law, on bankruptcy, on the behaviour of spendthrift young men or the practises of the medical profession. From this fact, they gain a quality of realism which makes a heightened dramatic impact. *Idea* has no overall dramatic structure and development such as we find in Sidney, but of all the Elizabethan sonneteers, including even Shakespeare, Drayton is the master in the presentation of what Daniel calls 'a present passion' (*Defence*, 138). The famous anthology pieces 'Since ther's no helpe' (61), or 'You not alone' (11), or 'How many paltry, foolish, painted things' (6), or 'An evill spirit' (20), have a passionate intensity which no one but Shakespeare can rival in the sonnet. Moreover, this quality often appears in conjunction with the most elaborate conceit: 'You not alone, when You are still alone' (11), is based on the same kind of wordplay as the much slighter 'No and I' sonnet (5), the difference being that in sonnet 11, the wit is a means of analysing passion rather than an end in itself. In *Idea*, the sonnet comes nearest to the poetry of the Metaphysicals, and some of Drayton's sonnets, notably 8, 15, 52, are very close to Donne's anti-Petrarchan poems.

With Spenser's *Amoretti*, we are back once more, though with a difference, in the charmed circle of sonnet love. Where Sidney and Drayton allow the sonnet to spill over into everyday life and attract to itself the whole range of contemporary imagery and allusion, Spenser observes the strictest decorum of the amorous mode and excludes everything which is not a part of love's poetic world. The language itself is consciously poetical, never colloquial, and it is apparent in the *Amoretti* as in *The Faerie Queene* that we are dealing with a poet who, in Ben Jonson's sense of the words, 'writ no language'. The vocabulary is as archaic, the syntax as uncolloquial as anything in the heroic poem. Spenser creates structures of words which justify themselves as patterns in relation to each other rather than as accurate and precise reporting. One cannot imagine Sidney or Drayton getting away with words such as 'dumpish' (4, 4), or 'portly' (5, 2), unless they used them satirically); or using words as Spenser does in lines *10–12* of his sonnet 15 which have no other function than to sustain a structural pattern of anaphora, rhyme and poetic diction. The opening sonnet with its highly formal pattern of 'Happy ye leaves', 'happy lines', 'happy rymes', concentrates the attention on the fact of the poetry itself and is a manifesto of the poetic diction to come. Spenser is the poet's poet in every sense; and the fact that the first sonnet may originally have been written as an introduction to *The Faerie*

Queene itself only serves to emphasise this common quality shared by Spenser's different poetic modes.

Within the limits which he sets himself, however, Spenser finds room for a surprising degree of freedom and unorthodoxy. At the local level this appears in the liberties, greater than in any other sonnet writer, which he takes with the classical myths he uses so freely. Sonnets 23, 24, 28, 38, for example, show him changing the basic stories to suit his own purposes. But the originality goes deeper than this. The *Amoretti* is thoroughly orthodox in its central situation and story line: the lady is firmly on her pedestal and the sonnets are devoted to her praises more completely than, say, Astrophel's, which are mainly preoccupied with his own states of mind. Spenser's lady is described in all her beauty and her cruelty; and though she appears to relent from sonnets 65–78, a 'Venemous toung' has confounded the relationship once more by 86. Yet the prevalent state of mind is neither one of frustration nor of the platonic idealisation of forced abstinence, the two normal responses to the Petrarchan dilemma. Instead, the *Amoretti* offers a paeon in praise of sexual love in the context of Christian marriage, which goes serenely on, often in opposition to the story line or in a way which makes it irrelevant. The classical properties are consistently Christianised, as in sonnet 1 where Helicon is peopled with angels; or 9, where the divinity of the lady is almost blasphemously equated with that of God himself; or 22, where love's altar becomes the high altar at Easter day; or 15 and 70 with their unmistakable allusions to the Song of Songs. The shame which afflicts Shakespeare's sonnet lover in the presence of lust, and drives Astrophel to try and platonise away the hunger of the flesh, seems to present Spenser with no problem, as the contrast between his sonnet 84 and Sidney's 71 or 72 reveals. The only exception is perhaps *Amoretti* 72, which suggests some degree of moral ambiguity. Otherwise, Spenser consistently stresses the moral goodness of sexual love in Christian marriage and it is easy to miss the precision with which the Christian context is defined. In *Amoretti* 55, for example, after eliminating the four material elements as fit substances from which his lady could be created, Spenser is left with only the celestial fifth element, the sky, out of which she could be formed. Having established his hyperbolic compliment, he then turns it neatly in the last couplet into a plea for mercy:

> Then sith to heaven ye lykened are the best,
>   be lyke in mercy as in all the rest.

The 'mercy' to which he is referring, however, is not merely that which the medieval lover implores from his mistress, nor is it the mercy of God in general terms: Spenser is also alluding to the specific manifestation of that mercy in the form of the Incarnation, and he is pleading with the lady to take on human flesh as Christ did. The Incarnation is the basis of Spenser's belief in the holiness of sex and the human body, as expressed in Books III and IV of *The Faerie Queene* and in the *Epithalamion*. It dictates also the dominant tone of the *Amoretti* and causes him to Christianise the Petrarchan love sonnet as he Christianised the heroic poem.

For this reason many critics have complained, with justification, that the *Amoretti* is self-contradictory, and that the Petrarchan motif is at odds with the un-Petrarchan theme. This, I think, is true: the sonnet conventions ran counter to Spenser's basic sexual attitudes, and his awareness of this fact is apparent in his treatment of Britomart, Amoret and the two Florimels in *The Faerie Queene*, Books III and IV. What is interesting about the *Amoretti*, however, is how, having undertaken a Petrarchan cycle, Spenser sets about papering over the cracks. The lady's cruelty, for example, is softened by being described in mock-heroic terms:

> See how the Tyrannesse doth joy to see
>   the huge massacres which her eyes do make, (10)

and there is a similar flippancy in the address to his poems which she has torn up:

> Innocent paper whom too cruell hand
>   did make the matter to avenge her yre, (48)

In this case the normal poetic diction of the *Amoretti* is exploited to give a touch of comedy to the situation. But the most potent force in the *Amoretti* is the Spenserean sonnet form itself with its interlocking quatrains used consistently throughout the whole sequence. The effect is to carry the statement forward without a break, and in this way to discourage the possibility of drama and play down the sense of conflict. By this means the whole cycle takes on a deceptive unity of tone not unlike that of Tennyson's *In Memoriam*, and for the same reasons. Spenser's sonnet drama comes out as a sustained piece of lyric with its discordant elements scarcely apparent.

For this reason, the conjunction of the *Amoretti* with the *Epithalamion* seems to me right, though technically they belong to opposing genres; and the legend that Spenser wrote both of them as a wedding present to his new wife is a reasonable one. The evidence of the sonnets suggests that he felt that she, too, deserved her proper tribute of a sonnet cycle, however inappropriate a poem of frustration might be to a happy marriage; and though, as a passionate humanist, he was not prepared to reshape the genre in a fundamental way, he did his best to turn it into something not wholly unsuitable to the situation. The result is a brilliant and strongly individual hybrid.

There is no need to say more than has been said in the notes about the shorter Petrarchan sequences included in this volume, but a further comment may be added on the *Gullinge Sonnets* of Sir John Davies, since these represent a major shift in taste at the end of the century. A form as idiosyncratic and a fashion as rampant as that of the sonnet inevitably lead to parody in the end, especially when more erotic modes of love poetry exist and at times even infiltrate the sonnet itself. *Hero and Leander* or *Venus and Adonis* represent a very different tradition in love, and their values can be seen in Barnes's sonnet 63 or Griffin's number 3, for example. Sidney's attack on the sonnet of his own times from the start set the precedent for further appeals for a return to nature, and Shakepeare's sonnet against sonnet hyperbole, 'My mistress' eyes are nothing like the sun' (130), is in the Sidneian tradition, not to mention the Bastard's outburst against the Dauphin's wooing of Blanche in sonnet terms – 'Drawn in the flattering table of her eye' (King John, II, *i*), or the whole of *Love's Labours Lost*. Shakespeare was anti-Petrarchan from the beginning, but by the late 1590s everyone felt that way, and the satirists such as Hall and Marston were in full cry against the sonneteers:

> Then poures he forth in patched Sonettings
> His love, his lust, and loathsome flatterings: . . .
> Then can he terme his durtie ill-fac'd bride
> Lady and Queene and Virgin deifide . . .
> (Hall, *Virgidemiarum*, 1, 7)

It is easier, however, to denounce the sonnet than to parody it, since a pyrotechnic display of rhetoric is part of the sonnet's quality, and its very excesses can be its virtues. Davies's legal conceits (7, 8, 9), are less extravagant and far less interesting than those of *Zepheria* which he sets out to parody, just as number 5 is less elaborate than some of the poems in the *Old Arcadia*. He is at his best when he finds a common sonnet conceit which it is still possible to stretch further than ever before, as in the case of 3 and 6.

The reader who hopes to taste the full flavour of the minor Elizabethan sonnet should read the exquisite miniature editions of the 1590s in the British Library. The arbitrary nature of the spelling and punctuation, generally attributable to the compositor rather than the author himself; the elegance of the printing, the elaborate capitals and decorative patterns of layout, give a stronger sense of the individuality of each than any modern edition can hope to do. I have tried to retain something of that flavour by avoiding a standardised and uniform presentation of the varying texts; but the reader who takes one of the original octavos in his hand will feel something of the excitement which a new book of poems must have produced in the relative infancy of printing, and be unusually conscious that he is handling an artefact. It is an experience peculiarly relevant to the reading of the sonnet.

MAURICE EVANS

REVISER'S NOTE

I have added to Maurice Evans's edition sonnets by Lady Mary Wroth, Richard Barnfield, and Sir Robert Sidney. To Spenser's *Amoretti* has been added *Epithalamion* (but not the brief anacreontics). Biographical detail and brief critical comment appears at the head of the notes on these poets, while in the introduction to the notes on Spenser number symbolism in his and other sonnet sequences is touched upon.

Adding the one woman writer of a sonnet sequence and, Shakespeare apart, the one homoerotic sonneteer of the period to the original array reflects the current scholarly interest in 'suppressed voices'. How effectively suppressed can be estimated from the treatment of the two writers in the relevant volumes of *The Oxford History of English Literature*. C. S. Lewis at least does show he read Barnfield, but displays his usual uneasiness with sexual matters in a dismissive by-blow at 'the least interesting of all misfortunes'. Douglas Bush, in the volume covering the earlier seventeenth century, mentions Lady Wroth twice in general remarks, but her writings are undiscussed and she is excluded from the bibliographical list of authors.

These two inclusions may be *bien pensant*, but raise the issue of literary value, for it is, finally, biographical circumstance which sustains interest in these two sequences. When the old trick (particularly favoured by the Victorian editors) of switching the sex of the fair beloved in Shakespeare's sonnets is played, they are still, though diminished, great poems. A heterosexualised 'Certaine Sonnets', or Lady Wroth's sequence cross-dressed as 'Amphilanthus to Pamphilia' would have lost almost everything. The interest is in seeing writers for whom the form was not facilitating (a way of writing when you have no subject, as it seems to have been for minor writers like William Smith and Giles Fletcher), but needed to be re-made, or indeed betrays the writer. Petrarchan pastoral let Barnfield write in feeble erotic reverie, but he could surpass himself, and 'If Musique and sweet Poetrie agree', an occasional poem included here, can be seen in the context of his other works, as one of the great pieces of homosexual love poetry in the period. Lady Wroth is repetitious, as sequence writing encouraged a writer to be, but has sometimes a Wyatt-like intensity of introspection.

Jane Austen made by implication a pointed comment on the form: 'for though she could not write sonnets, she brought herself to read them' – that is, even the highly impressionable Catherine Morland, apparently an ideal sonnet-consumer, has to steel herself to face them in numbers (*Northanger Abbey* Chap. 1). Back in the 1590s, there was a lot of merely fashionable writing of sonnets. Barnfield and, later, Wroth were doing more than that. Their variations give some purchase of attention upon repetitions of 'poore *Petrarch*'s long deceased woes', and will help readers to make their own judgements, comparisons and contrasts.

It should be noted by those who want to read more of Lady Wroth that the sequence printed here as 'Pamphilia to Amphilanthus' consists of the numbered first 55 (after this Lady Wroth continued with unnumbered poems) sonnets and songs from the 103 poems appended to her *Urania*. In Josephine Roberts's edition of Wroth's complete *Poems*, editorial re-numbering obscures the way poems 1–55 function as a complete, and, as my notes on the arrangement of the sonnets indicate, artistically well-shaped sequence. The poems which follow include a 'Crowne of Sonetts dedicated to Love' and a shorter sonnet sequence of complaints by another character in her romance, 'Lindamira'. Essentially, Lady Wroth's zeal to imitate her uncle had led her to publish a prose fiction broken off in mid-sentence, and do everything to put out a volume which looks as much as possible like the Countess of Pembroke's 1598 collected works of Philip Sidney, which had just had its fifth printing. In Lady Wroth's 1621 publication the first 55 poems are her equivalent to 'Astrophel and Stella', the rest her 'Certaine Sonnets'.

Once Lady Mary Wroth's poems had been added here to the sonnets of her uncle, to add at least a selection of the third Sidney, Sir Robert, her father, was irresistible, especially as he can be rather good. The mystery is why this apparently happily married man, who seems to have piqued himself on his own fidelity, develops such acute, intensified images of pain. He perhaps represents that aspect of the sonnet which registers in its octave and sestet the poetic equivalent of an emotional blow and the sufferer's sigh, the sonnet sequence's neurotic repetition of erotic suffering. The form is so attuned to suffering that it can be seen as finding its final expression in Wordsworth's 14 sonnets (a kind of sonnet of sonnets, or sonnet squared) on the death penalty, 'Sonnets Upon the Punishment of Death' (1839), with their ghastly parody of the Petrarchan notion that suffering ennobles the sufferer.

Adding *Epithalamion* to the *Amoretti* should make this edition a more convenient text for teachers and students.

In working on this revision, I had to hand my student copy of the text, since used often in teaching. Editions should be updated in the light of recent developments in scholarship (evidenced in *Suggestions for Further Reading*), but Maurice Evans's full-length introduction rightly remains, being still the best introduction to this now widening field of study. No texts have been dropped from his original selection.

ROY J. BOOTH

NOTE ON THE AUTHORS

BARNABE BARNES (*c.* 1569–1609) was the son of a bishop, Oxford educated, and (according to Nashe) an aspirant courtier laughed out of the royal presence for appearing there in 'a codpisse as big as a Bolognian sawsedge'. Attempted murder of the Recorder of Berwick with poisoned claret, 1598. Other literary productions include an anti-Catholic tragedy, *The Devil's Charter* and *A divine century of spirituall sonnets* (1595).

RICHARD BARNFIELD (1574–1627) was minor gentry. Oxford BA 1592, sought to establish a range of patrons in his publications of 1594–8, retired to the life of a country gentleman in Staffordshire. Married, one son 1604.

MARK ALEXANDER BOYD (1563–1601) was educated in Glasgow, travelled abroad, wrote mainly in Latin. Letters and poems published in Bordeaux (1590) and Antwerp (1592).

HENRY CONSTABLE (1562–1613) came from a distinguished family. BA Cambridge 1580, spent much time abroad as a spy, converted to Catholicism *c.* 1590, religious sonnets (unpublished by Constable) written after his conversion, returned from exile 1603, arrested 1604, lived in poverty until banished 1610, died in Liege (meditating on the crucifix for several days in his final illness) 9 October 1613.

SAMUEL DANIEL (1562–1619) was the son of a music master, born in Taunton, educated at Magdalen Hall, Oxford. Minor court official, and tutor to William Herbert (Third Earl of Pembroke, qv under **Wroth**); enjoyed the patronage of Fulke Greville and the Earl of Devonshire. Lost the king's favour after his tragedy *Philotas* (1605) was read as sympathetic to the rebellion of the Earl of Essex. Lyric, historical and dramatic poet, also a history of England in prose; *The Whole Workes* 1623.

SIR JOHN DAVIES (1569–1626), born Wiltshire, educated Queen's College, Oxford and Middle Temple, 1587. Expelled from Middle Temple 1597 after violent quarrel with Richard Martin, previously his friend and fellow wit. Re-admitted, elected MP 1601, Solicitor General for Ireland and knighted 1603, Lord Chief Justice 1626. Wrote *Orchestra* 1596, epigrams, satires, acrostic *Hymnes of Astraea* on the Queen 1599, philosophical poem *Nosce Teipsum* 1599.

MICHAEL DRAYTON (1563–1631) came from minor Warwickshire gentry, page in household of Sir Henry Goodyere, then in service of Lucy, Countess of Bedford. Playwright 1597–1602, 1603 esquire to Sir Walter Aston. Pastoral, historical, satirical and topographical poet, publishing from 1591. In his later years, lived under the patronage of the 4th Earl of Dorset. Buried in Westminster Abbey.

GILES FLETCHER (the Elder) (*c.* 1546–1611) was educated at Eton and King's, Cambridge, becoming a fellow of the College. Envoy to Russia 1588, and wrote an account *Of the Russe common wealth*. Uncle of John Fletcher the dramatist, father of Giles the Younger.

BARTHOLOMEW GRIFFIN (d. 1602): *Fidessa, more chaste than kind* was his sole publication.

THOMAS LODGE (1558–1625) was born the son of the Lord Mayor of London, Merchant Taylor's School and Trinity, Oxford. Privateering adventures to America, Catholic convert, studied medicine MD 1603, *A Treatise of the Plague* 1603. Wrote also Euphuistic romances, *Rosalynde* 1590 being the source text for *As You Like It*, a Defence of Plays and the first epyllion, *Scillaes metamorphosis*, 1589.

SIR PHILIP SIDNEY (1554–1586), born Penshurst, educated Shrewsbury and Christ Church, Oxford. European tour 1572–1575, Ambassador to German Emperor 1577, knighted 1583, married Frances Walsingham September 1583, Governor of Flushing November 1585; wounded in a skirmish at Zutphen, died 17 October 1586 aged 31. Wrote the *Arcadia* 1577–›, revised version 1586–›. Sonnets to Penelope Rich *c.* 1581, also *Defence of Poetry*, psalm translations, translations from du Bartas. Collected works in 1598, edited by Mary Sidney.

SIR ROBERT SIDNEY (1563–1626): younger brother of Philip and Mary. Educated at Christ Church, Oxford, travelled abroad 1579–82. Served as Governor of Flushing after the death of Philip, until 1616. Married a Welsh heiress, Barbara Gamage (1584), father of Lady Mary Wroth. Baronet 1603, Viscount 1605, Earl of Leicester 1618. Published none of his writings.

WILLIAM SMITH (fl. 1596): his published verses link him to Spenser and, possibly, the Countess of Pembroke, dedicatee of his *A newyeares' Guifte*. Also poems in *The Phoenix-Nest* 1595 and *England's Helicon* 1596.

EDMUND SPENSER (*c.* 1552–1599) was born London, educated Pembroke Hall, Cambridge. First publication 1569. Briefly in the Earl of Leicester's household, went to Ireland 1580 as secretary to Arthur, Lord Grey de Wilton. *Faerie Queene* Books I–III 1590, for which granted life pension 1591. Married 1594. His *View of the Present State of Ireland*, advocating one final winter campaign against the Irish, was refused a licence for publication in 1598. His settlement at Kilcolman burned in 1598. Sent to England by the Munster colonists to appeal for help, died in London 13 January 1599, the Earl of Essex paying for his funeral.

LADY MARY WROTH (1586 or 1587–*c.* 1653) was the eldest child of Sir Robert Sidney, educated in the Sidney household to high standards of performance in music, dancing and letters. Unhappy arranged marriage to Sir Robert Wroth, after his death, William Herbert, 3rd Earl of Pembroke became her lover, had two children by him. A long second part of her *Urania* remained unpublished after the scandal caused by the topical and personal allusions of the first part. Also wrote a dramatic entertainment, *Loves Victorie*.

ELIZABETHAN SONNETS

Sonnet to the Reader

Thou find'st not heere, neither the furious alarmes,
Of the pride of Spaine, or subtilnes of France:
Nor of the rude English, or mutine Almanes:
Nor neither of Naples, noble men of armes.
No, an Infant, and that yet surmounteth Knights:
Hath both vanquished me, and also my Muse,
And were it not: this is a lawfull excuse.
If thou hearst not the report, of their great fights,
Thou shalt see no death of any valiant soldier,
And yet I sing the beauty of a fierce warrier.
And amore alone I must strike on my Leer,
And but Eroto I knowe no other Muse.
And harke all you that are lyke us amourous.
And you that are not, goe read some otherwhere.

K. SOOWTHERN
Sonnets to his mystresse Diana, 1584

SIR PHILIP SIDNEY

Astrophel and Stella

1 Loving in truth, and faine in verse my love to show,
   That she (deare she) might take some pleasure of my paine;
   Pleasure might cause her reade, reading might make her
       know,
   Knowledge might pitie winne, and pitie grace obtaine,
   I sought fit words to paint the blackest face of woe,
   Studying inventions fine her wits to entertaine;
   Oft turning others' leaves, to see if thence would flow
   Some fresh and fruitfull showers upon my sunne-burn'd
       braine.
       But words came halting forth, wanting Invention's stay;
   Invention, Nature's child, fled step-dame Studie's blowes,
   And others' feete still seem'd but strangers in my way.
   Thus great with child to speake, and helplesse in my throwes,
       Biting my trewand pen, beating my selfe for spite,
       'Foole,' said my Muse to me, 'looke in thy heart and
           write.'

2 Not at the first sight, nor with a dribbed shot
       Love gave the wound, which while I breathe will
           bleed:
       But knowne worth did in mine of time proceed,
   Till by degrees it had full conquest got.
   I saw and liked, I liked but loved not,
       I loved, but straight did not what *Love* decreed:
       At length to *Love's* decrees I, forc'd, agreed,
   Yet with repining at so partiall lot.
       Now even that footstep of lost libertie
   Is gone, and now like slave-borne *Muscovite*,
   I call it praise to suffer Tyrannie;
   And now employ the remnant of my wit
       To make my selfe beleeve that all is well,
       While with a feeling skill I paint my hell.

3   Let daintie wits crie on the Sisters nine,
    That bravely maskt, their fancies may be told:
    Or *Pindare's* Apes, flaunt they in phrases fine,
    Enam'ling with pied flowers their thoughts of gold:
    Or else let them in statelier glorie shine,
    Ennobling new found Tropes with problemes old:
    Or with strange similies enrich each line,
    Of herbes or beastes, which *Inde* or *Afrike* hold.
        For me in sooth, no Muse but one I know:
        Phrases and Problemes from my reach do grow,
    And strange things cost too deare for my poore sprites.
        How then? Even thus: in *Stella's* face I reed
        What Love and Beautie be; then all my deed
    But Copying is what in her Nature writes.

4   *Vertue*, alas, now let me take some rest,
    Thou setst a bate betweene my will and wit:
    If vaine love have my simple soule opprest,
    Leave what thou likest not, deale not thou with it.
    Thy scepter use in some old *Catoe's* brest;
    Churches or schooles are for thy seate more fit:
    I do confesse; pardon a fault confest:
    My mouth too tender is for thy hard bit.
        But if that needs thou wilt usurping be
        The litle reason that is left in me,
    And stil th'effect of thy perswasions prove,
        I sweare, my heart such one shall shew to thee
        That shrines in flesh so true a Deitie,
    That, *Vertue*, thou thy selfe shalt be in love.

5   It is most true that eyes are form'd to serve
    The inward light, and that the heavenly part
    Ought to be king, from whose rules who do swerve,
        Rebels to Nature, strive for their owne smart.
        It is most true, what we call *Cupid's* dart,
    An image is, which for our selves we carve,
    And, fooles, adore in temple of our hart,
    Till that good God make Church and Churchman starve.
        True, that true Beautie Vertue is indeed,
    Whereof this Beautie can be but a shade
    Which elements with mortall mixture breed:

True, that on earth we are but pilgrims made,
  And should in soule up to our countrey move:
  True, and yet true that I must *Stella* love.

6   Some Lovers speake when they their Muses entertaine,
     Of hopes begot by feare, of wot not what desires;
     Of force of heav'nly beames, infusing hellish paine;
       Of living deaths, deare wounds, faire stormes and freesing
         fires:
     Some one his song in *Jove*, and *Jove's* strange tales attires,
     Brodered with buls and swans, powdred with golden raine:
     Another humbler wit to shepheard's pipe retires,
     Yet hiding royall bloud full oft in rurall vaine.
       To some a sweetest plaint a sweetest stile affords,
         While teares powre out his inke, and sighs breathe out his
           words:
     His paper, pale dispaire, and paine his pen doth niove.
       I can speake what I feele, and feele as much as they,
       But thinke that all the Map of my state I display,
     When trembling voice brings forth that I do *Stella* love.

7   When Nature made her chief worke, *Stella's* eyes,
     In colour blacke why wrapt she beames so bright?
     Would she in beamie blacke, like painter wise,
     Frame daintiest lustre, mixt of shades and light?
     Or did she else that sober hue devise
     In object best to knit and strength our sight,
     Least if no vaile these brave gleames did disguise,
     They sun-like should more dazle then delight?
       Or would she her miraculous power show,
     That whereas blacke seems Beautie's contrary,
     She even in blacke doth make all beauties flow?
     Both so and thus: she, minding love should be
       Placcd cver there, gave him this mourning weed,
       To honor all their deaths who for her bleed.

8   *Love* borne in *Greece*, of late fled from his native place,
       Forc'd by a tedious proofe that Turkish hardned hart
       Is no fit marke to pierce with his fine pointed dart;
     And pleasd with our soft peace, staid here his flying race.
     But finding these North clymes do coldly him embrace,

Not usde to frozen clips, he strave to find some part
Where with most ease and warmth he might employ his
     art:
At length he perch'd himself in *Stella's* joyfull face,
     Whose faire skin, beamy eyes, like morning sun on snow,
Deceiv'd the quaking boy, who thought from so pure light
Effects of lively heat must needs in nature grow.
But she, most faire, most cold, made him thence take his
     flight
     To my close heart, where while some firebrands he did lay,
     He burnt unwares his wings, and cannot fly away.

9   Queene *Vertue's* court, which some call *Stella's* face,
          Prepar'd by Nature's choisest furniture,
          Hath his front built of Alablaster pure;
     Gold is the covering of that stately place.
     The doore, by which sometimes comes forth her Grace,
          Red Porphir is, which locke of pearle makes sure;
          Whose porches rich (which name of cheekes endure)
     Marble mixt red and white do enterlace.
          The windowes now through which this heav'nly guest
     Looks over the world, and can find nothing such
     Which dare claime from those lights the name of best,
     Of touch they are that without touch doth touch,
          Which *Cupid's* selfe from Beautie's mine did draw:
          Of touch they are, and poore I am their straw.

10   Reason, in faith thou art well serv'd, that still
     Wouldst brabling be with sence and love in me:
     I rather wisht thee clime the Muses' hill,
          Or reach the fruite of Nature's choisest tree,
          Or seeke heavn's course, or heavn's inside to see:
     Why shouldst thou toyle our thornie soile to till?
     Leave sense, and those which sense's objects be:
     Deale thou with powers of thoughts; leave love to will.
          But thou wouldst needs fight both with love and sence,
     With sword of wit giving wounds of dispraise,
     Till downe-right blowes did foyle thy cunning fence:
     For soone as they strake thee with *Stella's* rayes,
          Reason, thou kneel'dst, and offeredst straight to prove
          By reason good, good reason her to love.

11   In truth, O love, with what a boyish kind
          Thou doest proceed in thy most serious wayes:
          That when the heav'n to thee his best displayes,
      Yet of that best thou leav'st the best behind.
      For like a child that some faire booke doth find,
          With guilded leaves or colourd Velume playes,
          Or at the most on some fine picture stayes,
      But never heeds the fruit of writer's mind:
          So when thou saw'st in Nature's cabinet
      Stella, thou straight lookst babies in her eyes,
      In her cheeke's pit thou didst thy pitfould set,
      And in her breast bopeepe or couching lyes,
          Playing and shining in each outward part:
          But, foole, seekst not to get into her hart.

12   *Cupid*, because thou shin'st in *Stella's* eyes,
          That from her lockes, thy day-nets, none scapes free,
          That those lips swell, so full of thee they bee,
      That her sweete breath makes oft thy flames to rise,
      That in her breast thy pap well sugred lies,
          That her Grace gracious makes thy wrongs, that she,
          What words so ere she speake, perswades for thee,
      That her cleare voyce lifts thy fame to the skies;
          Thou countest *Stella* thine, like those whose powers
      Having got up a breach by fighting well,
      Crie, 'Victorie, this faire day all is ours.'
      O no, her heart is such a Cittadell,
          So fortified with wit, stor'd with disdaine,
          That to win it is all the skill and paine.

13   *Phœbus* was Judge between *Jove*, *Mars*, and *Love*,
          Of those three gods, whose armes the fairest were:
          Jove's golden shield did Eagle sables beare,
      Whose talents held young *Ganimed* above:
      But in Vert field *Mars* bare a golden speare,
      Which through a bleeding heart his point did shove:
      Each had his creast: *Mars* caried *Venus'* glove;
          Jove on his helme the thunderbolt did reare.
      Cupid then smiles, for on his crest there lies
          Stella's faire haire; her face he makes his shield,
          Where roses gueuls are borne in silver field.

Phœbus drew wide the curtaines of the skies
   To blaze these last, and sware devoutly then,
   The first, thus matcht, were scantly Gentlemen.

14   Alas have I not paine enough, my friend,
     Upon whose breast a fiercer Gripe doth tire
     Then did on him who first stale downe the fire,
While *Love* on me doth all his quiver spend,
But with your Rubarb words you must contend
     To grieve me worse, in saying that Desire
     Doth plunge my wel-form'd soule even in the mire
Of sinfull thoughts, which do in ruine end?
     If that be sinne which doth the maners frame,
Well staid with truth in word and faith of deed,
Readie of wit and fearing nought but shame:
If that be sinne which in fixt hearts doth breed
     A loathing of all loose unchastitie,
     Then Love is sinne, and let me sinfull be.

15   You that do search for everie purling spring
     Which from the ribs of old *Parnassus* flowes,
     And everie floure, not sweet perhaps, which growes
Neare thereabouts, into your Poesie wring;
You that do Dictionaries' methode bring
     Into your rimes, running in ratling rowes:
     You that poore *Petrarch's* long deceased woes,
With new-borne sighes and denisend wit do sing;
     You take wrong waies; those far-fet helpes be such
     As do bewray a want of inward tuch;
And sure at length stolne goods do come to light.
     But if (both for your love and skill) your name
     You seeke to nurse at fullest breasts of Fame,
Stella behold, and then begin to endite.

16   In nature apt to like when I did see
     Beauties, which were of manie Carrets fine,
     My boiling sprites did thither soone incline,
And, Love, I thought that I was full of thee:
But finding not those restlesse flames in me
     Which others said did make their soules to pine,
     I thought those babes of some pinne's hurt did whine,

By my soule judging what Love's paine might be.
   But while I thus with this young Lyon plaid,
Mine eyes (shall I say curst or blest?) beheld
Stella: now she is nam'd, need more be said?
In her sight I a lesson new have speld;
   I now have learn'd Love right, and learn'd even so,
   As who by being poisond doth poison know.

17   His mother deare *Cupid* offended late,
   Because that *Mars*, growne slacker in her love,
   With pricking shot he did not throughly move
To keep the pace of their first loving state.
The boy refusde for feare of *Marse's* hate,
   Who threatned stripes, if he his wrath did prove:
   But she in chafe him from her lap did shove,
Brake bow, brake shafts, while *Cupid* weeping sate:
   Till that his grandame *Nature* pittying it,
Of *Stella's* browes made him two better bowes,
And in her eyes of arrowes infinit.
O how for joy he leapes, O how he crowes,
   And straight therewith, like wags new got to play,
   Fals to shrewd turnes, and I was in his way.

18   With what sharpe checkes I in my selfe am shent,
   When into Reason's audite I do go,
   And by just counts my selfe a banckrout know
Of all those goods, which heav'n to me hath lent;
Unable quite to pay even Nature's rent,
   Which unto it by birthright I do ow:
   And which is worse, no good excuse can show,
But that my wealth I have most idly spent.
   My youth doth waste, my knowledge brings forth toyes;
My wit doth strive those passions to defend
Which for reward spoile it with vaine annoyes.
I see my course to loose my selfe doth bend:
   I see and yet no greater sorrow take
   Then that I loose no more for *Stella's* sake.

19   On *Cupid's* bow how are my heart-strings bent,
   That see my wracke, and yet embrace the same!
   When most I glorie, then I feele most shame:
I willing run, yet while I run, repent.

My best wits still their owne disgrace invent:
   My verie inke turnes straight to *Stella's* name;
   And yet my words, as them my pen doth frame,
Avise themselves that they are vainely spent.
   For though she passe all things, yet what is all
That unto me, who fare like him that both
Lookes to the skies, and in a ditch doth fall?
O let me prop my mind, yet in his growth,
   And not in Nature for best fruits unfit:
   'Scholler,' saith *Love*, 'bend hitherward your wit.'

20   Flie, fly, my friends, I have my death wound; fly,
See there that boy, that murthring boy, I say,
Who like a theefe, hid in darke bush doth ly,
Till bloudie bullet get him wrongfull pray.
So Tyran he no fitter place could spie,
Nor so faire levell in so secret stay,
As that sweete blacke which vailes the heav'nly eye:
There himselfe with his shot he close doth lay.
   Poore passenger, passe now thereby I did,
And staid pleasd with the prospect of the place,
While that blacke hue from me the bad guest hid:
But straight I saw motions of lightning grace,
   And then descried the glistring of his dart:
   But ere I could flie thence, it pierc'd my heart.

21   Your words, my friend (right healthfull caustiks) blame
   My young mind marde, whom *Love* doth windlas so,
   That mine owne writings like bad servants show
My wits, quicke in vaine thoughts, in vertue lame;
That *Plato* I read for nought, but if he tame
   Such coltish gyres; that to my birth I owe
   Nobler desires, least else that friendly foe,
Great expectation, weare a traine of shame.
   For since mad March great promise made of me,
If now the May of my yeares much decline,
What can be hoped my harvest time will be?
Sure you say well; your wisdome's golden mine
   Dig deepe with learning's spade; now tell me this,
   Hath this world ought so faire as *Stella* is?

22   In highest way of heav'n the Sunne did ride,
       Progressing then from faire twinnes' gold'n place;
       Having no scarfe of clowds before his face,
    But shining forth of heate in his chiefe pride;
    When some faire Ladies, by hard promise tied,
       On horsebacke met him in his furious race,
       Yet each prepar'd, with fanne's wel-shading grace,
    From that foe's wounds their tender skinnes to hide.
    Stella alone with face unarmed marcht,
       Either to do like him, which open shone,
       Or carelesse of the wealth because her owne:
    Yet where the hid and meaner beauties parcht,
       Her daintiest bare went free; the cause was this,
       The Sunne, which others burn'd, did her but kisse.

23   The curious wits, seeing dull pensivenesse
       Bewray it selfe in my long setled eyes,
       Whence those same fumes of melancholy rise
    With idle paines, and missing ayme, do guesse.
    Some that know how my spring I did addresse,
       Deem that my Muse some fruit of knowledge plies:
       Others, because the Prince my service tries,
    Thinke that I thinke state errours to redresse.
       But harder Judges judge ambition's rage,
    Scourge of it selfe, still climing slipprie place,
    Holds my young braine captiv'd in golden cage.
    O fooles, or over-wise, alas the race
       Of all my thoughts hath neither stop nor start,
       But only *Stella's* eyes and *Stella's* hart.

24   Riche fooles there be, whose base and filthy hart
    Lies hatching still the goods wherein they flow;
    And damning their owne selves to *Tantal's* smart,
    Wealth breeding want, more blist, more wretched grow.
    Yet to those fooles heav'n such wit doth impart,
    As what their hands do hold, their heads do know,
    And knowing, love, and loving, lay apart
    As sacred things, far from all daunger's show.
       But that rich foole, who by blind Fortune's lot
    The richest gemme of Love and life enjoyes,
    And can with foule abuse such beauties blot;
    Let him, deprived of sweet but unfelt joyes,

(Exil'd for ay from those high treasures, which
He knowes not) grow in only follie rich.

25   The wisest scholler of the wight most wise,
By *Phœbus'* doome, with sugred sentence sayes
That Vertue, if it once met with our eyes,
Strange flames of *Love* it in our soules would raise;
But for that man with paine this truth descries,
Whiles he each thing in sense's ballance wayes,
And so nor will, nor can, behold those skies
Which inward sunne to *Heroicke* minde displaies,
    Vertue of late, with vertuous care to ster
Love of her selfe, tooke *Stella's* shape, that she
To mortall eyes might sweetly shine in her.
It is most true, for since I her did see,
    Vertue's great beautie in that face I prove,
    And find th'effect, for I do burne in love.

26   Though dustie wits dare scorne Astrologie,
And fooles can thinke those Lampes of purest light,
Whose numbers, wayes, greatnesse, eternitie,
Promising wonders, wonder do invite,
To have for no cause birthright in the skie,
But for to spangle the blacke weeds of night;
Or for some brawle, which in that chamber hie,
They should still daunce to please a gazer's sight:
    For me, I do Nature unidle know,
And know great causes great effects procure:
And know those Bodies high raigne on the low.
And if these rules did faile, proofe makes me sure,
    Who oft fore-judge my after-following race
    By only those two starres in *Stella's* face.

27   Because I oft in darke abstracted guise
    Seeme most alone in greatest companie,
    With dearth of words, or answers quite awrie,
To them that would make speech of speech arise,
They deeme, and of their doome the rumour flies,
    That poison foule of bubling pride doth lie
    So in my swelling breast that only I
Fawne on my self, and others do despise:

Yet pride I thinke doth not my soule possesse,
Which lookes too oft in his unflattring glasse:
But one worse fault, *Ambition*, I confesse,
That makes me oft my best friends overpasse,
    Unseene, unheard, while thought to highest place
    Bends all his powers, even unto *Stella's* grace.

28   You that with allegorie's curious frame
    Of others' children changelings use to make,
    With me those paines for God's sake do not take:
I list not dig so deepe for brasen fame.
When I say '*Stella*', I do meane the same
    Princesse of Beautie, for whose only sake
    The raines of *Love* I love, though never slake,
And joy therein, though Nations count it shame.
    I beg no subject to use eloquence,
Nor in hid wayes do guide Philosophie:
Looke at my hands for no such quintessence;
But know that I, in pure simplicitie,
    Breathe out the flames which burne within my heart,
    Love onely reading unto me this art.

29   Like some weake Lords, neighbord by mighty kings,
    To keepe themselves and their chiefe cities free,
    Do easly yeeld that all their coasts may be
Ready to store their campes of needfull things;
So *Stella's* heart, finding what power *Love* brings,
    To keepe it selfe in life and liberty
    Doth willing graunt that in the frontiers he
Use all, to helpe his other conquerings:
    And thus her heart escapes, but thus her eyes
Serve him with shot, her lips his heralds arre,
Her breasts his tents, legs his triumphall carre,
Her flesh his food, her skin his armour brave;
    And I, but for because my prospect lies
Upon that coast, am giv'n up for a slave.

30   Whether the Turkish new-moone minded be
    To fill his hornes this yeare on Christian coast;
    How *Poles'* right king meanes, without leave of hoast,
To warme with ill-made fire cold *Moscovy*:
If French can yet three parts in one agree;

What now the Dutch in their full diets boast;
    How *Holland* hearts, now so good townes be lost,
Trust in the shade of pleasing *Orange* tree;
    How *Ulster* likes of that same golden bit,
Wherewith my father once made it halfe tame;
If in the Scottishe Court be weltring yet;
These questions busie wits to me do frame;
    I, cúmbred with good maners, answer do,
    But know not how, for still I thinke of you.

31   With how sad steps, O Moone, thou climb'st the skies,
         How silently, and with how wanne a face;
         What, may it be that even in heav'nly place
     That busie archer his sharpe arrowes tries?
     Sure, if that long-with-*Love*-acquainted eyes
         Can judge of *Love*, thou feel'st a Lover's case;
         I reade it in thy lookes; thy languisht grace
     To me that feele the like, thy state descries.
         Then ev'n of fellowship, O Moone, tell me
     Is constant *Love* deem'd there but want of wit?
     Are Beauties there as proud as here they be?
     Do they above love to be lov'd, and yet
         Those Lovers scorne whom that *Love* doth possesse?
         Do they call *Vertue* there ungratefulnesse?

32   *Morpheus*, the lively sonne of deadly sleepe,
         Witnesse of life to them that living die;
         A Prophet oft, and oft an historie,
     A poet eke, as humours fly or creepe;
     Since thou in me so sure a power doest keepe,
         That never I with clos'd-up sense do lie,
         But by thy worke my *Stella* I descrie,
     Teaching blind eyes both how to smile and weepe,
         Vouchsafe of all acquaintance this to tell,
     Whence hast thou Ivorie, Rubies, pearle and gold,
     To shew her skin, lips, teeth and head so well?
     'Foole,' answers he, 'no *Indes* such treasures hold,
         But from thy heart, while my sire charmeth thee,
         Sweet *Stella's* image I do steale to mee.'

33   I might, unhappie word, O me, I might,
     And then would not, or could not see my blisse:

Till now, wrapt in a most infernall night,
I find how heav'nly day, wretch, I did misse.
Hart, rent thy selfe, thou doest thy selfe but right;
No lovely *Paris* made thy *Hellen* his:
No force, no fraud, robd thee of thy delight,
Nor Fortune of thy fortune author is:
    But to my selfe my selfe did give the blow,
While too much wit (forsooth) so troubled me,
That I respects for both our sakes must show:
And yet could not by rising Morne foresee
    How faire a day was neare. O punisht eyes,
    That I had bene more foolish or more wise.

34   Come let me write. 'And to what end?' To ease
    A burthned hart. 'How can words ease, which are
    The glasses of thy dayly vexing care?'
Oft cruell fights well pictured forth do please.
'Art not asham'd to publish thy disease?'
    Nay, that may breed my fame, it is so rare.
    'But will not wise men thinke thy words fond ware?'
Then be they close, and so none shall displease.
    'What idler thing then speake and not be hard?'
What harder thing then smart and not to speake?
Peace, foolish wit, with wit my wit is mard.
Thus write I while I doubt to write, and wreake
    My harmes on Ink's poore losse: perhaps some find
    Stella's great powrs, that so confuse my mind.

35   What may words say, or what may words not say,
Where truth it selfe must speake like flatterie?
Within what bounds can one his liking stay,
Where Nature doth with infinite agree?
What *Nestor's* counsell can my flames alay,
Since Reason's selfe doth blow the cole in me?
And ah, what hope that hope should once see day,
Where *Cupid* is sworne page to Chastity?
    Honour is honour'd that thou doest possesse
Him as thy slave, and now long needy Fame
Doth even grow rich, naming my *Stella's* name.
    Wit learnes in thee perfection to expresse:
Not thou by praise, but praise in thee is raisde:
It is a praise to praise, when thou art praisde.

36 *Stella*, whence doth this new assault arise,
  A conquerd, yelden, ransackt heart to winne?
  Whereto long since, through my long-battred eyes,
  Whole armies of thy beauties entred in.
  And there long since, *Love* thy Lieutenant lies,
  My forces razde, thy banners raisd within:
  Of conquest, do not these effects suffice,
  But wilt now warre upon thine owne begin?
   With so sweete voice, and by sweete Nature so,
  In sweetest strength, so sweetly skild withall,
  In all sweete stratagems sweete Arte can show,
  That not my soule, which at thy foot did fall,
   Long since forc'd by thy beames, but stone nor tree
   By Sence's priviledge, can scape from thee.

37 My mouth doth water, and my breast doth swell,
   My tongue doth itch, my thoughts in labour be:
   Listen then, Lordings, with good eare to me,
  For of my life I must a riddle tell.
  Towardes *Aurora's* Court a Nymph doth dwell,
   Rich in all beauties which man's eye can see;
   Beauties so farre from reach of words, that we
  Abase her praise, saying she doth excell:
  Rich in the treasure of deserv'd renowne,
  Rich in the riches of a royall hart,
  Rich in those gifts which give th'eternall crowne;
  Who, though most rich in these and everie part
   Which make the patents of true wordly blisse,
   Hath no misfortune, but that Rich she is.

38 This night, while sleepe begins with heavy wings
   To hatch mine eyes, and that unbitted thought
   Doth fall to stray, and my chiefe powres are brought
  To leave the scepter of all subject things,
  The first that straight my fancie's error brings
   Unto my mind is *Stella's* image, wrought
   By *Love's* owne selfe, but with so curious drought,
  That she, me thinks, not onely shines but sings.
   I start, looke, hearke, but what in closde-up sence
  Was held, in opend sense it flies away,
  Leaving me nought but wailing eloquence:

I, seeing better sights in sight's decay,
　　Cald it anew, and wooed sleepe againe:
　　But him, her host, that unkind guest had slaine.

39　　Come sleepe, O sleepe, the certaine knot of peace,
　　The baiting place of wit, the balme of woe,
　　The poore man's wealth, the prisoner's release,
　　Th'indifferent Judge betweene the high and low;
　　With shield of proofe shield me from out the prease
　　Of those fierce darts dispaire at me doth throw:
　　O make in me those civill warres to cease;
　　I will good tribute pay if thou do so.
　　　　Take thou of me smooth pillowes, sweetest bed,
　　A chamber deafe to noise, and blind to light;
　　A rosie garland, and a wearie hed;
　　And if these things, as being thine by right,
　　　　Move not thy heavy grace, thou shalt in me,
　　　　Livelier then else-where, *Stella's* image see.

40　　As good to write as for to lie and grone.
　　　　O *Stella* deare, how much thy power hath wrought,
　　　　That hast my mind, none of the basest, brought
　　My still kept course, while others sleepe, to mone.
　　Alas, if from the height of Vertue's throne
　　　　Thou canst vouchsafe the influence of a thought
　　　　Upon a wretch that long thy grace hath sought,
　　Weigh then how I by thee am overthrowne:
　　　　And then, thinke thus: although thy beautie be
　　　　Made manifest by such a victorie,
　　Yet noblest Conquerours do wreckes avoid.
　　　　Since then thou hast so farre subdued me
　　　　That in my heart I offer still to thee,
　　O do not let thy Temple be destroyd.

41　　Having this day my horse, my hand, my launce
　　　　Guided so well that I obtain'd the prize,
　　　　Both by the judgement of the English eyes,
　　And of some sent from that sweet enemie *Fraunce*;
　　Horsemen my skill in horsemanship advaunce,
　　　　Towne-folkes my strength; a daintier judge applies
　　　　His praise to sleight, which from good use doth rise:

Some luckie wits impute it but to chaunce:
    Others, because of both sides I do take
My bloud from them, who did excell in this,
Thinke Nature me a man of armes did make.
How farre they shoote awrie! The true cause is
    Stella lookt on, and from her heav'nly face
    Sent forth the beames which made so faire my race.

42   O eyes, which do the Spheares of beautie move,
Whose beames be joyes, whose joyes all vertues be,
Who while they make *Love* conquer, conquer *Love*,
The schooles where *Venus* hath learn'd Chastitie:
O eyes, where humble lookes most glorious prove,
Only lov'd Tyrants just in cruelty,
Do not, O do not from poore me remove;
Keepe still my Zenith, ever shine on me.
    For though I never see them, but straight wayes
My life forgets to nourish languisht sprites,
Yet still on me, O eyes, dart downe your rayes;
And if from Majestie of sacred lights,
    Oppressing mortall sense, my death proceed,
    Wrackes Triumphs be, which *Love* (high set) doth breed.

43   Faire eyes, sweet lips, deare heart, that foolish I
Could hope by *Cupid's* helpe on you to pray,
Since to himselfe he doth your gifts apply
    As his maine force, choise sport, and easefull stay.
    For when he will see who dare him gainesay,
Then with those eyes he lookes: lo by and by
Each soule doth at *Love's* feet his weapons lay,
Glad if for her he give them leave to die.
    When he will play, then in her lips he is,
Where blushing red, that *Love's* selfe them doth love,
With either lip he doth the other kisse:
But when he will for quiet's sake remove
    From all the world, her heart is then his rome,
    Where well he knowes no man to him can come.

44   My words I know do well set forth my mind;
    My mind bemones his sense of inward smart;
    Such smart may pitie claime of any hart;

Her heart, sweete heart, is of no Tygre's kind:
And yet she heares, and yet no pitie I find;
   But more I crie, lesse grace she doth impart.
   Alas, what cause is there so overthwart,
That Noblenesse it selfe makes thus unkind?
   I much do guesse, yet find no truth save this,
That when the breath of my complaints doth tuch
Those daintie dores unto the Court of blisse,
The heav'nly nature of that place is such,
   That once come there, the sobs of mine annoyes
   Are metamorphosd straight to tunes of joyes.

45   *Stella* oft sees the verie face of wo
   Painted in my beclowded stormie face;
   But cannot skill to pitie my disgrace,
Not though thereof the cause her selfe she know:
Yet hearing late a fable, which did show
   Of Lovers never knowne a grievous case,
   Pitie thereof gate in her breast such place
That, from that sea deriv'd, teares' spring did flow.
   Alas, if Fancy drawne by imag'd things,
Though false, yet with free scope more grace doth breed
Then servant's wracke where new doubts honor brings,
Then thinke, my deare, that you in me do reed
   Of Lover's ruine some sad Tragedie:
   I am not I; pitie the tale of me.

46   I curst thee oft, I pitie now thy case,
   Blind-hitting boy, since she that thee and me
   Rules with a becke, so tyrannizeth thee,
That thou must want or food, or dwelling place.
For she protests to banish thee her face:
   Her face? O *Love*, a Rogue thou then shouldst be,
   If *Love* learne not alone to love and see,
Without desire to feed of further grace.
   Alas poore wag, that now a scholler art
To such a schoole-mistresse, whose lessons new
Thou needs must misse, and so thou needs must smart.
Yet Deare, let me this pardon get of you,
   So long (though he from booke myche to desire)
   Till without fewell you can make hot fire.

47　　What, have I thus betrayed my libertie?
　　　　Can those blacke beames such burning markes engrave
　　　　In my free side? or am I borne a slave,
　　　Whose necke becomes such yoke of tyranny?
　　　Or want I sense to feele my miserie?
　　　　Or sprite, disdaine of such disdaine to have,
　　　　Who for long faith, tho dayly helpe I crave,
　　　May get no almes but scorne of beggerie?
　　　　Vertue awake; Beautie but beautie is:
　　　I may, I must, I can, I will, I do
　　　Leave following that, which it is gaine to misse.
　　　Let her go. Soft, but here she comes. Go to,
　　　　Unkind, I love you not: O me, that eye
　　　　Doth make my heart give to my tongue the lie.

48　　Soule's joy, bend not those morning starres from me,
　　　　Where Vertue is made strong by Beautie's might,
　　　　Where *Love* is chastnesse, Paine doth learne delight,
　　　And Humblenesse growes one with Majestie.
　　　What ever may ensue, O let me be
　　　　Copartner of the riches of that sight:
　　　　Let not mine eyes be hel-driv'n from that light:
　　　O looke, O shine, O let me die and see.
　　　　For though I oft my selfe of them bemone,
　　　　That through my heart their beamie darts be gone,
　　　Whose curelesse wounds even now most freshly bleed;
　　　　Yet since my death-wound is already got,
　　　　Deare Killer, spare not thy sweet cruell shot:
　　　A kind of grace it is to slay with speed.

49　　I on my horse, and *Love* on me doth trie
　　　　Our horsmanships, while by strange worke I prove
　　　　A horsman to my horse, a horse to *Love*;
　　　And now man's wrongs in me, poore beast, descrie.
　　　The raines wherewith my Rider doth me tie
　　　　Are humbled thoughts, which bit of Reverence move,
　　　　Curb'd in with feare, but with guilt bosse above
　　　Of Hope, which makes it seeme faire to the eye.
　　　　The Wand is Will; thou Fancie, Saddle art,
　　　Girt fast by memorie, and while I spurre
　　　My horse, he spurres with sharpe desire my hart:

He sits me fast, how ever I do sturre;
   And now hath made me to his hand so right,
   That in the Manage myselfe takes delight.

50   *Stella*, the fulnesse of my thoughts of thee
Cannot be staid within my panting breast,
But they do swell and struggle forth of me,
Till that in words thy figure be exprest.
And yet as soone as they so formed be,
According to my Lord *Love's* owne behest,
With sad eyes I their weake proportion see,
To portrait that which in this world is best.
   So that I cannot chuse but write my mind,
And cannot chuse but put out what I write,
While those poore babes their death in birth do find:
And now my pen these lines had dashed quite,
   But that they stopt his furie from the same,
   Because their forefront bare sweet *Stella's* name.

51   Pardon mine eares, both I and they do pray,
   So may your tongue still fluently proceed
   To them that do such entertainment need,
So may you still have somewhat new to say.
On silly me do not the burthen lay
   Of all the grave conceits your braine doth breed;
   But find some *Hercules* to beare, in steed
Of *Atlas* tyr'd, your wisedome's heav'nly sway.
   For me, while you discourse of courtly tides,
Of cunningst fishers in most troubled streames,
Of straying wayes, when valiant errour guides;
Meane while my heart confers with *Stella's* beames,
   And is even irkt that so sweet Comedie
   By such unsuted speech should hindred be.

52   A strife is growne between *Vertue* and *Love*,
   While each pretends that *Stella* must be his:
   Her eyes, her lips, her all, saith *Love*, do this,
Since they do weare his badge, most firmely prove.
But *Vertue* thus that title doth disprove:
   That *Stella* (O deare name) that *Stella* is
   That vertuous soule, sure heire of heav'nly blisse,

Not this faire outside, which our hearts doth move:
   And therefore, though her beautie and her grace
Be *Love's* indeed, in *Stella's* selfe he may
By no pretence claime any maner place.
Well *Love*, since this demurre our sute doth stay,
   Let *Vertue* have that *Stella's* selfe; yet thus,
   That *Vertue* but that body graunt to us.

53   In Martiall sports I had my cunning tride,
   And yet to breake more staves did me addresse,
   While with the people's shouts, I must confesse,
Youth, lucke, and praise, even fild my veines with pride;
When *Cupid*, having me, his slave, descride
   In *Marse's* liverie, prauncing in the presse,
   'What now, sir foole,' said he, 'I would no lesse:
Looke here, I say.' I look'd, and *Stella* spide,
   Who hard by made a window send forth light.
My heart then quak'd, then dazled were mine eyes,
One hand forgat to rule, th'other to fight.
Nor trumpets' sound I heard, nor friendly cries;
   My Foe came on, and beat the aire for me,
   Till that her blush taught me my shame to see.

54   Because I breathe not love to everie one,
   Nor do not use set colours for to weare,
   Nor nourish speciall lockes of vowed haire,
Nor give each speech a full point of a grone,
The courtly Nymphs, acquainted with the mone
   Of them, who in their lips *Love's* standerd beare,
   'What he?' say they of me, 'now I dare sweare,
He cannot love: no, no, let him alone.'
   And thinke so still, so *Stella* know my mind.
Professe in deed I do not *Cupid's* art;
But you, faire maides, at length this true shall find,
That his right badge is but worne in the hart:
   Dumbe Swannes, not chatring Pies, do Lovers prove;
   They love indeed who quake to say they love.

55   Muses, I oft invoked your holy ayde,
   With choisest flowers my speech to engarland so,
   That it, despisde in true but naked shew,

Might winne some grace in your sweet grace arraid;
And oft whole troupes of saddest words I staid,
   Striving abroad a-foraging to go,
   Untill by your inspiring I might know
How their blacke banner might be best displaid.
   But now I meane no more your helpe to trie,
Nor other sugring of my speech to prove,
But on her name incessantly to crie:
For let me but name her whom I do love,
   So sweete sounds straight mine eare and heart do hit,
   That I well find no eloquence like it.

56   Fy, schoole of Patience, Fy, you lesson is
   Far far too long to learne it without booke:
   What, a whole weeke without one peece of looke,
And thinke I should not your large precepts misse?
When I might reade those letters faire of blisse,
   Which in her face teach vertue, I could brooke
   Somewhat thy lead'n counsels, which I tooke
As of a friend that meant not much amisse:
   But now that I, alas, do want her sight,
What, dost thou thinke that I can ever take
In thy cold stuffe a flegmatike delight?
No, Patience, if thou wilt my good, then make
   Her come and heare with patience my desire,
   And then with patience bid me beare my fire.

57   Wo, having made with many fights his owne
   Each sence of mine, each gift, each power of mind,
   Growne now his slaves, he forst them out to find
The thorowest words, fit for woe's selfe to grone,
Hoping that when they might find *Stella* alone,
   Before she could prepare to be unkind,
   Her soule, arm'd but with such a dainty rind,
Should soone be pierc'd with sharpnesse of the mone.
   She heard my plaints, and did not only heare,
But them (so sweete is she) most sweetly sing,
With that faire breast making woe's darknesse cleare:
A pretty case! I hoped her to bring
   To feele my griefes, and she with face and voice
   So sweets my paines that my paines me rejoyce.

58   Doubt there hath bene, when with his golden chaine
        The Oratour so farre men's harts doth bind,
        That no pace else their guided steps can find
     But as he them more short or slacke doth raine,
     Whether with words this soveraignty he gaine,
        Cloth'd with fine tropes, with strongest reasons lin'd,
        Or else pronouncing grace, wherewith his mind
     Prints his owne lively forme in rudest braine.
        Now judge by this: in piercing phrases late,
        Th'anatomy of all my woes I wrate;
     Stella's sweete breath the same to me did reed.
        O voice, O face, maugre my speeche's might
        Which wooed wo, most ravishing delight
     Even those sad words even in sad me did breed.

59   Deare, why make you more of a dog then me?
        If he do love, I burne, I burne in love:
        If he waite well, I never thence would move:
     If he be faire, yet but a dog can be.
     Litle he is, so litle worth is he;
        He barks; my songs thine owne voyce oft doth prove:
        Bid'n, perhaps he fetcheth thee a glove,
     But I, unbid, fetch even my soule to thee.
        Yet while I languish, him that bosome clips,
     That lap doth lap, nay lets, in spite of spite,
     This sowre-breath'd mate tast of those sugred lips.
     Alas, if you graunt only such delight
        To witlesse things, then *Love* I hope (since wit
        Becomes a clog) will soone ease me of it.

60   When my good Angell guides me to the place,
        Where all my good I do in *Stella* see,
        That heav'n of joyes throwes onely downe on me
     Thundred disdaines and lightnings of disgrace:
     But when the ruggedst step of Fortune's race
        Makes me fall from her sight, then sweetly she
        With words, wherein the Muses' treasures be,
     Shewes love and pitie to my absent case.
        Now I, wit-beaten long by hardest Fate,
     So dull am that I cannot looke into
     The ground of this fierce *Love* and lovely hate:

Then some good body tell me how I do,
    Whose presence, absence, absence presence is;
    Blist in my curse, and cursed in my blisse.

61   Oft with true sighes, oft with uncalled teares,
    Now with slow words, now with dumbe eloquence
    I *Stella's* eyes assayll, invade her eares;
    But this at last is her sweet breath'd defence:
    That who indeed infelt affection beares
    So captives to his Saint both soule and sence
    That, wholly hers, all selfnesse he forbeares;
     Thence his desires he learnes, his live's course thence.
      Now since her chast mind hates this love in me,
        With chastned mind, I straight must shew that she
    Shall quickly me from what she hates remove.
        O Doctor *Cupid*, thou for me reply,
        Driv'n else to graunt by Angel's sophistrie,
    That I love not, without I leave to love.

62   Late tyr'd with wo, even ready for to pine
    With rage of *Love*, I cald my Love unkind;
    She in whose eyes *Love*, though unfelt, doth shine,
    Sweet said that I true love in her should find.
    I joyed, but straight thus watred was my wine,
    That love she did, but loved a Love not blind,
    Which would not let me, whom she loved, decline
    From nobler course, fit for my birth and mind:
        And therefore by her Love's authority,
        Wild me these tempests of vaine love to flie,
    And anchor fast my selfe on *Vertue's* shore.
        Alas, if this the only mettall be
        Of *Love*, new-coind to helpe my beggery,
    Deare, love me not, that you may love me more.

63   O Grammer rules, O now your vertues show;
        So children still reade you with awfull eyes,
        As my young Dove may, in your precepts wise,
    Her graunt to me by her owne vertue know.
    For late with heart most high, with eyes most low,
        I crav'd the thing which ever she denies:
        She, lightning *Love*, displaying *Venus'* skies,

Least once should not be heard, twise said, 'No, No.'
   Sing then, my Muse, now *Io Pean* sing;
   Heav'ns, envy not at my high triumphing,
But Grammer's force with sweet successe confirme;
   For Grammer sayes (O this, deare *Stella*, weighe,)
   For Grammer sayes (to Grammer who sayes nay?)
That in one speech two Negatives affirme.

First song
Doubt you to whom my Muse these notes entendeth,
Which now my breast orecharg'd to Musicke lendeth?
To you, to you, all song of praise is due,
Only in you my song begins and endeth.

Who hath the eyes which marrie state with pleasure,
Who keepes the key of Nature's chiefest treasure?
To you, to you, all song of praise is due,
Only for you the heav'n forgate all measure.

Who hath the lips, where wit in fairenesse raigneth,
Who womankind at once both deckes and stayneth?
To you, to you, all song of praise is due,
Onely by you *Cupid* his crowne maintaineth.

Who hath the feet, whose step all sweetnesse planteth,
Who else for whom *Fame* worthy trumpets wanteth?
To you, to you, all song of praise is due,
Onely to you her Scepter *Venus* granteth.

Who hath the breast whose milke doth passions nourish,
Whose grace is such, that when it chides doth cherish?
To you, to you, all song of praise is due,
Onelie through you the tree of life doth flourish.

Who hath the hand which without stroke subdueth,
Who long dead beautie with increase reneweth?
To you, to you, all song of praise is due,
Onely at you all envie hopelesse rueth.

Who hath the haire which, loosest, fastest tieth,
Who makes a man live then glad when he dieth?

To you, to you, all song of praise is due:
Only of you the flatterer never lieth.

Who hath the voyce, which soule from sences sunders,
Whose force but yours the bolts of beautie thunders?
To you, to you, all song of praise is due:
Only with you not miracles are wonders.

Doubt you to whom my Muse these notes intendeth,
Which now my breast orecharg'd to Musicke lendeth?
To you, to you, all song of praise is due:
Only in you my song begins and endeth.

64   No more, my deare, no more these counsels trie,
         O give my passions leave to run their race:
         Let Fortune lay on me her worst disgrace,
      Let folke orecharg'd with braine against me crie;
      Let clouds bedimme my face, breake in mine eye,
         Let me no steps but of lost labour trace;
         Let all the earth with scorne recount my case,
      But do not will me from my *Love* to flie.
         I do not envie *Aristotle's* wit,
      Nor do aspire to *Cæsar's* bleeding fame,
      Nor ought do care, though some above me sit,
      Nor hope, nor wishe another course to frame,
         But that which once may win thy cruell hart:
         Thou art my Wit, and thou my Vertue art.

65   Love, by sure proofe I may call thee unkind,
      That giv'st no better eare to my just cries;
      Thou whom to me such my good turnes should bind,
      As I may well recount, but none can prize:
      For when, nak'd boy, thou couldst no harbour find
      In this old world, growne now so too too wise,
      I lodg'd thee in my heart, and being blind
      By Nature borne, I gave to thee mine eyes:
         Mine eyes, my light, my heart, my life, alas:
      If so great services may scorned be,
      Yet let this thought thy tygrish courage passe,
      That I perhaps am somewhat kinne to thee;
         Since in thine armes, if learnd fame truth hath spread,
         Thou bear'st the arrow, I the arrow head.

66   And do I see some cause a hope to feede,
      Or doth the tedious burd'n of long wo
      In weakened minds quicke apprehending breed
      Of everie image which may comfort show?
      I cannot brag of word, much lesse of deed;
      Fortune wheeles still with me in one sort slow,
      My wealth no more, and no whit lesse my need;
      Desire still on the stilts of feare doth go.
        And yet amid all feares a hope there is
      Stolne to my heart, since last faire night, nay day,
      Stella's eyes sent to me the beames of blisse,
      Looking on me, while I lookt other way:
        But when mine eyes backe to their heav'n did move,
        They fled with blush, which guiltie seem'd of love.

67   Hope, art thou true, or doest thou flatter me?
        Doth *Stella* now begin with piteous eye
        The ruines of her conquest to espie?
      Will she take time, before all wracked be?
      Her eye's-speech is translated thus by thee:
        But failst thou not in phrase so heav'nly hie?
        Looke on again, the faire text better trie:
      What blushing notes doest thou in margine see?
        What sighes stolne out, or kild before full borne?
      Hast thou found such and such like arguments?
      Or art thou else to comfort me forsworne?
      Well, how so thou interpret the contents,
        I am resolv'd thy errour to maintaine,
        Rather then by more truth to get more paine.

68   *Stella*, the onely Planet of my light,
        Light of my life, and life of my desire,
        Chiefe good, whereto my hope doth only aspire,
      World of my wealth, and heav'n of my delight;
      Why doest thou spend the treasures of thy sprite,
        With voice more fit to wed *Amphion's* lyre,
        Seeking to quench in me the noble fire,
      Fed by thy worth, and kindled by thy sight?
        And all in vaine, for while thy breath most sweet,
      With choisest words, thy words with reasons rare,
      Thy reasons firmly set on *Vertue's* feet,

Labour to kill in me this killing care,
   O thinke I then, what paradise of joy
   It is, so faire a Vertue to enjoy.

69   O joy, too high for my low stile to show:
   O blisse, fit for a nobler state then me:
   Envie, put out thine eyes, least thou do see
What Oceans of delight in me do flow.
My friend, that oft saw through all maskes my wo,
   Come, come, and let me powre my selfe on thee;
   Gone is the winter of my miserie,
My spring appeares; O see what here doth grow.
   For *Stella* hath with words where faith doth shine,
Of her high heart giv'n me the monarchie:
I, I, O I may say that she is mine.
And though she give but thus conditionly
   This realme of blisse, while vertuous course I take,
   No kings be crown'd, but they some covenants make.

70   My Muse may well grudge at my heav'nly joy,
If still I force her in sad rimes to creepe:
She oft hath drunke my teares, now hopes to enjoy
Nectar of Mirth, since I *Jove's* cup do keepe.
Sonets be not bound prentise to annoy:
Trebles sing high, as well as bases deepe:
Griefe but *Love's* winter liverie is; the Boy
Hath cheekes to smile, as well as eyes to weepe.
   Come then my Muse, shew thou height of delight
In well raisde notes; my pen the best it may
Shall paint out joy, though but in blacke and white.
Cease, eager Muse; peace pen, for my sake stay;
   I give you here my hand for truth of this,
   Wise silence is best musicke unto blisse.

71   Who will in fairest booke of Nature know
   How Vertue may best lodg'd in beautie be,
   Let him but learne of *Love* to reade in thee,
Stella, those faire lines which true goodnesse show.
There shall he find all vices' overthrow,
   Not by rude force, but sweetest soveraigntie
   Of reason, from whose light those night-birds flie,

That inward sunne in thine eyes shineth so:
   And not content to be Perfection's heire
Thy selfe, doest strive all minds that way to move,
Who marke in thee what is in thee most faire.
So while thy beautie drawes the heart to love,
   As fast thy Vertue bends that love so good:
   'But ah,' Desire still cries, 'give me some food.'

72   Desire, though thou my old companion art,
   And oft so clings to my pure Love, that I
   One from the other scarcely can descrie,
While each doth blow the fier of my hart;
Now from thy fellowship I needs must part;
   Venus is taught with *Dian's* wings to flie:
   I must no more in thy sweet passions lie:
Vertue's gold now must head my *Cupid's* dart.
   Service and Honor, wonder with delight,
Feare to offend, will worthie to appeare,
Care shining in mine eyes, faith in my sprite,
These things are left me by my only Deare;
   But thou, Desire, because thou wouldst have all,
   Now banisht art, but yet alas how shall?

Second song
Have I caught my heav'nly jewell,
Teaching sleepe most faire to be?
Now will I teach her that she,
When she wakes, is too too cruell.

Since sweet sleep her eyes hath charmed,
The two only darts of *Love*,
Now will I with that boy prove
Some play, while he is disarmed.

Her tongue waking still refuseth,
Giving frankly niggard 'No':
Now will I attempt to know,
What 'No' her tongue sleeping useth.

See the hand which waking gardeth,
Sleeping, grants a free resort:

Now will I invade the fort;
Cowards *Love* with losse rewardeth.

But O foole, thinke of the danger
Of her just and high disdaine:
Now will I alas refraine;
Love feares nothing else but anger.

Yet those lips so sweetly swelling,
Do invite a stealing kisse:
Now will I but venture this:
Who will read must first learne spelling.

Oh sweet kisse, but ah she is waking;
Lowring beautie chastens me:
Now will I away hence flee:
Foole, more foole, for no more taking.

73   *Love* still a boy, and oft a wanton is,
     School'd onely by his mother's tender eye:
     What wonder then if he his lesson misse,
     When for so soft a rod deare play he trie?
     And yet, my Starre, because a sugred kisse
     In sport I suckt, while she asleepe did lie,
     Doth lowre, nay, chide; nay, threat for only this:
     Sweet, it was saucie *Love*, not humble I.
         But no scuse serves, she makes her wrath appeare
         In Beautie's throne; see now who dares come neare
     Those scarlet judges, threatning bloudy paine?
         O heav'nly foole, thy most kisse-worthie face
         Anger invests with such a lovely grace,
     That Anger' selfe I needs must kisse againe.

74   I never dranke of *Aganippe* well,
     Nor ever did in shade of *Tempe* sit:
     And Muses scorne with vulgar braines to dwell;
     Poor Layman I, for sacred rites unfit.
     Some do I heare of Poets' furie tell,
     But (God wot) wot not what they meane by it:
     And this I sweare by blackest brooke of hell,
     I am no pick-purse of another's wit.

How falles it then, that with so smooth an ease
My thoughts I speake, and what I speake doth flow
In verse, and that my verse best wits doth please?
Guesse we the cause: 'What, is it thus?' Fie no:
'Or so?' Much lesse: 'How then?' Sure thus it is:
    My lips are sweet, inspired with *Stella's* kisse.

75   Of all the kings that ever here did raigne,
    Edward named fourth, as first in praise I name,
    Not for his faire outside, nor well-lined braine,
      Although lesse gifts impe feathers oft on Fame;
      Nor that he could young-wise, wise valiant frame
    His Sire's revenge, joyn'd with a kingdome's gaine
    And gain'd by *Mars*, could yet mad *Mars* so tame,
    That Ballance weigh'd what sword did late obtaine;
      Nor that he made the Flouredeluce so fraid,
    Though strongly hedg'd of bloudy Lyon's pawes,
    That wittie *Lewis* to him a tribute paid:
    Nor this, nor that, nor any such small cause,
      But only for this worthy knight durst prove
      To lose his Crowne, rather then faile his Love.

76   She comes, and streight therewith her shining twins do move
      Their rayes to me, who in her tedious absence lay
      Benighted in cold wo, but now appeares my day,
    The onely light of joy, the onely warmth of *Love*.
    She comes with light and warmth, which like *Aurora* prove
      Of gentle force, so that mine eyes dare gladly play
      With such a rosie morne, whose beames most freshly gay
    Scortch not, but onely do darke chilling sprites remove.
      But lo, while I do speake, it groweth noone with me;
    Her flamie glistring lights increase with time and place;
    My heart cries 'ah, it burnes'; mine eyes now dazled be:
    No wind, no shade can coole; what helpe then in my case,
      But with short breath, long lookes, staid feet and walking
        hed,
      Pray that my sunne go downe with meeker beames to bed.

77   Those lookes, whose beames be joy, whose motion is delight,
    That face, whose lecture shewes what perfect beautie is;
    That presence, which doth give darke hearts a living light;

That grace, which *Venus* weepes that she her selfe doth misse;
That hand, which without touch holds more then *Atlas*
    might;
Those lips, which make death's pay a meane price for a kisse;
That skin, whose passe-praise hue scorns this poore terme of
    white;
Those words, which do sublime the quintessence of blisse;
    That voyce, which makes the soule plant himselfe in the
    eares;
That conversation sweet, where such high comforts be,
As consterd in true speech, the name of heav'n it beares,
Makes me in my best thoughts and quietst judgement see
    That in no more but these I might be fully blest:
    Yet ah, my Mayd'n Muse doth blush to tell the best.

78   O how the pleasant aires of true love be
        Infected by those vapours, which arise
        From out that noysome gulfe, which gaping lies
Betweene the jawes of hellish Jealousie.
A monster, others' harme, selfe-miserie,
        Beautie's plague, Vertue's scourge, succour of lies;
        Who his owne joy to his owne hurt applies,
And onely cherish doth with injurie;
        Who since he hath, by Nature's speciall grace,
        So piercing pawes as spoyle when they embrace,
So nimble feet as stirre still, though on thornes;
        So manie eyes ay seeking their owne woe,
        So ample eares as never good newes know:
It is not evill that such a Devill wants hornes?

79   Sweet kisse, thy sweets I faine would sweetly endite,
        Which even of sweetnesse sweetest sweetner art:
        Pleasingst consort, where each sence holds a part,
Which, coupling Doves, guides *Venus'* chariot right;
Best charge, and bravest retrait in *Cupid's* fight,
        A double key, which opens to the heart,
        Most rich, when most his riches it impart;
Neast of young joyes, schoolmaster of delight,
        Teaching the meane at once to take and give;
The friendly fray, where blowes both wound and heale,
The prettie death, while each in other live;

Poore hope's first wealth, ostage of promist weale,
   Breakefast of *Love* – but lo, lo, where she is:
   Cease we to praise, now pray we for a kisse.

80   Sweet swelling lip, well maist thou swell in pride,
   Since best wits thinke it wit thee to admire;
   Nature's praise, Vertue's stall, *Cupid's* cold fire,
Whence words, not words, but heav'nly graces slide:
The new *Pernassus*, where the Muses bide,
   Sweetner of musicke, wisedome's beautifier:
   Breather of life, and fastner of desire,
Where Beautie's blush in Honour's graine is dide.
   Thus much my heart compeld my mouth to say,
   But now spite of my heart my mouth will stay,
Loathing all lies, doubting this Flatterie is;
   And no spurre can his resty race renew,
   Without how farre this praise is short of you,
Sweet lip, you teach my mouth with one sweet kisse.

81   O kisse, which doest those ruddie gemmes impart,
Or gemmes, or frutes of new-found *Paradise*,
Breathing all blisse and sweetning to the heart,
   Teaching dumbe lips a nobler exercise:
   O kisse, which soules, even soules together ties
By linkes of *Love*, and only Nature's art;
How faine would I paint thee to all men's eyes,
Or of thy gifts at least shade out some part.
   But she forbids; with blushing words, she sayes
   She builds her fame on higher seated praise:
But my heart burnes, I cannot silent be.
   Then since (deare life) you faine would have me peace,
   And I, mad with delight, want wit to cease,
Stop you my mouth with still still kissing me.

82   Nymph of the gard'n, where all beauties be;
   Beauties which do in excellencie passe
   His who till death lookt in a watrie glasse,
Of hers whom naked the *Trojan* boy did see:
Sweet gard'n Nymph, which keepes the Cherrie tree,
   Whose fruit doth farre th'*Esperian* tast surpasse:
   Most sweet-faire, most faire-sweet, do not, alas,

From comming neare those Cherries banish me:
  For though full of desire, emptie of wit,
Admitted late by your best-graced grace,
I caught at one of them a hungrie bit;
Pardon that fault, once more graunt me the place,
    And I do sweare even by the same delight,
    I will but kisse, I never more will bite.

83   Good brother *Philip*, I have borne you long;
    I was content you should in favour creepe,
    While craftily you seem'd your cut to keepe,
As though that faire soft hand did you great wrong.
I bare (with Envie) yet I bare your song,
    When in her necke you did *Love* ditties peepe;
    Nay, more foole I, oft suffered you to sleepe
In Lillies' neast, where *Love's* selfe lies along.
    What, doth high place ambitious thoughts augment?
    Is sawcinesse reward of curtesie?
Cannot such grace your silly selfe content,
But you must needs with those lips billing be,
    And through those lips drinke Nectar from that toong?
    Leave that, sir *Phip*, least off your necke be wroong.

Third song
If *Orpheus'* voyce had force to breathe such musicke's love
Through pores of sencelesse tree, as it could make them move:
If stones good measure daunc'd, the *Theban* walles to build,
To cadence of the tunes, which *Amphyon's* lyre did yeeld,
More cause a like effect at leastwise bringeth:
O stones, O trees, learne hearing: *Stella* singeth.

If Love might sweet'n so a boy of shepheard' brood,
To make a Lyzard dull to taste Love's daintie food;
If Eagle fierce could so in *Grecian* Mayd delight,
As his light was her eyes, her death his endlesse night;
Earth gave that Love; heav'n, I trow, Love refineth:
O birds, O beasts, looke, love; lo, *Stella* shineth.

The birds, beasts, stones and trees feele this, and feeling, love:
And if the trees, nor stones stirre not the same to prove,
Nor beasts, nor birds do come unto this blessed gaze,

Know, that small Love is quicke, and great Love doth amaze:
They are amaz'd, but you with reason armed,
O eyes, O eares of men, how are you charmed!

84 Highway since you my chiefe *Pernassus* be,
        And that my Muse, to some eares not unsweet,
        Tempers her words to trampling horse's feet
    More oft then to a chamber melodie;
    Now blessed you, beare onward blessed me
        To her, where I my heart safeliest shall meet.
        My Muse and I must you of dutie greet
    With thankes and wishes, wishing thankfully.
        Be you still faire, honoured by publike heed,
    By no encrochment wrongd, nor time forgot;
    Nor blam'd for bloud, nor sham'd for sinfull deed:
    And that you know I envy you no lot
        Of highest wish, I wish you so much blisse,
        Hundreds of yeares you *Stella's* feet may kisse.

85 I see the house; my heart thy selfe containe;
        Beware full sailes drowne not thy tottring barge,
        Least joy, by Nature apt sprites to enlarge,
    Thee to thy wracke beyond thy limits straine:
    Nor do like Lords, whose weake confused braine,
        Not pointing to fit folkes each undercharge,
        While everie office themselves will discharge,
    With doing all, leave nothing done but paine.
        But give apt servants their due place, let eyes
    See Beautie's totall summe summ'd in her face;
    Let eares heare speech, which wit to wonder ties;
    Let breath sucke up those sweetes, let armes embracc
        The globe of weale, lips *Love's* indentures make:
        Thou but of all the kingly Tribute take.

Fourth song
Onely joy, now here you are,
Fit to heare and ease my care:
Let my whispering voyce obtaine
Sweete reward for sharpest paine:
Take me to thee, and thee to me.
'No, no, no, no, my Deare, let be.'

Night hath closd all in her cloke,
Twinckling starres Love-thoughts provoke:
Danger hence good care doth keepe,
Jealousie it selfe doth sleepe:
Take me to thee, and thee to me.
'No, no, no, no, my Deare, let be.'

Better place no wit can find,
Cupid's yoke to loose or bind:
These sweet flowers on fine bed too,
Us in their best language woo:
Take me to thee, and thee to me.
'No, no, no, no, my Deare, let be.'

This small light the Moone bestowes,
Serves thy beames but to disclose,
So to raise my hap more hie:
Feare not else, none can us spie:
Take me to thee, and thee to me.
'No, no, no, no, my Deare, let be.'

That you heard was but a Mouse,
Dumbe sleepe holdeth all the house:
Yet asleep, me thinkes they say,
Yong folkes, take time while you may:
Take me to thee, and thee to me.
'No, no, no, no, my Deare, let be.'

Niggard Time threats, if we misse
This large offer of our blisse,
Long stay ere he graunt the same:
Sweet then, while each thing doth frame,
Take me to thee, and thee to me.
'No, no, no, no, my Deare, let be.'

Your faire mother is a bed,
Candles out, and curtaines spread:
She thinkes you do letters write:
Write, but first let me endite:
Take me to thee, and thee to me.
'No, no, no, no, my Deare, let be.'

Sweet alas, why strive you thus?
Concord better fitteth us:
Leave to *Mars* the force of hands,
Your power in your beautie stands:
Take me to thee, and thee to me.
'No, no, no, no, my Deare, let be.'

Wo to me, and do you sweare
Me to hate, but I forbeare?
Cursed be my destines all
That brought me so high to fall:
Soone with my death I will please thee.
'No, no, no, no, my Deare, let be.'

86 Alas, whence came this change of lookes? If I
   Have chang'd desert, let mine owne conscience be
   A still felt plague, to selfe-condemning me:
  Let wo gripe on my heart, shame loade mine eye.
  But if all faith, like spotlesse Ermine ly
   Safe in my soule, which only doth to thee
   (As his sole object of felicitie)
  With wings of *Love* in aire of wonder flie,
   O ease your hand, treate not so hard your slave;
  In justice paines come not till faults do call:
  Or if I needs (sweet Judge) must torments have,
  Use something else to chast'n me withall
   Then those blest eyes, where all my hopes do dwell:
   No doome should make one's heav'n become his hell.

Fifth song   *Omitted*

Sixth song
O you that heare this voice,
O you that see this face,
Say whether of the choice
Deserves the former place:
Feare not to judge this bate,
For it is void of hate.

This side doth beauty take,
For that doth Musike speake,

Fit oratours to make
The strongest judgements weake:
The barre to plead their right,
Is only true delight.

Thus doth the voice and face,
These gentle Lawyers, wage,
Like loving brothers' case
For father's heritage,
That each, while each contends,
It selfe to other lends.

For beautie beautifies
With heavenly hew and grace
The heavenly harmonies;
And in this faultlesse face
The perfect beauties be
A perfect harmony.

Musicke more loftly swels
In speeches nobly placed:
Beauty as farre excels
In action aptly graced:
A friend each party drawes,
To countenance his cause:

Love more affected seemes
To beautie's lovely light,
And wonder more esteemes
Of Musick's wondrous might:
But both to both so bent,
As both in both are spent.

Musike doth witnesse call
The eare, his truth to trie:
Beauty brings to the hall
The judgement of the eye;
Both in their objects such,
As no exceptions tutch.

The common sence, which might
Be Arbiter of this,
To be, forsooth, upright,
To both sides partiall is:
He layes on this chiefe praise,
Chiefe praise on that he laies.

Then reason, Princesse hy,
Whose throne is in the mind,
Which Musicke can in sky
And hidden beauties find,
Say whether thou wilt crowne
With limitlesse renowne.

Seventh song
Whose senses in so evill consort their stepdame Nature laies,
That ravishing delight in them most sweete tunes do not raise;
Or if they do delight therein, yet are so closde with wit,
As with sententious lips to set a title vaine on it:
O let them heare these sacred tunes, and learne in wonder's
    schooles,
To be, in things past bounds of wit, fooles, if they be not
    fooles.

Who have so leaden eyes as not to see sweet beautie's show,
Or seeing, have so wodden wits as not that worth to know;
Or knowing, have so muddy minds as not to be in love;
Or loving, have so frothy thoughts as easly thence to move:
O let them see these heavenly beames, and in faire letters reede
A lesson fit, both sight and skill, love and firme love to breed.

Heare then, but then with wonder heare; see, but adoring see,
No mortall gifts, no earthly fruites now here descended be:
See, do you see this face? A face? Nay image of the skies,
Of which the two life-giving lights are figured in her eyes:
Heare you this soule-invading voice, and count it but a voice?
The very essence of their tunes, when Angels do rejoyce.

Eighth song
In a grove most rich of shade,
Where birds wanton musicke made,

May then yong his pide weedes showing,
New perfumed with flowers fresh growing,

Astrophel with *Stella* sweete,
Did for mutuall comfort meete,
Both within themselves oppressed,
But each in the other blessed.

Him great harmes had taught much care,
Her faire necke a foule yoke bare;
But her sight his cares did banish,
In his sight her yoke did vanish.

Wept they had, alas the while,
But now teares themselves did smile,
While their eyes by love directed,
Enterchangeably reflected.

Sigh they did, but now betwixt
Sighs of woes were glad sighs mixt,
With armes crost, yet testifying
Restlesse rest, and living dying.

Their eares hungry of each word
Which the deere tongue would afford,
But their tongues restrained from walking,
Till their harts had ended talking.

But when their tongues could not speake,
Love it selfe did silence breake;
Love did set his lips asunder,
Thus to speake in love and wonder:

'*Stella*, soveraigne of my joy,
Faire triumpher of annoy,
Stella, starre of heavenly fier,
Stella, loadstar of desier.

'*Stella*, in whose shining eyes
Are the lights of *Cupid's* skies,
Whose beames, where they once are darted,
Love therewith is streight imparted.

'*Stella*, whose voice when it speakes,
Senses all asunder breakes;
Stella, whose voice when it singeth,
Angels to acquaintance bringeth.

'*Stella*, in whose body is
Writ each character of blisse,
Whose face all, all beauty passeth,
Save thy mind which yet surpasseth:

'Graunt, O graunt — but speech, alas,
Failes me, fearing on to passe;
Graunt — O me, what am I saying?
But no fault there is in praying.

'Graunt, O deere, on knees I pray,'
(Knees on ground he then did stay)
'That not I, but since I love you,
Time and place for me may move you.

'Never season was more fit,
Never roome more apt for it;
Smiling ayre allowes my reason,
These birds sing, "Now use the season."

'This small wind which so sweete is,
See how it the leaves doth kisse,
Ech tree in his best attiring,
Sense of love to love inspiring.

'Love makes earth the water drinke,
Love to earth makes water sinke;
And if dumbe things be so witty,
Shall a heavenly grace want pitty?'

There his hands in their speech, faine
Would have made tongue's language plaine;
But her hands his hands repelling,
Gave repulse all grace excelling.

Then she spake; her speech was such
As not eares but hart did tuch,
While such wise she love denied
As yet love she signified.

'*Astrophel*' sayd she, 'my love
Cease in these effects to prove:
Now be still, yet still beleeve me,
Thy griefe more than death would grieve me.

'If that any thought in me
Can tast comfort but of thee,
Let me, fed with hellish anguish,
Joylesse, hopelesse, endlesse languish.

'If those eyes you praised be
Half so deere as you to me,
Let me home returne, starke blinded
Of those eyes, and blinder minded.

'If to secret of my hart
I do any wish impart
Where thou art not formost placed,
Be both wish and I defaced.

'If more may be sayd, I say,
All my blisse in thee I lay;
If thou love, my love content thee,
For all love, all faith is meant thee.

'Trust me, while I thee deny,
In my selfe the smart I try;
Tyran honour doth thus use thee;
Stella's selfe might not refuse thee.

'Therefore, Deere, this no more move,
Least, though I leave not thy love
Which too deep in me is framed,
I should blush when thou art named.'

Therewithall away she went,
Leaving him so passion rent
With what she had done and spoken,
That therewith my song is broken.

Ninth song
Go my flocke, go get you hence,
Seeke a better place of feeding,
Where you may have some defence
From the stormes in my breast breeding,
And showers from mine eyes proceeding.

Leave a wretch, in whom all wo
Can abide to keepe no measure;
Merry flocke, such one forgo,
Unto whom mirth is displeasure,
Only rich in mischiefe's treasure.

Yet alas before you go,
Heare your wofull maister's story,
Which to stones I els would show
Sorrow onely then hath glory,
When tis excellently sory.

Stella fiercest shepherdesse,
Fiercest but yet fairest ever;
Stella whom, O heavens, do blesse,
Tho against me shee persever,
Tho I blisse enherit never;

Stella hath refused me,
Stella who more love hath proved
In this caitife hart to be
Then can in good eawes be moved
Toward *Lamkins* best beloved.

Stella hath refused me:
Astrophel, that so wel served,
In this pleasant spring must see,
While in pride flowers be preserved,
Himselfe onely winter-sterved.

Why alas doth she then sweare
That she loveth me so dearely,
Seing me so long to beare
Coles of love that burne so clearely,
And yet leave me helplesse meerely?

Is that love? Forsooth I trow,
If I saw my good dog grieved,
And a helpe for him did know,
My love should not be beleeved
But he were by me releeved.

No, she hates me, wellaway,
Faining love, somewhat to please me;
For she knowes, if she display
All her hate, death soone would seaze me,
And of hideous torments ease me.

Then adieu, deere flocke, adieu:
But alas, if in your straying
Heavenly *Stella* meete with you,
Tell her in your piteous blaying,
Her poore slave's unjust decaying.

87   When I was forst from *Stella* ever deere,
      Stella food of my thoughts, hart of my hart,
      Stella whose eyes make all my tempests cleere,
          By iron lawes of duty to depart;
          Alas I found, that she with me did smart;
      I saw that teares did in her eyes appeare;
      I saw that sighes her sweetest lips did part,
      And her sad words my saddest sence did heare.
          For me, I wept to see pearles scattered so,
          I sighd her sighes, and wailed for her wo,
      Yet swam in joy, such love in her was seene.
          Thus while th' effect most bitter was to me,
          And nothing then the cause more sweet could be,
      I had bene vext, if vext I had not beene.

88   Out, traytour absence, darest thou counsell me
      From my deare Captainnesse to run away,

Because in brave array heere marcheth she,
That to win me oft shewes a present pay?
Is faith so weake? Or is such force in thee?
When Sun is hid, can starres such beames display?
Cannot heavn's food, once felt, keepe stomakes free
From base desire on earthly cates to pray?
   Tush, absence; while thy mistes eclipse that light,
   My Orphan sence flies to the inward sight,
Where memory sets foorth the beames of love;
   That where before hart loved and eyes did see,
   In hart both sight and love now coupled be;
United powers make each the stronger prove.

89   Now that of absence the most irksome night
     With darkest shade doth overcome my day;
     Since *Stella's* eyes, wont to give me my day,
Leaving my Hemisphere, leave me in night,
Each day seemes long, and longs for long-staid night;
     The night, as tedious, wooes th'approch of day;
     Tired with the dusty toiles of busie day,
Languisht with horrors of the silent night,
Suffering the evils both of the day and night,
     While no night is more darke then is my day,
     Nor no day hath lesse quiet then my night;
     With such bad mixture of my night and day,
That living thus in blackest winter night,
     I feele the flames of hottest sommer day.

90   *Stella,* thinke not that I by verse seeke fame,
     Who seeke, who hope, who love, who live but thee;
     Thine eyes my pride, thy lips my history:
If thou praise not, all other praise is shame.
Nor so ambitious am I, as to frame
     A nest for my yong praise in Lawrell tree:
     In truth I sweare, I wish not there should be
Graved in mine Epitaph a Poet's name:
     Ne if I would, could I just title make,
That any laud to me thereof should grow,
Without my plumes from others' wings I take.
For nothing from my wit or will doth flow,
     Since all my words thy beauty doth endite,
     And love doth hold my hand, and makes me write.

91   *Stella*, while now by honour's cruell might
      I am from you, light of my life, mis-led,
      And that faire you, my Sunne, thus overspred
   With absence' Vaile, I live in Sorowe's night;
   If this darke place yet shew, like candle light,
      Some beautie's peece, as amber-coloured hed,
      Milke hands, rose cheeks, or lips more sweet, more red,
   Or seeing jets, blacke, but in blacknesse bright:
      They please, I do confesse, they please mine eyes,
   But why? Because of you they models be,
   Models such be wood-globes of glistring skies.
   Deere, therefore be not jealous over me,
      If you heare that they seeme my hart to move;
      Not them, O no, but you in them I love.

92   Be your words made (good Sir) of Indian ware,
      That you allow me them by so small rate?
      Or do you cutted Spartanes imitate?
   Or do you meane my tender eares to spare,
   That to my questions you so totall are?
      When I demaund of *Phenix Stella's* state,
      You say, forsooth, you left her well of late.
   O God, thinke you that satisfies my care?
      I would know whether she did sit or walke,
   How cloth'd, how waited on, sighd she or smilde,
   Whereof, with whom, how often did she talke,
   With what pastime time's journey she beguilde,
      If her lips daignd to sweeten my poore name.
      Say all, and all well sayd, still say the same.

Tenth song
O Deare life, when shall it be
   That mine eyes thine eyes may see?
   And in them thy mind discover
   Whether absence have had force
   Thy remembrance to divorce
   From the image of thy lover?

O if I my selfe find not
   After parting ought forgot,
   Nor debard from beautie's treasure,

Let no tongue aspire to tell
In what high joyes I shall dwell;
Only thought aymes at the pleasure.

Thought therefore I will send thee
To take up the place for me;
Long I will not after tary.
There unseene thou maist be bold
Those faire wonders to behold,
Which in them my hopes do cary.

Thought, see thou no place forbeare,
Enter bravely every where;
Seaze on all to her belonging;
But if thou wouldst garded be,
Fearing her beames, take with thee
Strength of liking, rage of longing.

Think of that most gratefull time,
When my leaping hart will clime
In my lips to have his biding,
There those roses for to kisse
Which do breath a sugred blisse,
Opening rubies, pearles deviding.

Think of my most Princely power,
When I blessed shall devower
With my greedy licorous sences
Beauty, musicke, sweetnesse, love,
While she doth against me prove
Her strong darts but weake defences.

Thinke, thinke of those dalyings,
When with Dovelike murmurings,
With glad moning passed anguish,
We change eyes, and hart for hart,
Each to other do depart,
Joying till joy make us languish.

O my thought, my thoughts, surcease;
Thy delights my woes increase,

My life melts with too much thinking;
Thinke no more but die in me
Till thou shalt revived be,
At her lips my Nectar drinking.

93   O fate, O fault, O curse, child of my blisse,
     What sobs can give words grace my griefe to show?
     What inke is blacke inough to paint my wo?
  Through me, wretch me, even *Stella* vexed is.
  Yet truth (if Caitif's breath may call thee) this
     Witnesse with me, that my foule stumbling so
     From carelesnesse did in no maner grow,
  But wit confus'd with too much care did misse.
     And do I then my selfe this vaine scuse give?
  I have (live I and know this?) harmed thee;
  Tho worlds quite me, shall I my selfe forgive?
  Only with paines my paines thus eased be,
     That all thy hurts in my hart's wracke I reede;
     I cry thy sighs; my deere, thy teares I bleede.

94   Griefe, find the words, for thou hast made my braine
     So darke with misty vapors, which arise
     From out thy heavy mould, that inbent eyes
  Can scarce discerne the shape of mine owne paine.
  Do thou then (for thou canst) do thou complaine
     For my poore soule, which now that sicknesse tries
     Which even to sence, sence of it selfe denies,
  Though harbengers of death lodge there his traine:
     Or if thy love of plaint yet mine forbeares,
  As of a caitife worthy so to die,
  Yet waile thy selfe, and waile with causefull teares
  That though in wretchednesse thy life doth lie,
  Yet growest more wretched then thy nature beares,
  By being placed in such a wretch as I.

95   Yet sighs, deere sighs, indeede true friends you are,
     That do not leave your best friend at the wurst,
     But as you with my breast I oft have nurst,
  So gratefull now you waite upon my care.
  Faint coward joy no longer tarry dare,
     Seeing hope yeeld when this wo strake him furst:

Delight protests he is not for the accurst,
Though oft himselfe my mate-in-armes he sware.
   Nay, sorrow comes with such maine rage, that he
Kils his owne children, teares, finding that they
By love were made apt to consort with me.
Only true sighs, you do not go away,
      Thanke may you have for such a thankfull part,
      Thanke-worthiest yet when you shall breake my hart.

96   Thought with good cause thou likest so well the night,
          Since kind or chance gives both one liverie;
          Both sadly blacke, both blackly darkned be,
       Night bard from Sun, thou from thy owne sunne's light;
       Silence in both displaies his sullen might,
          Slow heaviness in both holds one degree,
          That full of doubts, thou of perplexity;
       Thy teares expresse night's native moisture right:
          In both a mazefull solitarinesse:
       In night, of sprites the gastly powers stur,
       In thee, or sprites or sprited gastlinesse:
       But, but (alas) night's side the ods hath fur,
          For that at length yet doth invite some rest,
          Thou, though still tired, yet still doost it detest.

97   *Dian* that faine would cheare her friend the Night,
          Shewes her oft at the full her fairest face,
          Bringing with her those starry Nimphs, whose chace
       From heavenly standing hits each mortall wight.
       But ah, poore Night, in love with *Phœbus'* light,
          And endlesly dispairing of his grace,
          Her selfe (to shew no other joy hath place)
       Silent and sad in mourning weedes doth dight:
          Even so (alas) a Lady, *Dian's* peere,
       With choise delights and rarest company,
       Would faine drive cloudes from out my heavy cheere.
       But wo is me, though joy it selfe were she,
          She could not shew my blind braine waies of joy,
          While I dispaire my Sunne's sight to enjoy.

98   Ah bed, the field where joye's peace some do see,
          The field where all my thoughts to warre be traind,

How is thy grace by my strange fortune staind!
How thy lee shores by my sighes stormed be!
With sweete soft shades thou oft invitest me
    To steale some rest, but wretch I am constrain'd,
    (Spurd with love's spur, though gald and shortly raind
With care's hard hand) to turne and tosse in thee,
    While the blacke horrors of the silent night
    Paint woe's blacke face so lively to my sight,
That tedious leasure marks each wrinckled line:
    But when *Aurora* leades out *Phœbus'* daunce,
    Mine eyes then only winke, for spite perchance,
That wormes should have their Sun, and I want mine.

99   When far spent night perswades each mortall eye,
        To whom nor art nor nature graunteth light,
        To lay his then marke-wanting shafts of sight,
    Clos'd with their quivers, in sleep's armory;
    With windowes ope then most my mind doth lie,
        Viewing the shape of darknesse and delight,
        Takes in that sad hue, which with th' inward night
    Of his mazde powers keepes perfit harmony:
        But when birds charme, and that sweete aire, which is
    Morne's messenger, with rose enameld skies
    Cals each wight to salute the floure of blisse,
    In tombe of lids then buried are mine eyes,
        Forst by their Lord, who is asham'd to find
        Such light in sense, with such a darkned mind.

100   O teares, no teares but raine from beautie's skies,
        Making those Lillies and those Roses grow,
        Which ay most faire, now more then most faire show,
    While gracefull pitty beauty beautifies:
    O honied sighs, which from that breast do rise,
        Whose pants do make unspilling creame to flow,
        Wing'd with whose breath so pleasing *Zephires* blow,
    As can refresh the hell where my soule fries:
        O plaints conserv'd in such a sugred phraise,
        That eloquence it selfe envies your praise,
    While sobd out words a perfect Musike give:
        Such teares, sighs, plaints, no sorrow is, but joy;
        Of if such heavenly signes must prove annoy,
    All mirth farewell, let me in sorrow live.

101   *Stella* is sicke, and in that sicke bed lies
      Sweetnesse, that breathes and pants as oft as she:
      And grace, sicke too, such fine conclusions tries,
      That sicknesse brags it selfe best graced to be.
      Beauty is sicke, but sicke in so faire guise,
      That in that palenesse beautie's white we see;
      And joy, which is inseperate from those eyes,
      Stella now learnes (strange case) to weepe in thee.
          Love moves thy paine, and like a faithfull page,
      As thy lookes sturre, runs up and downe to make
      All folkes prest at thy will thy paine to 'swage.
      Nature with care sweates for her darling's sake,
          Knowing worlds passe, ere she enough can find
          Of such heaven stuffe to cloath so heavenly mynde.

102   Where be those Roses gone, which sweetned so our eyes?
          Where those red cheeks, which oft with faire encrease did
              frame
          The height of honor in the kindly badge of shame?
      Who hath the crimson weeds stolne from my morning skies?
      How doth the colour vade of those vermillion dies
          Which Nature' selfe did make, and selfe engraind the same?
          I would know by what right this palenesse overcame
      That hue, whose force my hart still unto thraldome ties.
          Gallein's adoptive sonnes, who by a beaten way
          Their judgements hackney on, the fault on sicknesse lay,
      But feeling proofe makes me say they mistake it furre:
          It is but love, which makes his paper perfit white
          To write therein more fresh the story of delight,
      While beautie's reddest inke *Venus* for him doth sturre.

103   O happie Tems, that didst my *Stella* beare,
      I saw thy selfe with many a smiling line
      Upon thy cheerefull face, joye's livery weare,
      While those faire planets on thy streames did shine.
      The bote for joy could not to daunce forbeare,
      While wanton winds with beauties so devine
      Ravisht, staid not, till in her golden haire
      They did themselves (O sweetest prison) twine.
          And faine those *Æols'* youth there would their stay
      Have made, but forst by Nature still to flie,

First did with puffing kisse those lockes display.
She so discheveld, blusht; from window I
    With sight thereof cride out; 'O faire disgrace,
    Let honor's selfe to thee graunt highest place.'

104   Envious wits, what hath bene mine offence,
    That with such poysonous care my lookes you marke,
    That to each word, nay sigh of mine you harke,
As grudging me my sorrowe's eloquence?
Ah, is it not enough, that I am thence,
    Thence, so farre thence, that scarcely any sparke
    Of comfort dare come to this dungeon darke,
Where rigour's exile lockes up all my sense?
    But if I by a happy window passe,
If I but stars upon mine armour beare,
Sicke, thirsty, glad (though but of empty glasse:)
Your morall notes straight my hid meaning teare
    From out my ribs, and puffing prove that I
    Do *Stella* love. Fooles, who doth it deny?

Eleventh song
'Who is it that this darke night,
Underneath my window playneth?'
It is one who from thy sight,
Being (ah) exild, disdayneth
Every other vulgar light.

'Why alas, and are you he?
Be not yet those fancies changed?'
Deere, when you find change in me,
Though from me you be estranged
Let my chaunge to ruine be.

'Well in absence this will dy,
Leave to see, and leave to wonder.'
Absence sure will helpe, if I
Can learne how my selfe to sunder
From what in my hart doth ly.

'But time will these thoughts remove:
Time doth worke what no man knoweth.'

Time doth as the subject prove;
With time still th' affection groweth
In the faithfull Turtle dove.

'What if you new beauties see,
Will not they stir new affection?'
I will thinke theye pictures be,
(Image-like of Saints' perfection)
Poorely counterfeting thee.

'But your reason's purest light,
Bids you leave such minds to nourish.'
Deere, do reason no such spite,
Never doth thy beauty florish
More then in my reason's sight.

'But the wrongs love beares will make
Love at length leave undertaking.'
No, the more fooles it do shake,
In a ground of so firme making,
Deeper still they drive the stake.

'Peace, I thinke that some give eare:
Come no more, least I get anger.'
Blisse, I will my blisse forbeare,
Fearing (sweete) you to endanger,
But my soule shall harbour there.

'Well, be gone, be gone I say,
Lest that *Argus'* eyes perceive you.'
O unjustest fortune's sway,
Which can make me thus to leave you,
And from lowts to run away.

105   Unhappie sight, and hath she vanisht by
       So neere, in so good time, so free a place?
       Dead glasse, doost thou thy object so imbrace,
    As what my hart still sees thou canst not spie?
    I sweare by her I love and lacke, that I
       Was not in fault, who bent thy dazling race
       Onely unto the heav'n of *Stella's* face,

Counting but dust what in the way did lie.
    But cease mine eyes, your teares do witnesse well
That you, guiltlesse thereof, your Nectar mist:
Curst be the page from whome the bad torch fell,
Curst be the night which did your strife resist,
    Curst be the Cochman which did drive so fast,
    With no worse curse then absence makes me tast.

106   O absent presence! *Stella* is not here:
        False flattering hope, that with so faire a face
        Bare me in hand, that in this Orphane place
    Stella, I say, my *Stella*, should appeare;
    What saist thou now, where is that dainty cheere
        Thou toldst mine eyes should helpe their famisht case?
        But thou art gone, now that selfe felt disgrace
    Doth make me most to wish thy comfort neere.
        But heere I do store of faire Ladies meete,
        Who may with charme of conversation sweete
    Make in my heavy mould new thoughts to grow:
        Sure they prevaile as much with me, as he
        That bad his friend, but then new maim'd, to be
    Mery with him, and not thinke of his woe.

107   *Stella* since thou so right a Princesse art
        Of all the powers which life bestowes on me,
        That ere by them ought undertaken be,
    They first resort unto that soveraigne part;
    Sweete, for a while give respite to my hart,
        Which pants as though it still should leape to thee,
        And on my thoughts give thy Lieftenancy
    To this great cause, which needs both use and art.
        And as a Queene, who from her presence sends
    Whom she imployes, dismisse from thee my wit,
    Till it have wrought what thy owne will attends.
    On servants' shame oft Maister's blame doth sit;
        O let not fooles in me thy workes reprove,
        And scorning say, 'See, what it is to love!'

108   When sorrow (using mine owne fier's might)
        Melts downe his lead into my boyling brest,
        Through that darke fornace to my hart opprest,
    There shines a joy from thee my only light;

But soone as thought of thee breeds my delight,
    And my yong soule flutters to thee, his nest,
    Most rude dispaire, my daily unbidden guest,
Clips streight my wings, streight wraps me in his night,
    And makes me then bow downe my head, and say,
'Ah, what doth *Phœbus'* gold that wretch availe,
Whom iron doores do keepe from use of day?'
So strangely (alas) thy works in me prevaile,
    That in my woes for thee thou art my joy,
    And in my joyes for thee my only annoy.

From *Certaine Sonnets*
Thou blind man's marke, thou foole's selfe chosen snare,
Fond fancie's scum, and dregs of scattred thought,
Band of all evils, cradle of causelesse care,
    Thou web of will, whose end is never wrought:
    Desire, desire I have too dearely bought
With price of mangled mind thy worthlesse ware:
Too long, too long asleepe thou hast me brought,
Who should my mind to higher things prepare.
But yet in vaine thou hast my ruine sought,
    In vaine thou madest me to vaine things aspire,
    In vaine thou kindlest all thy smokie fire;
For vertue hath this better lesson taught,
    Within my selfe to seeke my onelie hire,
    Desiring nought but how to kill desire.

    Leave me, O Love, which reachest but to dust,
And thou, my mind, aspire to higher things:
Grow rich in that which never taketh rust:
What ever fades but fading pleasure brings.
    Draw in thy beames, and humble all thy might
To that sweet yoke, where lasting freedomes be,
Which breakes the clowdes and opens forth the light,
That doth both shine and give us sight to see.
    O take fast hold, let that light be thy guide,
In this small course which birth drawes out to death,
And thinke how evill becommeth him to slide,
Who seeketh heav'n, and comes of heav'nly breath.
    Then farewell world, thy uttermost I see:
    Eternall Love maintaine thy life in me.

SAMUEL DANIEL

To Delia

Sonnet 1
Unto the boundles Ocean of thy beautie
  Runs this poore river, charg'd with streams of zeale,
  Returning thee the trybute of my duty,
  Which heere my love, my youth, my plaints reveale.
Heere I unclaspe the booke of my charg'd soule,
  Where I have cast th'accounts of all my care:
  Heere have I summ'd my sighes; heere I enrole
  How they were spent for thee; looke what they are.
Looke on the deere expences of my youth,
  And see how just I reckon with thine eyes:
  Examine well thy beauty with my truth,
  And crosse my cares ere greater summes arise.
Reade it (sweete maide) though it be doone but slightly:
Who can shew all his love, doth love but lightly.

Sonnet 2
Goe, wayling verse, the Infants of my love,
  Minerva-lyke, brought foorth without a mother:
  Present the Image of the cares I prove,
  Witnes your Father's griefe exceedes all other.
Sigh out a story of her cruell deedes,
  With interrupted accents of dispaire:
  A monument that whosoever reedes,
  May justly praise, and blame my loveless Fayre
Say her disdaine hath dryed up my blood,
  And starved you, in succours still denying:
  Presse to her eyes, importune me some good;
  Waken her sleeping pitty with your crying.
Knock at her hard hart, beg till you have mov'd her,
And tell th'unkind, how deerely I have lov'd her.

Sonnet 3
If so it hap this of-spring of my care,
    These fatall! Antheames, sad and mournful songs,
    Come to their view who like afflicted are.
    Ah let them sigh theyr owne, and mone my wrongs.
But untoucht harts, with unaffected eye,
    Approch not to behold so great distresse:
    Cleer-sighted, you soone note what is awry,
    Whilst blinded ones mine errours never gesse.
You blinded soules whom youth and errors leade,
    You outcast Eaglets, dazeled with your sunne.
    Ah you, and none but you my sorrowes reade,
    You best can judge the wrongs that she hath done:
That she had done, the motive of my paine,
Who whilst I love, doth kill me with disdaine.

Sonnet 4
These plaintive verse, the Posts of my desire,
    Which haste for succour to her slowe regard,
    Beare not report of any slender fire,
    Forging a griefe to winne a fame's reward.
Nor are my passions lymned for outward hewe,
    For that no colours can depaint my sorrows:
    Delia her selfe, and all the world, may view
    Best in my face, where cares hath till'd deepe furrows.
No Bayes I seeke to deck my mourning brow,
    O cleer-eyde Rector of the holy Hill:
    My humble accents beare the Olive bough
    Of intercession to a tyrant's will.
These lines I use, t'unburthen mine owne hart;
My love affects no fame, nor steemes of art.

Sonnet 5
Whilst youth and error led my wandring minde,
    And sette my thoughts in heedles waies to range,
    All unawares a Goddesse chaste I finde,
    (*Diana*-like) to worke my suddaine change.
For her no sooner had mine eye bewraid,
    But with disdaine to see me in that place,
    With fairest hand, the sweet unkindest maid
    Casts water-cold disdaine upon my face:

Which turn'd my sport into a Hart's despaire,
　　Which still is chac'd, while I have any breath,
　　By mine owne thoughts, sette on mee by my faire;
　　My thoughts (like houndes) pursue me to my death.
Those that I fostred of mine owne accord
Are made by her to murder thus theyr Lord.

Sonnet 6

Fayre is my love, and cruell as sh'is fayre;
　　Her brow shades frowns, althogh her eyes are sunny;
　　Her smyles are lightning, though her pride, dispaire;
　　And her disdaines are gall, her favours hunny.
A modest mayde, deckt with a blush of honour,
　　Whose feete do tread greene pathes of youth and love;
　　The wonder of all eyes that looke upon her:
　　Sacred on earth, design'd a Saint above.
Chastity and Beauty, which were deadly foes,
　　Live reconciled friends within her brow:
　　And had she pitty to conjoyne with those,
　　Then who had heard the plaints I utter now?
O had she not been fayre, and thus unkind,
My Muse had slept, and none had knowne my minde.

Sonnet 7

O had shee not beene faire and thus unkind,
　　Then had no finger pointed at my lightnes:
　　The world had never knowne what I doe finde,
　　And clowdes obscure had shaded stil her brightnes.
Then had no Censor's eye these lynes survaide,
　　Nor graver browes have judg'd my Muse so vaine;
　　No sunne my blush and errour had bewraid,
　　Nor yet the world had heard of such disdaine.
Then had I walkt with bold erected face;
　　No down-cast looke had signified my misse:
　　But my degraded hopes, with such disgrace
　　Did force me grone out griefes, and utter this.
For being full, should I not then have spoken,
My sence, oppress'd, had faild, and hart had broken.

Sonnet 8

Thou poore hart, sacrifiz'd unto the fairest,
   Hast sent the incens of thy sighes to heaven;
   And still against her frownes fresh vowes repayrest,
   And made thy passions with her beauty even.
And you, mine eyes, the agents of my hart,
   Told the dumbe message of my hidden griefe;
   And oft with carefull turnes, with silent Arte,
   Did treate the cruell Fayre to yeeld reliefe.
And you, my verse, the Advocates of love,
   Have followed hard the processe of my case,
   And urg'd that tytle which doth plainly prove
   My faith should win, if justice might have place.
Yet though I see that nought we doe can move her,
Tis not disdaine must make me cease to love her.

Sonnet 9

If thys be love, to draw a weary breath,
   Paint on floods, till the shore, cry to th'ayre;
   With downward lookes still reading on the earth
   The sad memorials of my love's despayre:
If this be love, to warre against my soule,
   Lye downe to waile, rise up to sigh and grieve;
   The never-resting stone of care to roule,
   Still to complaine my griefes, whilst none relieve:
If this be love, to cloathe me with darke thoughts,
   Haunting untroden pathes to waile apart;
   My pleasures, horror; Musique, tragick notes;
   Teares in mine eyes, and sorrow at my hart:
If thys be love, to live a living death,
O then love I, and draw this weary breath.

Sonnet 10

O then love I, and draw this weary breath
   For her, the cruell Fayre, within whose brow
   I written finde the sentence of my death,
   In unkinde letters, wrought she cares not how.
O thou that rul'st the confines of the night,
   Laughter-loving goddesse, worldly plesures' Queen,
   Intenerat that hart that sets so light
   The truest love that ever yet was seene;

And cause her leave to tryumph in this wise
    Uppon the prostrate spoyle of that poore hart
    That serves a Trophey to her conquering eyes,
    And must theyr glory to the world impart.
Once let her know, sh'hath done enough to prove me,
And let her pitty if she cannot love me.

Sonnet 11

Teares, vowes, and prayers winne the hardest hart;
    Teares, vowes, and prayers have I spent in vaine:
    Teares cannot soften Flint, nor vowes convart;
    Prayers prevaile not with a quaint disdaine.
I lose my teares, where I have lost my love;
    I vowe my faith, where faith is not regarded;
    I pray in vaine, a merciles to move:
    So rare a faith ought better be rewarded.
Yet though I cannot win her will with teares,
    Though my soule's Idoll scorneth all my vowes,
    Though all my prayers be to so deafe eares,
    No favour though the cruell faire allowes;
Yet will I weepe, vowe, pray to cruell shee;
Flint, frost, disdaine, weares, melts, and yeelds, we see.

Sonnet 12

My spotlesse love hoovers with purest wings
    About the temple of the proudest frame,
    Where blaze those lights, fayrest of earthly things,
    Which cleer our clowded world with brightest flame.
M'ambitious thoughts, confined in her face,
    Affect no honour but what she can give:
    My hopes doe rest in limits of her grace;
    I weigh no comfort unlesse she relieve.
For she that can my hart imparadize,
    Holds in her fairest hand what deerest is:
    My fortune's wheele's the circle of her eyes,
    Whose rowling grace deigne once a turne of blis.
All my live's sweet consists in her alone,
So much I love the most unloving one.

Sonnet 13
Behold what hap *Pigmalion* had to frame
  And carve his propper griefe upon a stone:
  My heavie fortune is much like the same;
  I worke on Flint, and that's the cause I mone.
For haplesse loe, even with mine owne desires,
  I figured on the Table of mine hart
  The fairest forme that all the world admires,
  And so did perrish by my proper arte.
And still I toyle to change the Marble breast
  Of her, whose sweetest grace I doe adore,
  Yet cannot finde her breathe unto my rest;
  Hard is her hart and woe is me therefore.
O happie he that joy'd his stone and arte;
Unhappy I, to love a stony harte.

Sonnet 14
Those snary locks are those same nets (my Deere)
  Where-with my libertie thou didst surprize:
  Love was the flame that fired me so neere;
  The Dart transpearsing were those Christall eyes.
Strong is the net and fervent is the flame;
  Deepe is the wounde, my sighes doe well report:
  Yet doe I love, adore, and praise the same
  That holds, that burnes, that wounds me in this sort.
And list not seeke to breake, to quench, to heale,
  The bonde, the flame, the wound that festreth so,
  By knife, by liquor, or by salve to deale;
  So much I please to perrish in my woe.
Yet least long travailes be above my strength,
Good *Delia*, lose, quench, heale me now at length.

Sonnet 15
If that a loyall hart and fayth unfained,
  If a sweete languish with a chast desire,
  If hunger-starven thoughts so long retained,
  Fed but with smoake, and cherisht but with fire,
And if a brow with cares' characters painted,
  Bewraies my love, with broken words halfe spoken,
  To her that sits in my thought's Temple sainted,
  And layes to view my Vultur-gnawne hart open:

If I have done due homage to her eyes,
   And had my sighes styll tending on her name,
   If on her love my life and honour lyes,
   And shee (th'unkindest mayd) still scornes the same;
Let this suffice, that all the world may see
The fault is hers, though mine the hurt must bee.

Sonnet 16
Happy in sleepe, waking content to languish,
   Imbracing clowdes by night, in day time mourne,
   My joyes but shadowes, touch of truth my anguish,
   Griefes ever springing, comforts never borne:
And still expecting when she will relent,
   Growne hoarce with crying 'Mercy, mercy gyve';
   So many vowes and prayers having spent,
   That weary of myselfe, I loathe to lyve.
And yet the Hydra of my cares renewes
   Still new-borne sorrowes of her fresh disdaine:
   And still my hope the sommer windes pursues,
   Finding no end nor period of my paine.
This is my state; my griefes doe touch so neerely,
And thus I live because I love her deerely.

Sonnet 17
Why should I sing in verse, why should I frame
   These sad neglected notes for her deere sake?
   Why should I offer up unto her name
   The sweetest sacrifice my youth can make?
Why should I strive to make her live for ever,
   That never deignes to give me joy to live?
   Why should m'afflicted Muse so much endevour
   Such honour unto crueltie to give?
If her defects have purchast her this fame,
   What should her vertues doe, her smiles, her love?
   If this her worst, how should her best inflame?
   What passions would her milder favours move?
Favours (I thinke) would sence quite over-come,
And that makes happy Lovers ever dombe.

Sonnet 18
Since the first looke that led me to this error,
    To this thoughts-maze, to my confusion tending,
    Still have I liv'd in griefe, in hope, in terror,
    The circle of my sorrowes never ending,
Yet cannot leave her love that holds me hatefull;
    Her eyes exact it, though her hart disdaines me:
    See what reward he hath that serves th'ungratefull;
    So true and loyall love no favour gaines mee.
Still must I whet my young desires abated
    Upon the Flint of such a hart rebelling;
    And all in vaine; her pride is so innated,
    She yeeldes no place at all for pittye's dwelling.
Oft have I tolde her that my soule did love her,
(And that with teares) yet all this will not move her.

Sonnet 19
Restore thy tresses to the golden Ore,
    Yeeld *Citherea's* sonne those Arkes of love;
    Bequeath the heavens the starrs that I adore,
    And to th'Orient doe thy Pearles remove.
Yeeld thy hands' pride unto th'Ivory white,
    T'*Arabian* odors give thy breathing sweet:
    Restore thy blush unto *Aurora* bright,
    To *Thetis* give the honour of thy feete.
Let *Venus* have thy graces, her resign'd,
    And thy sweete voyce give backe unto the Spheares:
    But yet restore thy fierce and cruell minde
    To *Hyrcan* Tygers, and to ruthles Beares.
Yeelde to the Marble thy hard hart againe;
So shalt thou cease to plague, and I to paine.

Sonnet 20
If Beauty thus be clowded with a frowne,
    That pitty shines no comfort to my blis,
    And vapours of disdaine so over-growne
    That my live's light thus wholy darkned is,
Why should I more molest the world with cryes,
    The ayre with sighes, the earth below with teares,
    Sith I live hatefull to those ruthlesse eyes,
    Vexing with untun'd moane her dainty eares?

If I have lov'd her deerer then my breath,
   My breath that calls the heavens to witnes it,
   And still must holde her deere till after death,
   And if that all this cannot move a whit,
Yet let her say that she hath done me wrong
To use me thus and know I lov'd so long.

Sonnet 21

Come Death, the anchor-hold of all my thoughts,
   My last resort whereto my soule appeales,
   For all too-long on earth my fancy dotes,
   Whilst age upon my wasted body steales.
That hart, being made the prospective of horror,
   That honored hath the cruelst faire that lives,
   The cruelst faire, that sees I languish for her,
   Yet never mercy to my merrite gives:
Thys is her Lawrell and her triumphe's prize,
   To tread me downe with foote of her disgrace,
   Whilst I did builde my fortune in her eyes,
   And layd my live's rest on so faire a face:
Which rest I lost, my love, my life and all:
So high attempts to low disgraces fall.

Sonnet 22

These sorrowing sighes, the smoakes of mine annoy,
   These teares, which heate of sacred flame distils,
   Are those due tributes that my faith doth pay
   Unto the Tyrant whose unkindnes kils.
I sacrifize my youth and blooming yeeres
   At her proude feete, and she respects not it:
   My flowre untimely's withred with my teares,
   And Winter woes, for spring of youth unfit.
She thinkes a looke may recompence my care,
   And so with lookes prolongs my long-lookt ease:
   As short that blisse, so is the comfort rare,
   Yet must that blisse my hungry thoughts appease.
Thus she returns my hopes so fruitlesse ever:
Once let her love indeede, or eye me never.

Sonnet 23
False hope prolongs my ever certaine griefe,
   Traytour to me and faithfull to my Love:
   A thousand times it promis'd me reliefe,
   Yet never any true effect I prove.
Oft when I finde in her no truth at all,
   I bannish her, and blame her trecherie;
   Yet soone againe I must her backe recall,
   As one that dyes without her companie.
Thus often as I chase my hope from mee,
   Straight way she hastes her unto *Delia's* eyes;
   Fed with some pleasing looke there shall she bee,
   And so sent backe, and thus my fortune lyes.
Lookes feede my Hope, Hope fosters me in vaine;
Hopes are unsure, when certaine is my paine.

Sonnet 24
Looke in my griefes, and blame me not to mourne,
   From care to care that leades a life so bad;
   Th'Orphan of Fortune, borne to be her scorne,
   Whose clowded brow doth make my dayes so sad.
Long are their nights whose cares doe never sleepe,
   Lothsome their dayes, whome no sunne ever joyd:
   Her fairest eyes doe penetrate so deepe,
   That thus I live both day and night annoyd.
But sith the sweetest roote doth yeeld thus much,
   Her praise from my complaint I may not part:
   I love th'effect for that the cause is such;
   I'le praise her face, and blame her flinty hart;
Whilst that wee make the world admire at us,
Her for disdaine, and me for loving thus.

Sonnet 25
Raigne in my thoughts, faire hande, sweete eye, rare voyce,
   Posses me whole, my hart's triumvirate:
   Yet heavy hart to make so hard a choyse
   Of such as spoile thy poore afflicted state.
For whilst they strive which shall be Lord of all,
   All my poore life by them is troden downe:
   They all erect their Trophies on my fall,
   And yeeld me nought that gives them their renowne.

When backe I looke, I sigh my freedome past,
   And waile the state wherein I present stand;
   And see my fortune ever like to last,
   Finding me rain'd with such a heavie hand.
What can I do but yeeld? And yeeld I doo,
And serve all three, and yet they spoyle me too.

Sonnet 26
Alluding to the sparrow pursued by a Hauke that flew
into the bosome of Zenocrates
Whilst by her eyes pursu'd, my poore hart flew it
   Into the sacred bosome of my deerest,
   She there in that sweete sanctuarie slew it,
   Where it presum'd his safetie to be neerest.
My priviledge of faith could not protect it,
   That was with blood and three yeres' witnes signed;
   In all which time she never could suspect it,
   For well she sawe my love, and how I pined.
And yet no comfort would her brow reveale mee,
   No lightning looke, which falling hopes erecteth:
   What bootes to lawes of succour to appeale mee?
   Ladies and Tyrants never lawes respecteth.
Then there I die, where hop'd I to have liven,
And by that hand, which better might have given.

Sonnet 27
Still in the trace of my tormented thought,
   My ceaseless cares must martch on to my death:
   Thy least regarde too deerelie have I bought,
   Who to my comfort never deign'st a breath.
Why should'st thou stop thine eares now to my cryes,
   Whose eyes were open, ready to oppresse me?
   Why shutt'st thou not the cause whence al did rise,
   Or heare me now, and seeke how to redress me?
Injurious *Delia*, yet I'le love thee still,
   Whilst that I breathe in sorrow of my smart:
   I'le tell the world that I deserv'd but ill,
   And blame my selfe for to excuse thy hart.
Then judge who sinnes the greater of us twaine,
I in my love, or thou in thy disdaine.

Sonnet 28

Oft do I mervaile, whether *Delia's* eyes
 Are eyes, or else two radiant starres that shine:
 For how could Nature ever thus devise
 Of earth on earth a substance so divine?
Starrs sure they are, whose motions rule desires,
 And calme and tempest follow their aspects:
 Their sweet appearing still such power inspires,
 That makes the world admire so strange effects.
Yet whether fixt or wandring starrs are they,
 Whose influence rule the Orbe of my poore hart,
 Fixt sure they are, but wandring make me stray,
 In endles errors whence I cannot part.
Starrs then, not eyes, move you with milder view
Your sweet aspect on him that honours you.

Sonnet 29

The starre of my mishap impos'd this paine,
 To spend the Aprill of my yeeres in wayling,
 That ever found my fortune on the wayne,
 With still fresh cares my present woes assayling.
Yet her I blame not, though for her 'tis done,
 But my desire's wings so high aspyring,
 Which now are melted by that glorious Sunne,
 That makes me fall from off my hie desiring.
And in my fall, I cry for helpe with speed:
 No pittying eye lookes backe upon my mourning;
 No succour finde I now when most I need;
 Th'Ocean of my teares must drowne me burning;
Whilst my distress shall christen her anew,
And give the *Cruell Fayre* this title due.

Sonnet 30

And yet I cannot reprehend the flight,
 Or blame th'attempt presuming so to sore:
 The mounting venter for a high delight
 Did make the honour of the fall the more.
For who gets wealth that puts not from the shore?
 Daunger hath honour, great designes their fame,
 Glorie doth follow, courage goes before.
 And though th'event oft aunswers not the same,

Suffise that high attempts have never shame.
   The Meane-observer, (whom base Safety keepes,)
   Lives without honour, dies without a name,
   And in eternall darkness ever sleepes.
And therefore, Delia, 'tis to me no blot
To have attempted, though attain'd thee not.

Sonnet 31
Raysing my hopes on hills of high desire,
   Thinking to scale the heaven of her hart,
   My slender meanes presum'd too high a part;
   Her thunder of disdaine forst me retyre,
And threw mee downe to paine in all this fire,
   Where, loe, I languish in so heavie smart,
   Because th'attempt was farre above my arte:
   Her pride brook'd not poore soules shold come so nie her.
Yet I protest my high aspyring will
   Was not to dispossesse her of her right:
   Her soveraignty should have remained still,
   I onely sought the blisse to have her sight.
Her sight, contented thus to see me spill,
Fram'd my desires fit for her eyes to kill.

Sonnet 32
O why doth *Delia* credite so her glasse,
   Gazing her beautie deign'd her by the skyes,
   And doth not rather looke on him (alas)
   Whose state best shewes the force of murthering eyes?
The broken tops of loftie trees declare
   The furie of a mercy-wanting storme;
   And of what force your wounding graces are,
   Upon my selfe you best may finde the forme.
Then leave your glasse, and gaze your selfe on mee:
   That Mirror shewes what power is in your face:
   To view your forme too much may daunger bee;
   Narcissus chang'd t'a flower in such a case.
And you are chang'd, but not t'a Hiacint;
I feare your eye hath turn'd your hart to flint.

Sonnet 33

I once may see when yeres shall wreck my wrong,
   When golden hayres shall change to silver wier:
   And those bright rayes that kindle all this fire
   Shall faile in force, their working not so stronge;
Then beautie (now the burthen of my song)
   Whose glorious blaze the world doth so admire,
   Must yeeld up all to tyrant Time's desire:
   Then fade those flowers that deckt her pride so long:
When, if she grieve to gaze her in the glasse,
   Which then presents her winter-withered hew,
   Goe you, my verse, goe tell her what she was,
   For what shee was shee best shall finde in you.
Your fierie heate lets not her glorie passe,
But (Phenix-like) shall make her live anew.

Sonnet 34

Looke, *Delia*, how wee steeme the half-blowne Rose,
   The image of thy blush, and Sommer's honour,
   Whilst in her tender greene shee doth inclose
   The pure sweet beauty Time bestowes upon her:
No sooner spreades her glory in the ayre,
   But straight her ful-blowne pride is in declining;
   Shee then is scorn'd, that late adorn'd the fayre:
   So clowdes thy beautie, after fairest shining.
No Aprill can revive thy withred flowers,
   Whose blooming grace adornes thy glory now:
   Swift speedy Time, feathred with flying howers,
   Dissolves the beautie of the fairest brow.
O let not then such riches waste in vaine;
But love whilst that thou maist be lov'd againe.

Sonnet 35

But love whilst that thou maist be lov'd againe,
   Now whilst thy May hath fill'd thy lap with flowers,
   Now whilst thy beauty beares without a staine,
   Now use thy Sommer smiles ere Winter lowers.
And whilst thou spread'st unto the rysing sunne
   The fairest flowre that ever sawe the light,
   Now joy thy time before thy sweet be done,
   And (*Delia*) thinke thy morning must have night;

And that thy brightnes sets at length to West,
    When thou wilt close up that which now thou showest;
    And thinke the same becomes thy fading best,
    Which then shall hide it most, and cover lowest.
Men doe not wey the stalke for that it was,
When once they finde her flowre, her glory passe.

Sonnet 36

When men shall finde thy flower, thy glory passe,
    And thou with carefull brow sitting alone
    Received hast this message from thy glasse,
    That tells the truth, and saies that all is gone;
Fresh shalt thou see in mee the wounds thou madest,
    Though spent thy flame, in mee the heate remaining:
    I that have lov'd thee thus before thou fadest,
    My faith shall waxe, when thou art in thy waining.
The world shall finde this myracle in mee,
    That fire can burne, when all the matter's spent:
    Then what my faith hath beene thy selfe shalt see,
    And that thou wast unkind thou maist repent.
Thou maist repent that thou hast scorn'd my teares,
When winter snowes upon thy golden haires.

Sonnet 37

When Winter snowes upon thy golden haires,
    And frost of age hath nipt thy flowers neere,
    When dark shal seeme thy day that never cleeres,
    And all lies withred that was held so deere;
Then take this picture which I heere present thee,
    Limned with a Pensill not all unworthy:
    Heere see the gifts that God and nature lent thee;
    Heare reade thy selfe, and what I suffred for thee.
This may remaine thy lasting monument,
    Which happily posteritie may cherrish:
    These colours with thy fading are not spent;
    These may remaine, when thou and I shall perrish.
If they remaine, then thou shalt live thereby.
They will remaine, and so thou canst not die.

Sonnet 38
Thou canst not die whilst any zeale abound
   In feeling harts, that can conceive these lynes:
   Though thou a *Laura* hast no *Petrarch* found,
   In base attyre yet cleerely Beauty shines.
And I (though borne within a colder clime)
   Doe feele mine inward heat as great, (I knowe it):
   Hee never had more faith, although more rime;
   I love as well, though he could better show it.
But I may add one feather to thy fame,
   To helpe her flight throughout the fairest Ile;
   And if my pen could more enlarge thy name,
   Then shouldst thou live in an immortall stile.
For though that *Laura* better limned bee,
Suffice, thou shalt be lov'd as well as shee.

Sonnet 39
O be not griev'd that these my papers should
   Bewray unto the world how faire thou art,
   Or that my wits have shewed the best they could,
   (The chastest flame that ever warmed hart).
Thinke not (sweet *Delia*) this shall be thy shame
   My Muse should sound thy praise with mournefull warble:
   How many live, the glory of whose name
   Shall rest in Ise, when thine is grav'd in Marble.
Thou maist in after ages live esteem'd,
   Unburied in these lines reserv'd in purenes;
   These shall intombe those eyes that have redeem'd
   Mee from the vulgar, thee from all obscurenes.
Although my carefull accents never moov'd thee,
Yet count it no disgrace that I have lov'd thee.

Sonnet 40
Delia, these eyes that so admireth thine
   Have seene those walls the which ambition rear'd
   To check the world, how they intombd have lyen
   Within themselves, and on them ploughes have ear'd.
Yet found I that no barbarous hand attaind
   The spoyle of fame deserv'd by vertuous men,
   Whose glorious actions luckily had gaind
   Th'eternall Annals of a happy pen.

Why then, though *Delia* fade, let that not move her,
 Though time doe spoile her of the fairest vaile
 That ever yet mortalitie did cover,
 Which must instarre the needle and the Raile.
That grace, that vertue, all that serv'd t'in-woman,
Dooth her unto eternitie assommon.

Sonnet 41

Fayre and lovely mayde, looke from the shore,
 See thy *Leander* striving in these waves,
 Poore soule quite spent, whose force can do no more;
 Now send forth hopes, for now calme pitty saves:
And waft him to thee with those lovely eyes,
 A happy convoy to a holy Lande:
 Now shewe thy power, and where thy vertue lyes;
 To save thine owne, stretch out the fairest hand.
Stretch out the fairest hand, a pledge of peace;
 That hand that dartes so right, and never misses:
 I shall forget old wrongs, my griefes shall cease,
 And that which gave me wounds, Ile give it kisses.
O then let th'Ocean of my care find shore,
That thou be pleas'd, and I may sigh no more.

Sonnet 42

Reade in my face a volume of dispayres,
 The wayling Iliads of my tragicke woe,
 Drawne with my blood, and printed with my cares,
 Wrought by her hand that I have honoured so:
Who whilst I burne, she sings at my soule's wrack,
 Looking aloft from Turret of her pride:
 There my soule's Tyrant joyes her, in the sack
 Of her owne seate, whereof I made her guide.
There doe these smoakes that from affliction rise
 Serve as an incense to a cruell Dame;
 A Sacrifice thrice-gratefull to her eyes,
 Because their powre serve to exact the same.
Thus ruines shee (to satisfie her will)
The Temple, where her name was honour'd still.

Sonnet 43
My *Delia* hath the waters of mine eyes
   The ready handmaids on her grace attending,
   That never fall to ebb, but ever rise,
   For to their flow she never grants an ending.
Th'Ocean never did attend more dulie
   Upon his soveraigne's course, the night's pale Queen,
   Nor paid the impost of his waves more truely
   Then mine unto her Deitie have been.
Yet nought the rock of that hard hart can move,
   Where beate these teares with zeale, and fury driveth:
   And yet I rather languish in her love
   Then I would joy the fairest shee that liveth.
I doubt to finde such pleasure in my gayning,
As now I taste in compasse of complayning.

Sonnet 44
How long shall I in mine affliction mourne,
   A burthen to my selfe, distrest in minde?
   When shall my interdicted hopes returne
   From out dispaire wherein they live confin'd?
When shall her troubled brow, charg'd with disdaine,
   Reveale the treasure which her smyles impart?
   When shall my faith the happines attaine,
   To breake the Ise that hath congeald her hart?
Unto herselfe, herselfe my love doth sommon,
   (If love in her hath any power to move)
   And let her tell me as shee is a woman,
   Whether my faith hath not deserv'd her love.
I know she cannot but must needs confesse it,
Yet deignes not with one simple signe t'expresse it.

Sonnet 45
Beautie (sweet Love) is like the morning dewe
   Whose short refresh upon the tender greene
   Cheeres for a time but till the Sunne doth shew,
   And straight tis gone as it had never beene.
Soone doth it fade that makes the fairest florish;
   Short is the glory of the blushing Rose:
   The hewe which thou so carefully dost nourish,
   Yet which at length thou must be forc'd to lose.

When thou surcharg'd with burthen of thy yeeres,
   Shalt bend thy wrinkles homeward to the earth;
   When time hath made a pasport for thy feares,
   Dated in age, the Kalends of our death –
But ah, no more, this hath beene often tolde,
And women grieve to thinke they must be olde.

Sonnet 46

I must not grieve my Love, whose eyes would reede
   Lynes of delight, whereon her youth might smyle:
   Flowers have a tyme before they come to seed,
   And shee is young and now must sport the while.
Ah sport (sweet Maide) in season of these yeeres,
   And learne to gather flowers before they wither:
   And where the sweetest blossoms first appeares,
   Let love and youth conduct thy pleasures thither.
Lighten forth smyles to cleere the clowded ayre,
   And calme the tempest which my sighes do rayse:
   Pittie and smiles doe best become the faire,
   Pittie and smiles shall yeeld thee lasting praise.
I hope to say, when all my griefes are gone,
Happie the hart that sigh'd for such a one.

Sonnet 47: At the Author's going into Italie.

O Whether (poore forsaken) wilt thou goe,
   To goe from sorrow, and thine owne distresse,
   When every place presents like face of woe,
   And no remove can make thy sorrowes lesse?
Yet goe (forsaken,) leave these woods, these playnes,
   Leave her and all, and all for her that leaves
   Thee and thy love forlorne, and both disdaines;
   And of both, wrongfull deemes, and ill conceaves.
Seeke out some place, and see if any place
   Can give the least release unto thy griefe:
   Convay thee from the thought of thy disgrace,
   Steale from thy selfe, and be thy care's own thiefe.
But yet what comfort shall I heereby gaine?
Bearing the wound, I needs must feele the paine.

Sonnet 48: —This Sonnet was made at the Author's being in Italie.
Drawne with th'attractive vertue of her eyes,
　My toucht hart turnes it to that happie cost,
　My joyfull North, where all my fortune lyes,
　The levell of my hopes desired most;
There, where my *Delia*, fairer than the Sunne,
　Deckt with her youth whereon the world doth smile,
　Joyes in that honour which her eyes have wonne,
　Th'eternall wonder of our happy Ile.
Florish, faire, *Albion*, glorie of the North,
　Neptune's best darling held betweene his armes,
　Devided from the world as better worth,
　Kept for himselfe, defended from all harmes.
Still let disarmed peace decke her and thee;
And Muse-foe *Mars* abroade farre fostred bee.

Sonnet 49
Care-charmer Sleepe, sonne of the sable Night,
　Brother to death, in silent darknes borne;
　Relieve my languish, and restore the light,
　With darke forgetting of my care's returne:
And let the day be time enough to mourne
　The shipwrack of my ill-adventred youth:
　Let waking eyes suffice to waile their scorne,
　Without the torment of the night's untruth.
Cease dreames, th'imag'ry of our day desires,
　To modell forth the passions of the morrow:
　Never let rysing Sunne approve you lyers,
　To adde more griefe to agravate my sorrow.
Still let me sleepe, imbracing clowdes in vaine,
And never wake to feele the daye's disdayne.

Sonnet 50
Let others sing of Knights and Palladines
　In aged accents and untimely words,
　Paint shadowes in imaginarie lines,
　Which wel the reach of their high wits records:
But I must sing of thee and those faire eyes;
　Autentique shall my verse in time to come,
　When yet th'unborne shall say, 'Loe, where she lyes,

Whose beauty made him speak that else was dombe.'
These are the Arkes, the Trophies I erect,
   That fortifie thy name against old age;
   And these thy sacred vertues must protect
   Against the darke, and Time's consuming rage.
Though th'error of my youth they shall discover,
Suffice, they shew I liv'd and was thy lover.

Sonnet 51

As to the Roman that would free his Land,
   His error was his honour and renowne,
   And more the fame of his mistaking hand,
   Then if he had the Tyrant over-throwne:
So *Delia*, hath mine errour made me knowne,
   And my deceiv'd attempt deserv'd more fame
   Then if I had the victory mine owne,
   And thy hard hart had yeelded up the same:
And so likewise, renowned is thy blame,
   Thy crueltie, thy glorie. O strange case,
   That errours should be grac'd that merrite shame,
   And sinne of frownes bring honor to the face.
Yet happy *Delia* that thou wast unkind,
But happier yet, if thou wouldst change thy minde.

Sonnet 52

Like as the Lute that joyes or els dislikes,
   As is his arte that playes upon the same,
   So sounds my Muse according as shee strikes
   On my hart strings, high tun'd unto her fame.
Her touch doth cause the warble of the sound,
   Which heere I yeeld in lamentable wise,
   A wailing deskant on the sweetest ground,
   Whose due reports give honour to her eyes.
Els harshe my stile, untunable my Muse,
   Hoarce sounds the voyce that praiseth not her name:
   If any pleasing relish heere I use,
   Then judge the world her beauty gives the same.
O happie ground that makes the musique such,
And blessed hand that gives so sweet a touch.

Sonnet 53

None other fame myne unambitious Muse
    Affected ever but t'eternize thee:
    All other honours doe my hopes refuse,
    Which meaner priz'd and momentarie be.
For God forbid I should my papers blot,
    With mercynarie lines, with servile pen;
    Praysing vertues in them that have them not,
    Basely attending on the hopes of men.
No, no, my verse respects nor Thames nor Theaters,
    Nor seekes it to be knowne unto the great:
    But *Avon* poore in fame, and poore in waters,
    Shall have my song, where *Delia* hath her seate.
Avon shall be my Thames, and shee my song;
I'le sound her name the River all along.

Sonnet 54

Unhappy pen and ill accepted papers,
    That intimate in vaine my chast desires,
    My chast desires, (the ever burning Tapers)
    Inkindled by her eyes' celestiall fires:
Celestiall fires and unrespecting powers,
    That deigne not viewe the glory of your might,
    In humble lines the worke of carefull howres,
    The sacrifice I offer to her sight.
But sith she scornes her owne, this rests for mee,
    I'le mone my selfe, and hide the wrong I have;
    And so content mee that her frownes should be
    To m'infant stile the cradle, and the grave.
What though my selfe no honour get thereby,
Each byrd sings to herselfe, and so will I.

Sonnet 55

Loe heere the impost of a faith unfayning,
    That love hath paid, and her disdaine extorted:
    Behold the message of my just complaining,
    That shewes the world how much my griefe imported.
These tributarie plaints fraught with desire
    I send those eyes, the cabinets of love,
    The Paradice whereto my hopes aspire,
    From out this hell, which mine afflictions prove:

Wherein I thus doe live cast downe from myrth,
   Pensive alone, none but dispaire about mee;
   My joyes abortive, perrisht at their birth,
   My cares long liv'd, and will not die without mee.
This is my state, and *Delia's* hart is such;
I say no more, I feare I said too much.

FINIS

MICHAEL DRAYTON

TO THE READER OF THESE SONNETS

Into these Loves, who but for Passion lookes,
At this first sight, here let him lay them by,
And seeke else-where, in turning other Bookes,
Which better may his labour satisfie.
No farre-fetch'd Sigh shall ever wound my Brest,
Love from mine Eye a Teare shall never wring,
Nor in Ah-mees my whyning Sonnets drest,
(A Libertine) fantastickly I sing:
My Verse is the true image of my Mind,
Ever in motion, still desiring change;
And as thus to Varietie inclin'd,
So in all Humors sportively I range:
　　My Muse is rightly of the English straine,
　　That cannot long one Fashion intertaine.

Idea in Sixtie Three Sonnets

1　　Like an adventurous Sea-farer am I
Who hath some long and dang'rous Voyage beene,
And call'd to tell of his Discoverie,
How farre he sayl'd, what Countries he had seene,
Proceeding from the Port whence he put forth,
Shewes by his Compasse how his Course he steer'd,
When East, when West, when South, and when by North,
As how the Pole to ev'ry place was rear'd;
What Capes he doubled, of what Continent
The Gulphes and Straits that strangely he had past,
Where most becalm'd, where with foule Weather spent,
And on what Rocks in perill to be cast:
　　Thus in my Love, Time calls me to relate
　　My tedious Travels and oft-varying Fate.

2   My heart was slaine, and none but you and I:
     Who should I thinke the Murther should commit?
     Since, but your selfe, there was no Creature by,
     But onely I, guiltlesse of murth'ring it.
     It slew it selfe: the Verdict on the view
     Doe quit the dead, and me not accessarie:
     Well, well, I feare it will be prov'd by you,
     Th'evidence so great a proofe doth carrie.
     But O, see, see, we need inquire no further;
     Upon your Lips the scarlet drops are found,
     And in your Eye, the Boy that did the Murther,
     Your Cheekes yet pale, since first he gave the Wound.
       By this I see, how-ever things be past,
       Yet Heav'n will still have Murther out at last.

3   Taking my Penne, with Words to cast my Woe,
     Duely to count the summe of all my cares,
     I finde, my Griefes innumerable growe,
     The reck'nings rise to millions of Despaires;
     And thus dividing of my fatall Houres,
     The paiments of my Love I read, and crosse;
     Substracting, set my Sweets unto my Sowres;
     My Joyes' arrerage leades me to my losse.
     And thus mine Eies a debtor to thine Eye
     Which by Extortion gaineth all their lookes;
     My heart hath paid such grievous Usurie,
     That all their Wealth lies in thy beautie's Bookes,
       And all is Thine which hath been due to Me,
       And I a Bankrupt, quite undone by Thee.

4   Bright starre of Beauty, on whose eye-lids sit
     A thousand Nimph-like and inamor'd Graces,
     The Goddesses of Memory and Wit,
     Which there in order take their severall places;
     In whose deare Bosome, sweet delicious Love
     Layes downe his Quiver, which he once did beare:
     Since he that blessed Paradise did prove,
     And leaves his Mother's lap to sport him there,
     Let others strive to entertaine with Words;
     My Soule is of a braver Mettle made;
     I hold that vile, which Vulgar wit affords;

In Me's that Faith which Time cannot invade.
   Let what I praise be still made good by you:
   Be you most worthy, whilst I am most true.

5   Nothing but No and I, and I and No:
How fals it out so strangely you reply?
I tell yee (Faire) I'le not be answered so,
With this affirming No, denying I.
I say, 'I Love'; you sleightly answere 'I':
I say, 'You Love'; you peule me out a No:
I say, 'I Die'; you Eccho me with 'I':
'Save mee', I Crie; you sigh me out a No.
Must Woe and I have naught but No and I?
No I am I, if I no more can have:
Answere no more; with Silence make reply,
And let me take my selfe what I doe crave;
   Let No and I with I and you be so:
   Then answere No and I, and I and No.

6   How many paltry, foolish, painted things,
That now in Coaches trouble ev'ry Street,
Shall be forgotten, whom no Poet sings,
Ere they be well wrap'd in their winding Sheet!
Where I to thee Eternitie shall give,
When nothing else remayneth of these dayes,
And Queenes hereafter shall be glad to live
Upon the Almes of thy superfluous prayse:
Virgins and Matrons reading these my Rimes,
Shall be so much delighted with thy story,
That they shall grieve they liv'd not in these Times,
To have seene thee, their Sexe's onely glory:
   So shalt thou flye above the vulgar Throng,
   Still to survive in my immortall Song.

7   Love, in a Humor, play'd the Prodigall,
And bad my Senses to a solemne Feast;
Yet more to grace the Company withall,
Invites my Heart to be the chiefest Ghest:
No other Drinke would serve this Glutton's turne
But precious Teares distilling from mine Eyne,
Which with my Sighes this Epicure doth burne,

Quaffing Carowses in this costly Wine;
Where, in his Cups o'rcome with foule Excesse,
Straightwayes he plays a swagg'ring Ruffin's part,
And at the Banquet, in his Drunkennesse,
Slew his deare Friend, my kind and truest Heart:
　　A gentle warning (Friends) thus may you see,
　　What 'tis to keepe a Drunkard companie.

8　　There's nothing grieves me, but that Age should haste,
That in my dayes I may not see thee old;
That where those two cleare sparkling Eyes are plac'd,
Onely two Loope-holes then I might behold.
That lovely, arched, yvorie, pollish'd Brow,
Defac'd with Wrinkles, that I might but see;
Thy daintie Hayre, so curl'd, and crisped now,
Like grizzled Mosse upon some aged Tree;
Thy Cheeke, now flush with Roses, sunke, and leane,
Thy Lips, with age, as any Wafer thinne;
Thy Pearly Teeth out of thy Head so cleane,
That when thou feed'st, thy Nose shall touch thy Chinne:
　　These Lines that now thou scorn'st, which should delight
　　　thee,
　　Then would I make thee read but to despight thee.

9　　As other Men, so I my selfe doe Muse,
Why in this sort I wrest Invention so,
And why these giddy Metaphors I use,
Leaving the Path the greater part doe goe.
I will resolve you; I am Lunaticke,
And ever this in Mad-men you shall finde,
What they last thought of, when the Braine grew sicke,
In most distraction they keepe that in Minde.
Thus talking idly in this Bedlam fit,
Reason and I (you must conceive) are twaine;
'Tis nine yeeres now since first I lost my Wit;
Beare with Me then, though troubled be my Braine:
　　With Diet and Correction Men distraught
　　(Not too farre past) may to their Wits be brought.

10　　To nothing fitter can I Thee compare
Then to the Sonne of some rich Penny-father,

Who having now brought on his end with Care,
Leaves to his Sonne all he had heap'd together.
This new rich Novice, lavish of his chest,
To one Man gives, doth on another spend,
Then heere he riots, yet amongst the rest
Haps to lend some to one true honest Friend.
Thy Gifts thou in Obscuritie doest waste,
False Friends thy kindnesse, borne but to deceive Thee,
Thy Love, that is on the unworthy plac'd;
Time hath thy Beautie, which with Age will leave thee;
   Onely that little which to Me was lent
   I give Thee backe, when all the rest is spent.

11   You not alone, when You are still alone,
O God from You, that I could private be;
Since You one were, I never since was one;
Since You in Me, my selfe since out of Me,
Transported from my Selfe, into Your being;
Though either distant, present yet to either,
Senselesse with too much Joy, each other seeing,
And onely absent, when Wee are together.
Give Me my Selfe, and take your Selfe againe;
Devise some meanes but how I may forsake You;
So much is Mine, that doth with You remaine,
That taking what is Mine, with Me I take You;
   You doe bewitch Me: O that I could flie,
   From my Selfe You, or from your owne Selfe I.

To the Soule
12   That learned Father, which so firmely proves
The Soule of Man immortall and divine,
And doth the sev'rall Offices define,

Anima	Gives her that Name, as she the Body moves;
Amor	Then is she Love, imbracing Charitie;
Animus	Moving a Will in us, it is the Mind;
Mens	Retayning Knowledge, still the same in kind;
Memoria	As intellectuall, it is Memorie;
Ratio	In judging, Reason onely is her Name;
Sensus	In speedie apprehension, it is Sense;
Conscientia	In Right or Wrong, they call her Conscience;
Spiritus	The Spirit, when it to God-ward doth inflame.

These of the Soule the sev'rall Functions bee,
Which my Heart, lightned by thy Love, doth see.

To the Shadow

13   Letters and Lines we see are soone defaced,
Metals doe waste, and fret with Canker's Rust,
The Diamond shall once consume to Dust,
And freshest Colours with foule staynes disgraced;
Paper and Inke can paint but naked Words;
To write with Bloud of force offends the Sight,
And if with Teares, I find them all too light,
And Sighes and Signes a silly Hope affords.
O sweetest Shadow, how thou serv'st my turne,
Which still shalt be, as long as there is Sunne;
Nor whilst the World is, never shall be done,
Whilst Moone shall shine, or any Fire shall burne:
    That ev'ry thing whence Shadow doth proceed,
    May in his Shadow my Love's storie read.

14   If he, from Heav'n that filch'd that living Fire,
Condemn'd by JOVE to endlesse Torment bee,
I greatly marvell, how you still goe free,
That farre beyond PROMETHEUS did aspire:
The Fire he stole, although of Heav'nly kind,
Which from above he craftily did take,
Of livelesse Clods us living Men to make,
He did bestow in temper of the Mind.
But you broke into Heav'n's immortall store,
Where Vertue, Honour, Wit, and Beautie lay;
Which taking thence, you have escap'd away,
Yet stand as free as ere you did before:
    Yet old PROMETHEUS punish'd for his Rape.
    Thus poore Theeves suffer, when the greater scape.

His Remedie for Love

15   Since to obtaine thee nothing me will sted,
I have a Med'cine that shall cure my Love:
The powder of her Heart dry'd, when she is dead,
That Gold nor Honour ne'r had pow'r to move;
Mix'd with her Teares, that ne'r her true-Love crost,
Nor at Fifteene ne'r long'd to be a Bride;

Boyl'd with her Sighes, in giving up the Ghost,
That for her late deceased Husband dy'd:
Into the same then let a Woman breathe,
That being chid, did never word replie,
With one thrice-marry'd's Pray'rs, that did bequeath
A Legacie to stale Virginitie.
　　If this Receit have not the pow'r to winne me,
　　Little I'le say, but thinke the Devill's in me.

An Allusion to the Phœnix

16　'Mongst all the Creatures in this spacious Round,
Of the Birds' kind, the Phœnix is alone,
Which best by you, of living Things, is knowne:
None like to that, none like to you is found:
Your Beautie is the hot and splend'rous Sunne;
The precious Spices be your chaste Desire,
Which being kindled by that heav'nly fire,
Your Life so like the Phœnix's begun;
Your selfe thus burned in that sacred flame,
With so rare sweetnesse all the Heav'ns perfuming,
Againe increasing as you are consuming,
Onely by dying, borne the very same:
　　And wing'd by Fame, you to the Starres ascend,
　　So you of Time shall live beyond the End.

To Time

17　Stay, speedy Time, behold, before thou passe,
From Age to Age what thou hast sought to see,
One, in whom all the Excellencies be,
In whom, Heav'n lookes it selfe as in a Glasse:
Time, looke thou too, in this Tralucent Glasse,
And thy Youth past in this pure Mirrour see,
As the World's Beautie in his Infancie,
What it was then, and thou before it was;
Passe on, and to Posteritie tell this,
Yet see thou tell, but truly, what hath beene;
Say to our Nephewes that thou once hast seene,
In perfect humane shape, all heav'nly Blisse;
　　And bid them mourne, nay more, despaire with thee,
　　That she is gone, her like againe to see.

To the Celestiall Numbers

18
To this our World, to Learning, and to Heaven,
Three Nines there are, to every one a Nine,
One number of the Earth, the other both Divine;
One Woman now makes three odde Numbers even:
Nine orders first of Angels be in Heaven;
Nine Muses doe with Learning still frequent,
These with the Gods are ever resident;
Nine worthie Women to the World were given:
My worthy, One to these Nine Worthies addeth,
And my faire Muse, one Muse unto the Nine,
And my good Angell (in my Soule divine)
With one more Order these nine Orders gladdeth:
    My Muse, my Worthy, and my Angel then
    Makes every One of these three Nines a Ten.

To Humour

19
You cannot love, my prettie Heart, and why?
There was a time, You told Me that you would,
But now againe You will the same denie;
If it might please You, would to God You could:
What, will You hate? Nay that You will not neither?
Nor Love, nor Hate, how then? What will You doe?
What, will You keepe a meane then betwixt either?
Or will You love Me, and yet hate Me too?
Yet serves not This. What next, what other Shift?
You Will, and Will not: what a coyle is here!
I see Your craft, now I perceive Your drift,
And all this while, I was mistaken there:
    Your Love and Hate is this, I now doe prove You,
    You love in Hate, by Hate to make Me love You.

20
An evill spirit, your beautie haunts Me still,
Where with (alas) I have beene long possest,
Which ceaseth not to tempt Me to each Ill,
Nor gives Me once but one poore minute's rest:
In Me it speakes, whether I Sleepe or Wake,
And when by Meanes to drive it out I try,
With greater Torments then it Me doth take,
And tortures Me in most extremity:
Before my Face it layes downe my Despaires,

And hastes Me on unto a sudden Death,
Now tempting Me to drowne my Selfe in teares,
And then in sighing, to give up my breath:
    Thus am I still provok'd to every Evill
    By this good wicked Spirit, sweet Angell Devill.

21   A witlesse Gallant a young Wench that woo'd,
      (Yet his dull Spirit her not one jot could move)
      Intreated me, as e'r I wish'd his good,
      To write him but one Sonnet to his Love:
      When I, as fast as e'r my Penne could trot,
      Powr'd out what first from quicke Invention came,
      Nor never stood one word thereof to blot,
      Much like his Wit, that was to use the same:
      But with my Verses he his Mistres wonne,
      Who doted on the Dolt beyond all measure.
      But see, for you to Heav'n for Phraze I runne,
      And ransacke all APOLLO's golden Treasure;
          Yet by my Froth, this Foole his Love obtaines,
          And I lose you, for all my Wit and Paines.

      To Folly
22   With Fooles and Children good Discretion beares;
      Then honest People, beare with Love and Me,
      Nor older yet, nor wiser made by yeeres,
      Amongst the rest of Fooles and Children be:
      Love still a Baby, playes with Gawdes and Toyes,
      And like a Wanton, sports with every Fether;
      And Ideots still are running after Boyes,
      Then Fooles and Children fitt'st to goe together:
      He still as young as when he first was borne,
      No wiser I then when as young as he.
      You that behold us, laugh us not to scorne;
      Give Nature thankes, you are not such as we:
          Yet Fooles and Children sometimes tell in play
          Some wise in shew, more Fooles indeed then they.

23   Love banish'd Heav'n, in Earth was held in scorne,
      Wand'ring abroad in Need and Beggerie;
      And wanting Friends, though of a Goddesse borne,
      Yet crav'd the Almes of such as passed by:

I, like a Man devout and charitable,
Clothed the Naked, lodg'd this wand'ring Ghest,
With Sighes and Teares still furnishing his Table,
With what might make the Miserable blest.
But this ungratefull, for my good desert,
Intic'd my Thoughts against me to conspire,
Who gave consent to steale away my Heart,
And set my Brest, his Lodging, on a fire.
   Well, well, my Friends, when Beggers grow thus bold,
   No marvell then though Charitie grow cold.

24   I heare some say, 'This Man is not in love:
Who? Can he love? A likely thing!' they say;
'Reade but his Verse, and it will eas'ly prove.'
O, judge not rashly (gentle Sir) I pray:
Because I loosely trifle in this sort,
As one that faine his Sorrowes would beguile,
You now suppose me all this time in sport,
And please your selfe with this Conceit the while:
Yee shallow Censures, sometime see yee not
In greatest Perils some Men pleasant be;
Where Fame by Death is onely to be got,
They resolute? So stands the case with me:
   Where other Men in depth of Passion crie,
   I laugh at Fortune, as in jest to die.

25   O, why should Nature niggardly restraine
That Foraine Nations rellish not our Tongue!
Else should my Lines glide on the Waves of *Rhene*,
And crowne the *Piren's* with my living Song.
But bounded thus, to *Scotland* get you forth,
Thence take you Wing unto the *Orcades*;
There let my Verse get glory in the North,
Making my Sighes to thaw the Frozen Seas:
And let the *Bards* within that *Irish* Ile,
To whom my Muse with fierie Wings shall passe,
Call backe the stiffe-neck'd Rebels from Exile,
And mollifie the slaught'ring *Galliglasse*;
   And when my flowing Numbers they rehearse,
   Let Wolves and Beares be charmed with my Verse.

To Despaire

26 I ever love where never Hope appeares,
Yet Hope drawes on my never-hoping Care,
And my Live's Hope would die but for Despaire.
My never-certaine Joy breeds ever-certaine Feares,
Uncertaine Dread gives Wings unto my Hope;
Yet my Hope's Wings are laden so with Feare,
As they cannot ascend to my Hope's Sphere:
Though Feare gives them more then a Heav'nly Scope,
Yet this large Roome is bounded with Despaire,
So my Love is still fett'red with vaine Hope,
And Liberty deprives him of his Scope,
And thus am I imprison'd in the Aire.
   Then, sweet Despaire, awhile hold up thy head,
   Or all my Hope for Sorrow will be dead.

27 Is not Love here as 'tis in other Clymes,
And diff'reth it as doe the sev'rall Nations?
Or hath it lost the Vertue with the Times,
Or in this Iland alt'reth with the Fashions?
Or have our Passions lesser pow'r then theirs
Who had lesse Art them lively to expresse?
Is Nature growne lesse pow'rfull in their Heires,
Or in our Fathers did she more transgresse?
I am sure my Sighes come from a Heart as true
As any Man's that Memory can boast,
And my Respects and Services to you
Equall with his that loves his Mistres most:
   Or Nature must be partiall in my Cause,
   Or onely you doe violate her Lawes.

28 To such as say Thy Love I over-prize,
And doe not sticke to terme my Prayses folly,
Against these Folkes, that thinke themselves so wise,
I thus oppose my Reason's forces wholly:
Though I give more then well affords my state,
In which expence the most suppose me vaine,
Which yeelds them nothing, at the easiest rate,
Yet at this price returnes me treble gaine.
They value not, unskilfull how to use,
And I give much, because I gaine thereby:

I that thus take, or they that thus refuse,
Whether are these deceived then, or I?
    In ev'ry thing I hold this Maxim still,
    The Circumstance doth make it good, or ill.

To the Senses

29   When conqu'ring Love did first my Heart assayle,
Unto mine aid I summon'd ev'ry Sense,
Doubting, if that proud Tyrant should prevayle,
My Heart should suffer for mine Eyes' Offence;
But he with Beautie first corrupted Sight,
My Hearing brib'd with her Tongue's Harmonie,
My Taste by her sweet Lips drawne with Delight,
My Smelling wonne with her Breath's Spicerie:
But when my Touching came to play his part,
(The King of Senses, greater then the rest)
He yeelds Love up the Keyes unto my Heart,
And tells the other how they should be blest.
    And thus by those of whom I hop'd for ayd
    To cruell Love my Soule was first betray'd.

To the Vestals

30   Those Priests which first the Vestall Fire begun,
Which might be borrow'd from no Earthly flame,
Devis'd a Vessell to receive the Sunne,
Being stedfastly opposed to the same;
Where, with sweet Wood, layd curiously by Art,
On which the Sunne might by reflection beat,
Receiving strength from ev'ry secret part,
The Fuell kindled with Celestiall Heat.
Thy blessed Eyes, the Sunne which lights this Fire;
My holy Thoughts, they be the Vestall flame;
The precious Odors be my chaste Desire;
My Brest's the Vessell which includes the same:
    Thou art my VESTA, thou my Goddesse art,
    Thy hallow'd Temple onely is my Heart.

To the Criticke

31   Methinkes I see some crooked Mimicke jeere,
And taxe my Muse with this fantasticke Grace,
Turning my Papers, askes, 'What have we heere?'

Making withall some filthy Antike Face.
I feare no censure, nor what thou canst say,
Nor shall my Spirit one jot of vigour lose.
Think'st thou my Wit shall keepe the pack-Horse Way
That ev'ry Dudgen low Invention goes?
Since Sonnets thus in Bundles are imprest,
And ev'ry Drudge doth dull our satiate Eare,
Think'st thou my Love shall in those Ragges be drest
That ev'ry Dowdy, ev'ry Trull doth weare?
   Up, to my Pitch, no common Judgement flyes;
   I scorne all Earthly Dung-bred Scarabies.

To the River Ankor

Our Flouds-Queen *Thames* for Ships & Swans is crowned,
And stately *Severne* for her Shoare is praysed;
The Crystall *Trent*, for Foords and Fish renowned,
And *Avon's* Fame to *Albion's* Cliffes is raysed;
Carlegion Chester vaunts her holy *Dee*,
Yorke many Wonders of her *Owse* can tell,
The *Peake* her *Dove*, whose Bankes so fertile be,
And *Kent* will say her *Medway* doth excell;
Cotswold commends her *Isis* to the *Tame*,
Our Northerne Borders boast of *Tweed's* faire Floud,
Our Westerne Parts extoll their *Wili's* Fame,
And the old *Lea* brags of the *Danish* Bloud:
   Arden's sweet *Ankor*, let thy glory bee
   That faire *Idea* onely lives by thee.

To Imagination

33 Whilst yet mine Eyes doe surfet with Delight,
My wofull Heart, imprison'd in my Brest,
Wisheth to be transformed to my Sight,
That it, like those, by looking might be blest:
But whilst mine Eyes thus greedily doe gaze,
Finding their Objects over-soone depart,
These now the other's Happinesse doe prayse,
Wishing themselves that they had beene my Heart;
That Eyes were Heart, or that the Heart were Eyes,
As covetous the other's use to have:
But finding Nature their request denyes,
This to each other mutually they crave,

That since the one cannot the other bee,
That Eyes could thinke or that my Heart could see.

To Admiration

34 Marvell not, Love, though I thy pow'r admire,
Ravish'd a World beyond the farthest Thought,
And knowing more then ever hath beene taught,
That I am onely starv'd in my desire:
Marvell not, Love, though I thy pow'r admire,
Ayming at things exceeding all perfection,
To Wisedome's selfe to minister direction,
That I am onely starv'd in my desire:
Marvell not, Love, though I thy pow'r admire,
Though my Conceit I further seeme to bend
Then possibly Invention can extend,
And yet am onely starv'd in my desire:
    If thou wilt wonder, here's the wonder, Love,
    That this to me doth yet no wonder prove.

To Miracle

35 Some misbeleeving and prophane in Love,
When I doe speake of Miracles by thee,
May say that thou art flattered by mee,
Who onely write, my skill in Verse to prove.
See Miracles, ye unbeleeving, see:
A dumbe-borne Muse made to expresse the Mind,
A cripple Hand to write, yet lame by Kind,
One by thy Name, the other touching thee:
Blind were mine Eyes till they were seene of thine,
And mine Eares deafe by thy Fame healed bee,
My Vices cur'd by Vertues sprung from thee,
My Hopes reviv'd which long in Grave had lyne:
    All uncleane Thoughts, foule Spirits, cast out in mee,
    Onely by Vertue that proceeds from thee.

Cupid *conjured*

36 Thou purblind Boy, since thou hast beene so slacke
To wound her Heart, whose Eyes have wounded me,
And suff'red her to glory in my Wracke,
Thus to my aid, I lastly conjure thee:
By Hellish *Styx* (by which the THUND'RER sweares)

By thy faire Mother's unavoided Power,
By HECAT's Names, by PROSERPINE's sad Teares,
When she was rapt to the infernall Bower;
By thine owne loved PSYCHE's, by the Fires
Spent on thine Altars, flaming up to Heav'n;
By all true Lovers' Sighes, Vowes, and Desires,
By all the Wounds that ever thou hast giv'n;
    I conjure thee by all that I have nam'd,
    To make her love, or CUPID be thou damn'd.

37 Deare, why should you command me to my Rest,
    When now the Night doth summon all to sleepe?
    Me thinkes this Time becommeth Lovers best;
    Night was ordayn'd together Friends to keepe.
    How happy are all other living Things,
    Which though the Day dis-joyne by sev'rall flight,
    The quiet Ev'ning yet together brings,
    And each returnes unto his Love at Night!
    O, Thou that art so courteous else to all!
    Why should'st thou, Night, abuse me onely thus,
    That ev'ry Creature to his kind do'st call,
    And yet 'tis thou do'st onely sever us?
        Well could I wish it would be ever Day,
        If when Night comes, you bid me goe away.

38 Sitting alone, Love bids me goe and write;
    Reason plucks back, commanding me to stay,
    Boasting that she doth still direct the way,
    Or else Love were unable to indite:
    Love growing angry, vexed at the Spleene,
    And scorning Reason's maymed Argument,
    Straight taxeth Reason wanting to invent
    Where she with Love conversing hath not beene:
    Reason, reproched with this coy Disdaine,
    Despiteth Love, and laugheth at her Folly;
    And Love, contemning Reason's reason wholly,
    Thought it in weight too light by many a Graine:
        Reason, put back, doth out of sight remove,
        And Love alone picks reason out of love.

39   Some, when in Ryme they of their Loves doe tell,
      With Flames and Lightnings their Exordiums paint;
      Some call on Heaven, some invocate on Hell,
      And Fates and Furies with their woes acquaint.
      Elizium is too high a seate for Me,
      I will not come in *Stix* or *Phlegeton*;
      The thrice-three Muses but too wanton be;
      Like they that Lust, I care not, I will none.
      Spightfull ERINNIS frights Me with her Lookes;
      My man-hood dares not with foule ATE mell;
      I quake to looke on HECAT's charming Bookes;
      I still feare Bug-beares in APOLLO's Cell.
          I passe not for MINERVA, nor ASTREA,
          Onely I call on my divine IDEA.

40   My Heart the Anvile where my Thoughts doe beate,
      My Words the Hammers, fashioning my desire,
      My Brest the Forge, including all the heate,
      Love is the Fewell, which maintaines the fire;
      My Sighes the Bellowes, which the Flame encreaseth,
      Filling mine Eares with Noise and Nightly groning;
      Toyling with Paine, my Labour never ceaseth,
      In grievous Passions my Woes still bemoning:
      My Eyes with Teares against the fire striving,
      Whose scorching gleed my heart to Cinders turneth;
      But with those Drops the Flame againe reviving,
      Still more and more it to my torment burneth:
          With SISIPHUS thus doe I role the stone,
          And turne the Wheele with damned IXION.

      Love's Lunacie
41   Why doe I speake of Joy, or write of Love,
      When my Heart is the very Den of Horror,
      And in my Soule the paines of hell I prove,
      With all his Torments and Infernall terror?
      What should I say? What yet remaines to doe?
      My Braine is drie with weeping all too long;
      My Sighes be spent in utt'ring of my Woe,
      And I want words wherewith to tell my Wrong:
      But still distracted in Love's Lunacie,
      And Bedlam-like, thus raving in my Griefe,

Now raile upon her Haire, then on her Eye;
Now call her Goddesse, then I call her Thiefe;
   Now I deny Her, then I doe confesse Her,
   Now doe I curse Her, then againe I blesse Her.

42   Some Men there be which like my Method well,
And much commend the strangenesse of my Vaine:
Some say I have a passing pleasing Straine,
Some say That in my Humor I excell;
Some, who not kindly rellish my Conceit,
They say (As Poets doe) I use to faine,
And in bare words paint out my Passion's paine;
Thus sundry Men their sundry Minds repeat:
I passe not, I, how Men affected bee,
Nor who commends or discommends my Verse;
It pleaseth me if I my Woes rehearse,
And in my Lines if she my love may see:
   Onely my comfort still consists in this,
   Writing her prayse, I cannot write amisse.

43   Why should your faire Eyes with such sov'raigne grace
Disperse their Rayes on ev'ry vulgar Spirit,
Whilst I in darknesse, in the selfe-same place,
Get not one glance, to recompence my Merit?
So doth the Plow-man gaze the wand'ring Starre,
And onely rest contented with the Light,
That never learn'd what Constellations are
Beyond the bent of his unknowing Sight.
O, why should Beautie (Custome to obey)
To their grosse Sense apply her selfe so ill!
Would God I were as ignorant as they,
When I am made unhappy by my skill;
   Onely compell'd on this poore good to boast,
   Heav'ns are not kind to them that know them most.

44   Whilst thus my Pen strives to eternize thee,
Age rules my Lines with Wrinkles in my Face,
Where, in the Map of all my Miserie,
Is model'd out the World of my Disgrace;
Whilst in despite of tyrannizing Times,
MEDEA-like, I make thee young againe,

Proudly thou scorn'st my World-out-wearing Rimes,
And murther'st Vertue with thy coy disdaine:
And though in youth my Youth untimely perish,
To keepe Thee from Oblivion and the Grave,
Ensuing Ages yet my Rimes shall cherish,
Where I, intomb'd, my better part shall save;
   And though this Earthly Body fade and die,
   My Name shall mount upon Eternitie.

45   Muses which sadly sit about my Chayre,
Drown'd in the Teares extorted by my Lines,
With heavie Sighes whilst thus I breake the Ayre,
Painting my Passions in these sad Designes;
Since she disdaines to blesse my happie Verse,
The strong-built Trophies to her living Fame,
Ever henceforth my Bosome be your Hearse,
Wherein the World shall now intombe her Name:
Inclose my Musike, you poore senselesse Walls,
Sith she is deafe, and will not heare my Mones;
Soften your selves with ev'ry Teare that falls,
Whilst I like ORPHEUS sing to Trees and Stones,
   Which with my plaint seeme yet with pittie moved,
   Kinder then she whom I so long have loved.

46   Plaine-path'd Experience, th'unlearned's guide,
Her simple Followers evidently shewes
Sometimes what Schoole-men scarcely can decide,
Nor yet wise Reason absolutely knowes:
In making tryall of a Murther wrought,
If the vile actors of the heynous deed
Neere the dead Body happily be brought,
Oft't'ath been prov'd, the breathlesse Coarse will bleed.
She comming neere, that my poore Heart hath slaine,
Long since departed (to the World no more)
Th'ancient Wounds no longer can containe,
But fall to bleeding, as they did before:
   But what of this? Should she to death be led,
   It furthers Justice, but helpes not the dead.

47   In pride of Wit, when high desire of Fame
Gave Life and Courage to my lab'ring Pen,

And first the sound and vertue of my Name
Wonne grace and credit in the Eares of Men;
With those the thronged Theaters that presse,
I in the Circuit for the Lawrell strove,
Where the full Prayse, I freely must confesse,
In heat of Bloud a modest Mind might move.
With Showts and Claps at ev'ry little pawse,
When the proud Round on ev'ry side hath rung
Sadly I sit, unmov'd with the Applause,
As though to me it nothing did belong:
    No publike Glorie vainely I pursue;
    All that I seeke is to enternize you.

48   Cupid, I hate thee, which I'de have thee know:
A naked Starveling ever may'st thou be.
Poore Rogue, goe pawne thy *Fascia* and thy Bow,
For some few Ragges wherewith to cover thee:
Or if thou'lt not, thy Archerie forbeare;
To some base Rustick doe thy selfe preferre,
And when Corne's sowne, or growne into the Eare,
Practise thy Quiver, and turne Crow-keeper;
Or being Blind (as fittest for the Trade)
Goe hyre thy selfe some bungling Harper's Boy:
They that are blind are Minstrels often made.
So may'st thou live, to thy faire Mother's Joy;
    That whilst with MARS she holdeth her old Way,
    Thou, her blind Sonne, may'st sit by them, and play.

49   Thou Leaden Braine, which censur'st what I write,
And say'st my Lines be dull and doe not move,
I marvell not thou feel'st not my Delight,
Which never felt'st my fierie touch of Love:
But thou, whose Pen hath like a Packe-Horse serv'd,
Whose Stomack unto Gall hath turn'd thy Food,
Whose Senses, like poore Pris'ners, hunger-starv'd,
Whose Griefe hath parch'd thy Body, dry'd thy Blood;
Thou which hast scorned Life, and hated Death,
And in a moment Mad, Sober, Glad, and Sorrie;
Thou which hast bann'd thy Thoughts, and curst thy Birth,
With thousand Plagues more then in Purgatorie:
    Thou, thus whose Spirit Love in his fire refines,
    Come thou and reade, admire, applaud my Lines.

50   As in some Countries, farre remote from hence,
The wretched Creature destined to die,
Having the Judgement due to his Offence,
By Surgeons beg'd, their Art on him to trie,
Which on the Living worke without remorse,
First make incision on each mast'ring Veine,
Then stanch the bleeding, then trans-pierce the Coarse,
And with the Balmes recure the Wounds againe;
Then Poyson, and with Physike him restore:
Not that they feare the hope-lesse Man to kill,
But their Experience to increase the more:
Ev'n so my Mistres workes upon my Ill,
    By curing me and killing me each How'r,
    Onely to shew her Beautie's Sov'raigne Pow'r.

51   Calling to minde, since first my Love begun,
Th'incertaine Times oft varying in their Course,
How Things still unexpectedly have runne,
As't please the Fates by their resistlesse force:
Lastly, mine Eyes amazedly have seene
ESSEX' great fall, TYRONE his Peace to gaine,
The quiet end of that Long-living Queene,
This King's faire Entrance, and our Peace with *Spaine*,
We and the *Dutch* at length our Selves to sever:
Thus the World doth, and evermore shall Reele;
Yet to my Goddesse am I constant ever,
How e're blind Fortune turne her giddie Wheele:
    Though Heaven and Earth prove both to me untrue,
    Yet am I still inviolate to You.

52   What do'st thou meane to Cheate me of my Heart,
To take all Mine, and give me none againe?
Or have thine Eyes such Magike or that Art,
That what They get They ever doe retaine?
Play not the Tyrant, but take some Remorse;
Rebate thy Spleene, if but for Pittie's sake;
Or, Cruell, if thou can'st not, let us scorse,
And for one piece of Thine, my whole heart take.
But what of Pitty doe I speake to Thee,
Whose Brest is proofe against Complaint or Prayer?
Or can I thinke what my Reward shall be

From that proud Beauty, which was my betrayer?
  What talke I of a Heart, when thou hast none,
  Or if thou hast, it is a flinty one?

Another to the River Ankor
53 Cleere *Ankor*, on whose Silver-sanded shore
My Soule-shrin'd Saint, my faire IDEA lies,
O blessed Brooke, whose milke-white Swans adore
Thy Cristall streame refined by her Eyes,
Where sweet Myrrh-breathing *Zephire* in the Spring
Gently distills his Nectar-dropping showres,
Where Nightingales in *Arden* sit and sing,
Amongst the daintie Dew-impearled flowres;
Say thus, faire Brooke, when thou shalt see thy Queene,
'Loe, heere thy Shepheard spent his wandring yeeres;
And in these Shades, deare Nymph, he oft hath beene,
And heere to Thee he sacrific'd his Teares.'
    Faire *Arden*, thou my *Tempe* art alone,
    And thou, sweet *Ankor*, art my *Helicon*.

54 Yet reade at last the storie of my Woe,
The drerie abstracts of my endlesse Cares,
With my Life's Sorrow interlined so,
Smoak'd with my Sighes, and blotted with my Teares;
The sad Memorialls of my Miseries,
Pen'd in the griefe of mine afflicted Ghost,
My Live's complaint in dolefull Elegies,
With so pure Love as Time could never boast;
Receive the Incense which I offer here,
By my strong Faith ascending to thy Fame,
My Zeale, my Hope, my Vowes, my Prayse, my Pray'r,
My Soule's Oblations to thy sacred Name:
    Which Name my Muse to highest Heav'ns shall rayse,
    By chaste Desire, true Love, and vertuous Prayse.

55 My faire, if thou wilt register my Love,
A World of Volumes shall thereof arise:
Preserve my Teares, and thou thy Selfe shalt prove
A second Floud, downe rayning from mine Eyes:
Note but my Sighes, and thine Eyes shall behold

The Sun-beames smothered with immortall Smoke;
And if by Thee my Prayers may be enrol'd
They Heaven and Earth to pitty shall provoke;
Looke Thou into my brest, and Thou shalt see
Chaste holy Vowes for my Soule's sacrifice,
That Soule (sweet Maid) which so hath honor'd Thee,
Erecting Trophies to thy Sacred Eyes;
    Those Eyes to my Heart shining ever bright,
    When Darknesse hath obscur'd each other Light.

An allusion to the Eaglets

56   When like an Eaglet I first found my Love,
For that the vertue I thereof would know,
Upon the Nest I set it forth, to prove
If it were of that Kingly kind, or no:
But it no sooner saw my Sunne appeare,
But on her Rayes with open Eyes it stood,
To shew that I had hatch'd it for the Ayre,
And rightly came from that brave mounting Brood:
And when the Plumes were summ'd with sweet desire,
To prove the Pynions, it ascends the Skyes:
Doe what I could, it needsly would aspire
To my Soule's Sunne, those two Celestiall Eyes:
    Thus from my Brest, where it was bred alone,
    It after thee is like an Eaglet flowne.

57   You best discern'd of my Mind's inward Eyes,
And yet your Graces outwardly Divine,
Whose deare remembrance in my Bosome lyes,
Too rich a Relique for so poore a Shrine:
You, in whom Nature chose her selfe to view,
When she her owne perfection would admire,
Bestowing all her Excellence on you,
At whose pure Eyes, Love lights his hallow'd Fire:
Ev'n as a Man that in some Trance hath seene
More then his wond'ring utt'rance can unfold,
That rapt in Spirit, in better Worlds hath beene,
So must your prayse distractedly be told;
    Most of all short, when I should shew you most,
    In your perfections so much am I lost.

58   In former times, such as had store of Coyne,
In Warres at home, or when for Conquests bound,
For feare that some their Treasure should purloyne,
Gave it to keepe to Spirits within the Ground;
And to attend it, them as strongly ty'd,
Till they return'd. Home when they never came,
Such as by Art to get the same have try'd,
From the strong Spirit by no meanes force the same;
Neerer Men come, That further flyes away,
Striving to hold it strongly in the Deepe.
Ev'n as this Spirit, so you alone doe play
With those rich Beauties Heav'n gives you to keepe:
    Pittie so left to th'coldnesse of your Blood,
    Not to availe you, nor doe others good.

To Proverbe

59   As love and I, late harbour'd in one Inne,
With Proverbs thus each other intertaine:
'*In Love there is no lack*,' thus I begin;
'*Faire words make Fooles*,' replyeth he againe;
'*Who spares to speake doth spare to speed*' (quoth I);
'*As well* (sayth he) *too forward, as too slow*.'
'*Fortune assists the boldest*,' I reply;
'*A hastie Man* (quoth he) *ne'r wanted Woe*.'
'*Labour is light, where Love* (quoth I) *doth pay*.'
(Saith he) '*Light Burthen's heavy, if farre borne*.'
(Quoth I) '*The Maine lost, cast the By away*.'
'*You have spunne a faire Thred*', he replyes in scorne.
    And having thus awhile each other thwarted,
    Fooles as we met, so Fooles againe we parted.

60   Define my Weale, and tell the joyes of Heaven;
Expresse my Woes, and shew the paines of Hell;
Declare what Fate unlucky Starres have given,
And aske a World upon my Life to dwell.
Make knowne the Faith that Fortune could not move;
Compare my Worth with others' base Desert;
Let Vertue be the Touch-stone of my Love,
So may the Heavens read wonders in my Heart.
Behold the Clouds which have eclips'd my Sunne,
And view the Crosses which my course doe let;

Tell Me, if ever since the World begunne,
So Faire a rising had so Foule a set:
   And see if Time (if he would strive to prove)
   Can shew a Second to so pure a Love.

61   Since ther's no helpe, Come let us kisse and part,
Nay, I have done: You get no more of Me,
And I am glad, yea glad with all my heart,
That thus so cleanly I my Selfe can free;
Shake hands for ever, Cancell all our Vowes,
And when We meet at any time againe,
Be it not seene in either of our Browes,
That We one jot of former Love reteyne:
Now at the last gaspe of Love's latest Breath,
When his Pulse fayling, Passion speechlesse lies,
When Faith is kneeling by his bed of Death,
And Innocence is closing up his eyes,
   Now if thou would'st, when all have given him over,
   From Death to Life thou might'st him yet recover.

62   When first I Ended, then I first Began,
Then more I Traveld, further from my Rest;
Where most I Lost, there most of all I Wan,
Pined with Hunger, rising from a Feast.
Me thinkes I Flie, yet want I legges to Goe;
Wise in Conceit, in Act a very sot;
Ravish'd with Joy amid'st a hell of Woe;
What most I Seeme, that surest am I Not.
I build my Hopes a world above the Skie,
Yet with the Mole I creepe into the Earth;
In plenty I am starv'd with Penurie,
And yet I Surfet in the greatest Dearth:
   I have, I want; Despaire, and yet Desire,
   Burn'd in a Sea of yce, and drown'd amidst a fire.

63   Truce, gentle Love, a Parly now I crave;
Me thinkes 'tis long since first these Warres begun;
Nor thou, nor I, the better yet can have:
Bad is the Match, where neither partie wonne.
I offer free Conditions of faire Peace,
My Heart for Hostage that it shall remaine;

Discharge our Forces, here let Malice cease,
So for my Pledge thou give me Pledge againe.
Or if no thing but Death will serve thy turne,
Still thirsting for subversion of my state,
Doe what thou canst, raze, massacre, and burne,
Let the World see the utmost of thy hate:
  I send defiance, since if overthrowne,
  Thou vanquishing, the Conquest is mine owne.

FINIS

EDMUND SPENSER

Amoretti

Sonnet 1

Happy ye leaves when as those lilly hands,
    which hold my life in their dead-doing might
    shall handle you and hold in love's soft bands,
    lyke captives trembling at the victor's sight.
And happy lines, on which with starry light
    those lamping eyes will deigne sometimes to look
    and reade the sorrowes of my dying spright,
    written with teares in hart's close bleeding book.
And happy rymes, bath'd in the sacred brooke
    of *Helicon* whence she derived is,
    when ye behold that Angel's blessed looke,
    my soule's long-lacked foode, my heaven's blis.
Leaves, lines, and rymes, seeke her to please alone,
    whom if ye please, I care for other none.

Sonnet 2

Unquiet thought, whom at the first I bred,
    of th'inward bale of my love-pined hart,
    and sithens have with sighes and sorrowes fed,
    till greater then my wombe thou woxen art;
Breake forth at length out of the inner part
    in which thou lurkest lyke to viper's brood,
    and seeke some succour both to ease my smart
    and also to sustayne thy selfe with food.
But if in presence of that fayrest proud
    thou chance to come, fall lowly at her feet,
    and with meeke humblesse and afflicted mood,
    pardon for thee, and grace for me intreat.
Which if she graunt, then live and my love cherish;
    if not, die soone, and I with thee will perish.

Sonnet 3

The soverayne beauty which I doo admyre,
    witnesse the world how worthy to be prayzed;
    the light wherof hath kindled heavenly fyre
    in my fraile spirit by her from basenesse raysed:
That being now with her huge brightnesse dazed,
    base thing I can no more endure to view,
    but looking still on her I stand amazed
    at wondrous sight of so celestiall hew.
So when my toung would speak her praises dew,
    it stopped is with thought's astonishment;
    and when my pen would write her titles true,
    it ravisht is with fancie's wonderment:
Yet in my hart I then both speake and write
    the wonder that my wit cannot endite.

Sonnet 4

New yeare forth looking out of Janus' gate,
    doth seeme to promise hope of new delight;
    and bidding th'old Adieu, his passed date
    bids all old thoughts to die in dumpish spright:
And calling forth out of sad Winter's night
    fresh love, that long hath slept in cheerlesse bower,
    wils him awake, and soone about him dight
    his wanton wings and darts of deadly power.
For lusty spring, now in his timely howre,
    is ready to come forth him to receive,
    and warnes the Earth with divers-colord flowre
    to decke hir selfe, and her faire mantle weave.
Then you, faire flowre, in whom fresh youth doth raine,
    prepare your selfe new love to entertaine.

Sonnet 5

Rudely thou wrongest my deare hart's desire,
    in finding fault with her too portly pride:
    the thing which I doo most in her admire
    is of the world unworthy most envide.
For in those lofty lookes is close implide
    scorn of base things, and sdeigne of foule dishonor,
    thretning rash eies which gaze on her so wide,
    that loosely they ne dare to looke upon her.

Such pride is praise, such portliness is honor,
   that boldned innocence beares in hir eies;
   and her faire countenance like a goodly banner
   spreds in defiaunce of all enemies.
Was never in this world ought worthy tride,
   without some spark of such self-pleasing pride.

Sonnet 6
Be nought dismayed that her unmoved mind
   doth still persist in her rebellious pride:
   such love not lyke to lusts of baser kynd,
   the harder wonne, the firmer will abide.
The durefull Oake, whose sap is not yet dride,
   is long ere it conceive the kindling fyre;
   but when it once doth burne, it doth divide
   great heat, and makes his flames to heaven aspire.
So hard it is to kindle new desire
   in gentle brest that shall endure for ever:
   deepe is the wound that dints the parts entire
   with chast affects, that naught but death can sever.
Then thinke not long in taking litle paine,
   to knit the knot, that ever shall remaine.

Sonnet 7
Fayre eyes, the myrrour of my mazed hart,
   what wondrous vertue is contaynd in you
   the which both lyfe and death forth from you dart
   into the object of your mighty view?
For when ye mildly looke with lovely hew,
   then is my soule with life and love inspired:
   but when ye lowre, or looke on me askew,
   then doe I die, as one with lightning fyred.
But since that lyfe is more than death desyred,
   looke ever lovely, as becomes you best,
   that your bright beams of my weak eies admyred,
   may kindle living fire within my brest.
Such life should be the honor of your light,
   such death the sad ensample of your might.

Sonnet 8

More then most faire, full of the living fire,
   kindled above unto the maker neere:
   no eies but joyes, in which al powers conspire
   that to the world naught else be counted deare:
Thrugh your bright beams doth not the blinded guest
   shoot out his darts to base affections' wound?
   but Angels come to lead fraile mindes to rest
   in chast desires on heavenly beauty bound.
You frame my thoughts and fashion me within;
   you stop my toung, and teach my hart to speake;
   you calme the storme that passion did begin,
   strong thrugh your cause, but by your vertue weak.
Dark is the world, where your light shined never;
   well is he borne, that may behold you ever.

Sonnet 9

Long-while I sought to what I might compare
   those powrefull eies, which lighten my dark spright,
   yet find I nought on earth to which I dare
   resemble th'ymage of their goodly light.
Not to the Sun: for they doo shine by night;
   nor to the Moone: for they are changed never;
   nor to the Starres: for they have purer sight;
   nor to the fire: for they consume not ever;
Nor to the lightning: for they still persever;
   nor to the Diamond: for they are more tender;
   nor unto Christall: for nought may them sever;
   nor unto glasse: such basenesse mought offend her;
Then to the Maker selfe they likest be,
   whose light doth lighten all that here we see.

Sonnet 10

Unrighteous Lord of love, what law is this,
   that me thou makest thus tormented be,
   the whiles she lordeth in licentious blisse
   of her freewill, scorning both thee and me?
See how the Tyrannesse doth joy to see
   the huge massacres which her eyes do make,
   and humbled harts brings captives unto thee,
   that thou of them mayst mightie vengeance take.

But her proud hart doe thou a little shake
   and that high look, with which she doth comptroll
   all this world's pride, bow to a baser make,
   and al her faults in thy black booke enroll;
That I may laugh at her in equal sort,
   as she doth laugh at me and makes my pain her sport.

Sonnet 11
Dayly when I do seeke and sew for peace,
   and hostages doe offer for my truth,
   she, cruell warriour, doth her selfe addresse
   to battell, and the weary war renew'th:
Ne wilbe moov'd with reason or with rewth
   to graunt small respit to my restlesse toile,
   but greedily her fell intent poursewth,
   of my poore life to make unpittied spoile.
Yet my poore life, all sorrowes to assoyle,
   I would her yield, her wrath to pacify:
   but then she seekes with torment and turmoyle
   to force me live and will not let me dy.
All paine hath end and every war hath peace,
   but mine no price nor prayer may surcease.

Sonnet 12
One day I sought with her hart-thrilling eies
   to make a truce and termes to entertaine,
   all fearelesse then of so false enimies,
   which sought me to entrap in treason's traine.
So as I then disarmed did remaine,
   a wicked ambush which lay hidden long
   in the close covert of her guilefull eyen,
   thence breaking forth, did thick about me throng.
Too feeble I t'abide the brunt so strong,
   was forst to yeeld my selfe into their hands:
   who me captiving streight with rigorous wrong
   have ever since me kept in cruell bands.
So Ladie now to you I doo complaine
   against your eies that justice I may gaine.

Sonnet 13
In that proud port, which her so goodly graceth,
   whiles her faire face she reares up to the skie,
   and to the ground her eie lids low embaseth,
   most goodly temperature ye may descry,
Myld humblesse mixt with awfull maiesty:
   for looking on the earth whence she was borne,
   her minde remembreth her mortalitie,
   what so is fayrest shall to earth returne:
But that same lofty countenance seemes to scorne
   base thing, and thinke how she to heaven may clime,
   treading downe earth as lothsome and forlorne,
   that hinders heavenly thoughts with drossy slime.
Yet lowly still vouchsafe to looke on me:
   such lowlinesse shall make you lofty be.

Sonnet 14
Retourne agayne, my forces late dismayd,
   unto the siege by you abandon'd quite:
   great shame it is to leave like one afrayd
   so fayre a peece for one repulse so light.
Gaynst such strong castles needeth greater might
   then those small forts which ye were wont belay;
   such haughty mynds enur'd to hardy fight
   disdayne to yield unto the first assay.
Bring therefore all the forces that ye may,
   and lay incessant battery to her heart,
   playnts, prayers, vowes, ruth, sorrow, and dismay;
   those engins can the proudest love convert.
And if those fayle, fall downe and dy before her;
   so dying live, and living do adore her.

Sonnet 15
Ye tradefull Merchants that with weary toyle
   do seeke most pretious things to make your gain,
   and both the Indias of their treasures spoile,
   what needeth you to seeke so farre in vaine?
For loe, my love doth in her selfe containe
   all this world's riches that may farre be found:
   if Saphyres, loe her eies be Saphyres plaine;
   if Rubies, loe hir lips be Rubies sound:

If Pearles, hir teeth be pearles both pure and round;
  if Yvorie, her forhead yvory weene;
  if Gold, her locks are finest gold on ground;
  if silver, her faire hands are silver sheene:
But that which fairest is, but few behold,
  her mind adornd with vertues manifold.

Sonnet 16

One day as I unwarily did gaze
  on those fayre eyes, my love's immortall light,
  the whiles my stonisht hart stood in amaze,
  through sweet illusion of her looke's delight;
I mote perceive how in her glauncing sight
  legions of loves with little wings did fly,
  darting their deadly arrowes fyry bright
  at every rash beholder passing by.
One of those archers closely I did spy,
  ayming his arrow at my very hart;
  when suddenly with twincle of her eye,
  the Damzell broke his misintended dart.
Had she not so doon, sure I had bene slayne,
  yet as it was, I hardly scap't with paine.

Sonnet 17

The glorious pourtraict of that Angel's face,
  made to amaze weake men's confused skil,
  and this world's worthlesse glory to embase,
  what pen, what pencill can expresse her fill?
For though he colours could devise at will
  and eke his learned hand at pleasure guide,
  least trembling it his workmanship should spill,
  yet many wondrous things there are beside.
The sweet eye-glaunces, that like arrowes glide,
  the charming smiles, that rob sence from the hart;
  the lovely pleasance and the lofty pride,
  cannot expressed be by any art.
A greater craftesman's hand thereto doth neede,
  that can expresse the life of things indeed.

Sonnet 18

The rolling wheele that runneth often round,
   the hardest steele in tract of time doth teare;
   and drizling drops that often doe redound,
   the firmest flint doth in continuance weare.
Yet cannot I with many a dropping teare
   and long intreaty soften her hard hart,
   that she will once vouchsafe my plaint to heare,
   or looke with pitty on my payneful smart.
But when I pleade, she bids me play my part,
   and when I weep, she sayes teares are but water:
   and when I sigh, she sayes I know the art,
   and when I waile, she turnes hir selfe to laughter.
So doe I weepe, and wayle, and pleade in vaine,
   whiles she as steele and flint doth still remayne.

Sonnet 19

The merry Cuckow, messenger of Spring,
   his trompet shrill hath thrise already sounded,
   that warnes al lovers wayt upon their king,
   who now is comming forth with girland crouned:
With noyse whereof the quyre of Byrds resounded
   their anthemes sweet devized of love's prayse,
   that all the woods theyr ecchoes back rebounded,
   as if they knew the meaning of their layes.
But mongst them all which did Love's honor rayse,
   no word was heard of her that most it ought,
   but she his precept proudly disobayes,
   and doth his ydle message set at nought.
Therefore O love, unlesse she turne to thee
   ere Cuckow end, let her a rebell be.

Sonnet 20

In vaine I seeke and sew to her for grace,
   and doe myne humbled hart before her poure;
   the whiles her foot she in my necke doth place,
   and tread my life downe in the lowly floure.
And yet the Lyon that is Lord of power,
   and reigneth over every beast in field,
   in his most pride disdeigneth to devoure
   the silly lambe that to his might doth yield.

But she more cruell and more salvage-wylde
    then either Lyon or the Lyonesse
    shames not to be with guiltlesse bloud defylde,
    but taketh glory in her cruelnesse.
Fayrer then fayrest, let none ever say,
    that ye were blooded in a yeelded pray.

Sonnet 21

Was it the worke of nature or of Art
    which tempred so the feature of her face,
    that pride and meeknesse, mixt by equall part,
    doe both appeare t'adorne her beautie's grace?
For with mild pleasance, which doth pride displace,
    she to her love doth lookers' eyes allure;
    and with sterne countenance back again doth chace
    their looser lookes that stir up lustes impure.
With such strange termes her eyes she doth inure,
    that with one looke she doth my life dismay,
    and with another doth it streight recure;
    her smile me drawes, her frowne me drives away.
Thus doth she traine and teach me with her lookes,
    such art of eyes I never read in bookes.

Sonnet 22

This holy season fit to fast and pray,
    men to devotion ought to be inclynd:
    therefore, I lykewise on so holy day,
    for my sweet Saynt some service fit will find.
Her temple fayre is built within my mind,
    in which her glorious ymage placed is,
    on which my thoughts doo day and night attend
    lyke sacred priests that never thinke amisse.
There I to her, as th'author of my blisse,
    will builde an altar to appease her yre;
    and on the same my hart will sacrifise,
    burning in flames of pure and chast desyre:
The which vouchsafe, O goddesse, to accept,
    amongst thy deerest relicks to be kept.

Sonnet 23
Penelope for her *Ulisses'* sake,
    deviz'd a Web her wooers to deceave;
    in which the worke that she all day did make
    the same at night she did againe unreave.
Such subtile craft my Damzell doth conceave,
    th'importune suit of my desire to shonne:
    for all that I in many dayes doo weave,
    in one short houre I find by her undonne.
So when I thinke to end that I begonne,
    I must begin and never bring to end;
    for with one looke she spils that long I sponne,
    and with one word my whole year's work doth rend.
Such labour like the Spyder's web I fynd,
    whose fruitlesse worke is broken with least wynd.

Sonnet 24
When I behold that beautie's wonderment,
    and rare perfection of each goodly part,
    of nature's skill the onely complement,
    I honor and admire the maker's art.
But when I feele the bitter balefull smart
    which her fayre eyes unwares doe worke in mee,
    that death out of theyr shiny beames doe dart,
    I thinke that I a new *Pandora* see;
Whom all the Gods in councell did agree
    into this sinfull world from heaven to send,
    that she to wicked men a scourge should bee,
    for all their faults with which they did offend.
But since ye are my scourge I will intreat,
    that for my faults ye will me gently beat.

Sonnet 25
How long shall this lyke-dying lyfe endure,
    and know no end of her owne mysery,
    but wast and weare away in termes unsure,
    twixt feare and hope depending doubtfully?
Yet better were attonce to let me die,
    and shew the last ensample of your pride,
    then to torment me thus with cruelty,
    to prove your powre, which I too wel have tride.

But yet if in your hardned brest ye hide
   a close intent at last to shew me grace,
   than all the woes and wrecks which I abide,
   as meanes of blisse I gladly wil embrace;
And wish that more and greater they might be,
   that greater meede at last may turne to mee.

Sonnet 26
Sweet is the Rose, but growes upon a brere;
   sweet is the Junipere, but sharpe his bough;
   sweet is the Eglantine, but pricketh nere;
   sweet is the firbloome, but his braunches rough.
Sweet is the Cypresse, but his rynd is tough;
   sweet is the nut, but bitter is his pill;
   sweet is the broome-flowre, but yet sowre enough;
   and sweet is Moly, but his root is ill.
So every sweet with soure is tempred still,
   that maketh it be coveted the more:
   for easie things that may be got at will,
   most sorts of men doe set but little store.
Why then should I accoumpt of little paine,
   that endlesse pleasure shall unto me gaine?

Sonnet 27
Faire proud, now tell me why should faire be proud,
   sith all world's glorie is but drosse uncleane,
   and in the shade of death it selfe shall shroud,
   how ever now thereof ye little weene.
That goodly Idoll now so gay beseene,
   shall doffe her fleshe's borowd fayre attyre,
   and be forgot as it had never beene,
   that many now much worship and admire.
Ne any then shall after it inquire,
   ne any mention shall thereof remaine,
   but what this verse, that never shall expyre,
   shall to you purchas with her thankles paine.
Faire be no lenger proud of that shall perish,
   but that which shal you make immortall, cherish.

Sonnet 28

The laurell leafe, which you this day doe weare,
   gives me great hope of your relenting mynd;
   for since it is the badg which I doe beare,
   ye bearing it doe seeme to me inclind:
The powre thereof, which ofte in me I find,
   let it lykewise your gentle brest inspire
   with sweet infusion, and put you in mind
   of that proud mayd, whom now those leaves attyre:
Proud *Daphne* scorning Phæbus' lovely fyre,
   on the Thessalian shore from him did flee;
   for which the gods in theyr revengefull yre
   did her transforme into a laurell tree.
Then fly no more, fayre love, from Phebus' chace,
   but in your brest his leafe and love embrace.

Sonnet 29

See how the stubborne damzell doth deprave
   my simple meaning with disdaynfull scorne,
   and by the bay which I unto her gave,
   accoumpts my selfe her captive quite forlorne.
The bay (quoth she) is of the victours borne,
   yielded them by the vanquisht as theyr meeds,
   and they therewith doe poetes' heads adorne,
   to sing the glory of their famous deedes.
But sith she will the conquest challeng needs,
   let her accept me as her faithfull thrall,
   that her great triumph which my skill exceeds,
   I may in trump of fame blaze over all.
Then would I decke her head with glorious bayes,
   and fill the world with her victorious prayse.

Sonnet 30

My love is lyke to yse, and I to fyre:
   how comes it then that this her cold so great
   is not dissolv'd through my so hot desyre,
   but harder growes the more I her intreat?
Or how comes it that my exceeding heat
   is not delayed by her hart frosen cold,
   but that I burne much more in boyling sweat,
   and feele my flames augmented manifold?

What more miraculous thing may be told
   that fire, which all thing melts, should harden yse:
   and yse which is congeald with sencelesse cold,
   should kindle fyre by wonderfull devyse?
Such is the powre of love in gentle mind
   that it can alter all the course of kynd.

Sonnet 31

Ah why hath nature to so hard a hart
   given so goodly giftes of beautie's grace,
   whose pryde depraves each other better part,
   and all those pretious ornaments deface;
Sith to all other beastes of bloody race
   a dreadfull countenaunce she given hath,
   that with theyr terrour al the rest may chace,
   and warne to shun the daunger of theyr wrath?
But my proud one doth worke the greater scath
   through sweet allurement of her lovely hew,
   that she the better may in bloody bath
   of such poore thralls her cruell hands embrew.
But did she know how ill these two accord,
   such cruelty she would have soone abhord.

Sonnet 32

The paynefull smith with force of fervent heat
   the hardest yron soone doth mollify,
   that with his heavy sledge he can it beat,
   and fashion to what he it list apply.
Yet cannot all these flames in which I fry
   her hart more harde then yron soft awhit,
   ne all the playnts and prayers with which I
   doe beat on th'andvyle of her stubberne wit:
But still the more she fervent sees my fit,
   the more she frieseth in her wilfull pryde,
   and harder growes the harder she is smit,
   with all the playnts which to her be applyde.
What then remaines but I to ashes burne,
   and she to stones at length all frosen turne?

Sonnet 33
Great wrong I doe, I can it not deny,
    to that most sacred Empresse, my dear dred,
    not finishing her Queene of faery,
    that mote enlarge her living prayses dead:
But Lodwick, this of grace to me aread:
    doe ye not thinck th'accomplishment of it
    sufficient worke for one man's simple head,
    all were it as the rest but rudely writ?
How then should I without another wit
    thinck ever to endure so taedious toyle,
    sins that this one is tost with troublous fit
    of a proud love, that doth my spirite spoyle?
Ceasse then, till she vouchsafe to grawnt me rest,
    or lend you me another living brest.

Sonnet 34
Lyke as a ship that through the Ocean wyde,
    by conduct of some star doth make her way,
    whenas a storme hath dimd her trusty guyde,
    out of her course doth wander far astray:
So I, whose star, that wont with her bright ray
    me to direct, with cloudes is overcast,
    doe wander now in darknesse and dismay,
    through hidden perils round about me plast.
Yet hope I well that when this storme is past
    my *Helice*, the lodestar of my lyfe,
    will shine again, and looke on me at last,
    with lovely light to cleare my cloudy grief.
Till then I wander carefull comfortlesse,
    in secret sorow and sad pensivenesse.

Sonnet 35
My hungry eyes, through greedy covetize
    still to behold the object of their paine,
    with no contentment can themselves suffize,
    but having pine and having not, complaine.
For lacking it, they cannot lyfe sustayne,
    and having it, they gaze on it the more;
    in their amazement lyke *Narcissus* vaine
    whose eyes him starv'd: so plenty makes me poore.

Yet are mine eyes so filled with the store
    of that faire sight, that nothing else they brooke,
    but lothe the things which they did like before,
    and can no more endure on them to looke.
All this world's glory seemeth vayne to me,
    and all their showes but shadowes saving she.

Sonnet 36

Tell me when shall these wearie woes have end,
    or shall their ruthlesse torment never cease;
    but al my dayes in pining languor spend,
    without hope of aswagement or release?
Is there no meanes for me to purchace peace,
    or make agreement with her thrilling eyes,
    but that their cruelty doth still increace,
    and dayly more augment my miseryes?
But when ye have shewed all extremityes,
    then thinke how litle glory ye have gayned
    by slaying him, whose lyfe though ye despyse,
    mote have your life in honour long maintayned.
But by his death which some perhaps will mone,
    ye shall condemned be of many a one.

Sonnet 37

What guyle is this, that those her golden tresses,
    she doth attyre under a net of gold,
    and with sly skill so cunningly them dresses,
    that which is gold or heare may scarse be told?
Is it that men's frayle eyes, which gaze too bold,
    she may entangle in that golden snare;
    and being caught, may craftily enfold
    theyr weaker harts, which are not wel aware?
Take heed therefore, myne eyes, how ye doe stare
    henceforth too rashly on that guilefull net,
    in which if ever ye entrapped are,
    out of her bands ye by no meanes shall get.
Fondnesse it were for any being free
    to covet fetters, though they golden bee.

Sonnet 38

Arion, when through tempest's cruel wracke,
    he forth was thrown into the greedy seas,
    through the sweet musick which his harp did make
    allur'd a Dolphin him from death to ease.
But my rude musick, which was wont to please
    some dainty eares, cannot with any skill
    the dreadfull tempest of her wrath appease,
    nor move the Dolphin from her stubborne will;
But in her pride she dooth persever still,
    all carelesse how my life for her decayse:
    yet with one word she can it save or spill:
    to spill were pitty, but to save were prayse.
Chose rather to be praysd for dooing good
    then to be blam'd for spilling guiltlesse blood.

Sonnet 39

Sweet smile, the daughter of the Queene of love,
    expressing all thy mother's powrefull art,
    with which she wonts to temper angry *Jove*,
    when all the gods he threats with thundring dart:
Sweet is thy vertue as thy selfe sweet art,
    for when on me thou shinedst late in sadnesse,
    a melting pleasance ran through every part,
    and me revived with hart-robbing gladnesse.
Whylest rapt with Joy resembling heavenly madnes,
    my soule was ravisht quite as in a traunce;
    and feeling thence no more her sorowe's sadnesse,
    fed on the fulnesse of that chearefull glaunce.
More sweet than Nectar or Ambrosiall meat
    seemd every bit, which thenceforth I did eat.

Sonnet 40

Mark when she smiles with amiable cheare,
    and tell me whereto can ye lyken it,
    when on each eyelid sweetly doe appeare
    an hundred Graces as in shade to sit.
Lykest it seemeth in my simple wit
    unto the fayre sunshine in somer's day,
    that when a dreadfull storme away is flit,
    thrugh the broad world doth spred his goodly ray:

At sight whereof each bird that sits on spray,
    and every beast that to his den was fled,
    comes forth afresh out of their late dismay,
    and to the light lift up theyr drouping hed.
So my storme-beaten hart likewise is cheared
    with that sunshine when cloudy looks are cleared.

Sonnet 41

Is it her nature or is it her will,
    to be so cruell to an humbled foe?
    if nature, then she may it mend with skill;
    if will, then she at will may will forgoe.
But if her nature and her wil be so,
    that she will plague the man that loves her most,
    and take delight t'encrease a wretche's woe,
    then all her nature's goodly guifts are lost:
And that same glorious beautie's ydle boast
    is but a bayt such wretches to beguile,
    as, being long in her love's tempest tost,
    she meanes at last to make her piteous spoyle.
O fayrest fayre let never it be named,
    that so fayre beauty was so fowly shamed.

Sonnet 42

The love which me so cruelly tormenteth
    so pleasing is in my extreamest paine,
    that all the more my sorrow it augmenteth,
    the more I love and doe embrace my bane.
Ne doe I wish (for wishing were but vaine)
    to be acquit fro my continuall smart,
    but joy her thrall for ever to remayne,
    and yield for pledge my poore captyved hart:
The which that it from her may never start,
    let her, yf please her, bynd with adamant chayne;
    and from all wandring loves which mote pervart
    his safe assurance, strongly it restrayne.
Onely let her abstaine from cruelty,
    and doe me not before my time to dy.

Sonnet 43
Shall I then silent be or shall I speake?
   and if I speake, her wrath renew I shall:
   and if I silent be, my hart will breake,
   or choked be with overflowing gall.
What tyranny is this both my hart to thrall,
   and eke my toung with proud restraint to tie,
   that nether I may speake nor thinke at all,
   but like a stupid stock in silence die!
Yet I my hart with silence secretly
   will teach to speak, and my just cause to plead;
   and eke mine eies with meeke humility,
   love-learned letters to her eyes to read:
Which her deep wit, that true hart's thought can spel,
   wil soone conceive, and learne to construe well.

Sonnet 44
When those renoumed noble Peres of Greece,
   thrugh stubborn pride amongst themselves did jar,
   forgetfull of the famous golden fleece,
   then *Orpheus* with his harp theyr strife did bar.
But this continuall cruell civill warre,
   the which my selfe against my selfe doe make,
   whilest my weak powres of passions warreid arre,
   no skill can stint nor reason can aslake.
But when in hand my tunelesse harp I take,
   then doe I more augment my foe's despight;
   and griefe renew, and passions doe awake,
   to battaile fresh against my self to fight:
Mongst whome the more I seeke to settle peace,
   the more I fynd their malice to increace.

Sonnet 45
Leave, lady, in your glasse of christall clene
   your goodly selfe for evermore to vew,
   and in my selfe, my inward selfe I meane,
   most lively-lyke behold your semblant trew.
Within my hart, though hardly it can shew
   thing so divine to vew of earthly eye,
   the fayre Idea of your celestiall hew
   and every part remaines immortally:

And were it not that through your cruelty
   with sorrow dimmed and deformd it were,
   the goodly ymage of your visnomy
   clearer then christall would therein appere.
But if your selfe in me ye playne will see,
   remove the cause by which your fayre beames darkned be.

Sonnet 46

When my abode's prefixed time is spent,
   my cruell fayre streight bids me wend my way:
   but then from heaven most hideous stormes are sent
   as willing me against her will to stay.
Whom then shall I or heaven or her obay?
   the heavens know best what is the best for me:
   but as she will, whose will my life doth sway,
   my lower heaven, so it perforce must bee.
But ye high hevens, that all this sorrowe see,
   sith all your tempests cannot hold me backe,
   aswage your stormes, or else both you and she
   will both together me too sorely wrack.
Enough it is for one man to sustaine
   the stormes, which she alone on me doth raine.

Sonnet 47

Trust not the treason of those smyling lookes,
   untill ye have theyr guylefull traynes well tryde;
   for they are lyke but unto golden hookes,
   that from the foolish fish theyr bayts doe hyde:
So she with flattring smyles weake harts doth guyde
   unto her love, and tempte to theyr decay,
   whome being caught, she kills with cruell pryde,
   and feeds at pleasure on the wretched pray:
Yet even whylst her bloody hands them slay,
   her eyes looke lovely and upon them smyle,
   that they take pleasure in her cruell play,
   and dying doe them selves of payne beguyle.
O mighty charm which makes men love theyr bane,
   and thinck they dy with pleasure, live with payne.

Sonnet 48
Innocent paper whom too cruell hand
    did make the matter to avenge her yre,
    and ere she could thy cause wel understand,
    did sacrifize unto the greedy fyre:
Well worthy thou to have found better hyre
    then so bad end for hereticks ordayned:
    yet heresy nor treason didst conspire,
    but plead thy maister's cause unjustly payned:
Whom she, all carelesse of his griefe, constrayned
    to utter forth th' anguish of his hart,
    and would not heare, when he to her complayned
    the piteous passion of his dying smart.
Yet live for ever, though against her will,
    and speake her good, though she requite it ill.

Sonnet 49
Fayre cruell, why are ye so fierce and cruell?
    is it because your eyes have powre to kill?
    then know, that mercy is the mightie's jewell,
    and greater glory thinke to save, then spill.
But if it be your pleasure and proud will
    to shew the powre of your imperious eyes,
    then not on him that never thought you ill,
    but bend your force against your enemyes.
Let them feele th'utmost of your crueltyes,
    and kill with looks, as Cockatrices doo:
    but him that at your footstoole humbled lies,
    with mercifull regard, give mercy too.
Such mercy shal you make admyred to be,
    so shall you live by giving life to me.

Sonnet 50
Long languishing in double malady
    of my hart's wound and of my bodie's greife,
    there came to me a leach that would apply
    fit medicines for my bodie's best reliefe.
'Vayne man' (quod I) 'that hast but little priefe,
    in deep discovery of the mynd's disease,
    is not the hart of all the body chiefe,
    and rules the members as it selfe doth please?

Then with some cordialls seeke first to appease
   the inward languour of my wounded hart,
   and then my body shall have shortly ease:
   but such sweet cordialls passe Physition's art.
Then, my lyfe's Leach, doe you your skill reveale,
   and with one salve both hart and body heale.'

Sonnet 51
Doe I not see that fayrest ymages
   of hardest Marble are of purpose made,
   for that they should endure through many ages,
   ne let theyr famous moniments to fade?
Why then doe I, untrainde in lover's trade,
   her hardnes blame which I should more commend,
   sith never ought was excellent assayde,
   which was not hard t'atchive and bring to end?
Ne ought so hard, but he that would attend,
   mote soften it and to his will allure:
   so doe I hope her stubborne hart to bend,
   and that it then more stedfast will endure.
Onely my paines wil be the more to get her,
   but having her, my joy wil be the greater.

Sonnet 52
So oft as homeward I from her depart,
   I goe lyke one that, having lost the field,
   is prisoner led away with heavy hart,
   despoyld of warlike armes and knowen shield.
So doe I now my selfe a prisoner yeeld
   to sorrow and to solitary paine,
   from presence of my dearest deare exylde,
   longwhile alone in languor to remaine.
There let no thought of joy or pleasure vaine
   dare to approch, that may my solace breed:
   but sudden dumps and drery sad disdayne
   of all world's gladnesse more my torment feed.
So I her absens will my penaunce make,
   that of her presens I my meed may take.

Sonnet 53
The Panther knowing that his spotted hyde
   doth please all beasts but that his looks them fray,
   within a bush his dreadfull head doth hide,
   to let them gaze whylest he on them may pray.
Right so my cruell fayre with me doth play:
   for with the goodly semblant of her hew,
   she doth allure me to mine owne decay,
   and then no mercy will unto me shew.
Great shame it is, thing so divine in view
   made for to be the world's most ornament,
   to make the bayte her gazers to embrew:
   good shames to be to ill an instrument.
But mercy doth with beautie best agree,
   as in theyr maker ye them best may see.

Sonnet 54
Of this world's Theatre in which we stay,
   my love lyke the Spectator ydly sits
   beholding me that all the pageants play,
   disguysing diversly my troubled wits.
Sometimes I joy when glad occasion fits,
   and mask in myrth lyke to a Comedy:
   soone after when my joy to sorrow flits,
   I waile and make my woes a Tragedy.
Yet she beholding me with constant eye,
   delights not in my merth nor rues my smart:
   but when I laugh she mocks, and when I cry
   she laughes, and hardens evermore her hart.
What then can move her? if nor merth nor mone,
   she is no woman, but a sencelesse stone.

Sonnet 55
So oft as I her beauty doe behold,
   and therewith doe her cruelty compare,
   I marvaile of what substance was the mould
   the which her made attonce so cruell-faire.
Not earth; for her high thoghts more heavenly are:
   not water; for her love doth burne like fyre:
   not ayre; for she is not so light or rare:
   not fyre; for she doth friese with faint desire.

Then needs another Element inquire
   whereof she mote be made; that is the skye:
   for to the heaven her haughty lookes aspire,
   and eke her mind is pure immortall hye.
Then sith to heaven ye lykened are the best,
   be lyke in mercy as in all the rest.

Sonnet 56

Fayre ye be sure, but cruell and unkind,
   as is a Tygre that with greedinesse
   hunts after bloud, when he by chance doth find
   a feeble beast, doth felly him oppresse.
Fayre be ye sure, but proud and pittilesse,
   as is a storme, that all things doth prostrate,
   finding a tree alone all comfortlesse,
   beats on it strongly it to ruinate.
Fayre be ye sure, but hard and obstinate,
   as is a rocke amidst the raging floods,
   gaynst which a ship, of succour desolate,
   doth suffer wreck both of her selfe and goods.
That ship, that tree, and that same beast am I,
   whom ye doe wreck, doe ruine, and destroy.

Sonnet 57

Sweet warriour, when shall I have peace with you?
   high time it is, this warre now ended were,
   which I no lenger can endure to sue,
   ne your incessant battry more to beare:
So weake my powres, so sore my wounds appeare,
   that wonder is how I should live a jot,
   seeing my hart through-launched every where
   with thousand arrowes, which your eies have shot.
Yet shoot ye sharpely still, and spare me not,
   but glory thinke to make these cruel stoures.
   ye cruell one, what glory can be got
   in slaying him that would live gladly yours?
Make peace therefore, and graunt me timely grace,
   that al my wounds wil heale in little space.

Sonnet 58
By her that is most assured to her selfe.
Weake is th'assurance that weake flesh reposeth
  in her owne powre, and scorneth other's ayde:
  that soonest fals when as she most supposeth
  her selfe assurd, and is of nought affrayd.
All flesh is frayle, and all her strength unstayd,
  like a vaine bubble blowen up with ayre:
  devouring tyme and changeful chance have prayd
  her glorie's pride that none may it repayre.
Ne none so rich or wise, so strong or fayre,
  but fayleth, trusting on his owne assurance:
  and he that standeth on the hyghest stayre
  fals lowest, for on earth nought hath enduraunce.
Why then doe ye, proud fayre, misdeeme so farre,
  that to your selfe ye most assured arre?

Sonnet 59
Thrise happie she, that is so well assured
  unto her selfe and setled so in hart;
  that nether will for better be allured,
  ne feard with worse to any chaunce to start;
But like a steddy ship doth strongly part
  the raging waves and keepes her course aright;
  ne ought for tempest doth from it depart,
  ne ought for fayrer weather's false delight.
Such selfe assurance need not feare the spight
  of grudging foes, ne favour seek of friends,
  but in the stay of her owne stedfast might,
  nether to one her selfe nor other bends.
Most happy she that most assured doth rest,
  but he most happy who such one loves best.

Sonnet 60
They that in course of heavenly spheares are skild,
  to every planet point his sundry yeare,
  in which her circle's voyage is fulfild,
  as Mars in three score yeares doth run his spheare.
So since the winged God his planet cleare
  began in me to move, one yeare is spent:
  the which doth longer unto me appeare
  then al those fourty which my life outwent.

Then by that count, which lovers' books invent,
 the spheare of Cupid fourty yeares containes,
 which I have wasted in long languishment,
 that seemd the longer for my greater paines.
But let my love's fayre Planet short her wayes
 this yeare ensuing, or else short my dayes.

Sonnet 61

The glorious image of the maker's beautie,
 my soverayne saynt, the Idoll of my thought,
 dare not henceforth above the bounds of dewtie,
 t'accuse of pride, or rashly blame for ought.
For being as she is divinely wrought,
 and of the brood of Angels' hevenly borne,
 and with the crew of blessed Saynts upbrought,
 each of which did her with theyr guifts adorne;
The bud of joy, the blossome of the morne,
 the beame of light, whom mortal eyes admyre:
 what reason is it then but she should scorne
 base things that to her love too bold aspire?
Such heavenly formes ought rather worshipt be
 then dare be lov'd by men of meane degree.

Sonnet 62

The weary yeare his race now having run,
 the new begins his compass course anew:
 with shew of morning mylde he hath begun,
 betokening peace and plenty to ensew.
So let us, which this chaunge of weather vew,
 chaunge eeke our mynds and former lives amend;
 the old yeare's sinnes forepast let us eschew,
 and fly the faults with which we did offend.
Then shall the new yeare's joy forth freshly send
 into the glooming world his gladsome ray;
 and all these stormes which now his beauty blend,
 shall turne to caulmes and tymely cleare away.
So likewise love cheare you your heavy spright,
 and chaunge old yeare's annoy to new delight.

Sonnet 63
After long stormes and tempests' sad assay,
  which hardly I endured heretofore,
  in dread of death and daungerous dismay,
  with which my silly barke was tossed sore;
I doe at length descry the happy shore,
  in which I hope ere long for to arryve:
  fayre soyle it seemes from far and fraught with store
  of all that deare and daynty is alyve.
Most happy he that can at last atchyve
  the joyous safety of so sweet a rest,
  whose least delight sufficeth to deprive
  remembrance of all paines which him opprest.
All paines are nothing in respect of this,
  all sorrowes short that gaine eternall blisse.

Sonnet 64
Comming to kisse her lyps, (such grace I found)
  me seemd I smelt a gardin of sweet flowres,
  that dainty odours from them threw around
  for damzels fit to decke their lovers' bowres.
Her lips did smell lyke unto Gillyflowers,
  her ruddy cheekes lyke unto Roses red;
  her snowy browes lyke budded Bellamoures,
  her lovely eyes lyke Pincks but newly spred;
Her goodly bosome lyke a Strawberry bed,
  her neck lyke to a bounch of Cullambynes;
  her brest lyke lillyes, ere theyr leaves be shed,
  her nipples lyke yong blossom'd Jessemynes:
Such fragrant flowres doe give most odorous smell,
  but her sweet odour did them all excell.

Sonnet 65
The doubt which ye misdeeme, fayre love, is vaine,
  that fondly feare to loose your liberty,
  when loosing one, two liberties ye gayne,
  and make him bond that bondage earst dyd fly.
Sweet be the bands, the which true love doth tye,
  without constraynt or dread of any ill:
  the gentle birde feeles no captivity
  within her cage, but singes and feeds her fill.

There pride dare not approch, nor discord spill
    the league twixt them, that loyal love hath bound;
    but simple truth and mutuall good will
    seekes with sweet peace to salve each other's wound:
There fayth doth fearlesse dwell in brasen towre,
    and spotlesse pleasure builds her sacred bowre.

Sonnet 66

To all those happy blessings which ye have
    with plenteous hand by heaven upon you thrown,
    this one disparagement they to you gave,
    that ye your love lent to so meane a one.
Yee whose high worth's surpassing paragon,
    could not on earth have found one fit for mate,
    ne but in heaven matchable to none,
    why did ye stoup unto so lowly state?
But ye thereby much greater glory gate,
    then had ye sorted with a prince's pere;
    for now your light doth more it selfe dilate,
    and in my darknesse greater doth appeare.
Yet since your light hath once enlumind me,
    with my reflex yours shall encreased be.

Sonnet 67

Lyke as a huntsman after weary chace,
    seeing the game from him escapt away,
    sits downe to rest him in some shady place,
    with panting hounds beguiled of their pray:
So after long pursuit and vaine assay,
    when I all weary had the chace forsooke,
    the gentle deare returnd the selfe-same way,
    thinking to quench her thirst at the next brooke.
There she beholding me with mylder looke,
    sought not to fly, but fearelesse still did bide;
    till I in hand her yet halfe trembling tooke,
    and with her owne goodwill hir fyrmely tyde.
Strange thing me seemd to see a beast so wyld,
    so goodly wonne with her owne will beguyld.

Sonnet 68
Most glorious Lord of lyfe that on this day
   didst make thy triumph over death and sin,
   and having harrowd hell didst bring away
   captivity thence captive us to win:
This joyous day, deare Lord, with joy begin,
   and grant that we for whom thou diddest dye,
   being with thy deare blood clene washt from sin,
   may live for ever in felicity:
And that thy love we weighing worthily,
   may likewise love thee for the same againe;
   and for thy sake that all lyke deare didst buy,
   with love may one another entertayne.
So let us love, deare love, lyke as we ought:
   love is the lesson which the Lord us taught.

Sonnet 69
The famous warriors of the anticke world
   used Trophees to erect in stately wize,
   in which they would the records have enrold
   of theyr great deeds and valarous emprize.
What trophee then shall I most fit devize,
   in which I may record the memory
   of my love's conquest, peerelesse beautie's prise,
   adorn'd with honour, love, and chastity?
Even this verse vowd to eternity
   shall be thereof immortall moniment;
   and tell her prayse to all posterity,
   that may admire such world's rare wonderment:
The happy purchase of my glorious spoile,
   gotten at last with labour and long toyle.

Sonnet 70
Fresh spring, the herald of love's mighty king,
   in whose cote-armour richly are displayd
   all sorts of flowers the which on earth do spring
   in goodly colours gloriously arrayd:
Goe to my love, where she is carelesse layd,
   yet in her winter's bowre not well awake:
   tell her the joyous time wil not be staid
   unlesse she doe him by the forelock take.

Bid her therefore her selfe soone ready make,
  to wayt on love amongst his lovely crew,
  where every one that misseth then her make,
  shall be by him amearst with penance dew.
Make hast therefore, sweet love, whilest it is prime,
  for none can call againe the passed time.

Sonnet 71

I joy to see how in your drawen work,
  your selfe unto the Bee ye doe compare;
  and me unto the Spyder that doth lurke
  in close awayt to catch her unaware.
Right so your selfe were caught in cunning snare
  of a deare foe, and thralled to his love;
  in whose streight bands ye now captived are
  so firmely, that ye never may remove.
But as your worke is woven all above
  with woodbynd flowers and fragrant Eglantine,
  so sweet your prison you in time shall prove,
  with many deare delights bedecked fyne.
And all thensforth eternall peace shall see,
  betweene the Spyder and the gentle Bee.

Sonnet 72

Oft when my spirit doth spred her bolder winges,
  in mind to mount up to the purest sky,
  it down is weighd with thoght of earthly things
  and clogd with burden of mortality;
Where when that soverayne beauty it doth spy,
  resembling heaven's glory in her light,
  drawne with sweet pleasure's bayt, it back doth fly,
  and unto heaven forgets her former flight.
There my fraile fancy fed with full delight,
  doth bath in blisse and mantleth most at ease;
  ne thinks of other heaven, but how it might
  her hart's desire with most contentment please.
Hart need not wish none other happinesse,
  but here on earth to have such heven's blisse.

Sonnet 73

Being my selfe captyved here in care,
   my hart, whom none with servile bands can tye
   but the fayre tresses of your golden hayre,
   breaking his prison forth to you doth fly.
Lyke as a byrd that in one's hand doth spy
   desired food, to it doth make his flight,
   even so my hart, that wont on your fayre eye
   to feed his fill, flyes backe unto your sight.
Doe you him take, and in your bosome bright
   gently encage, that he may be your thrall:
   perhaps he there may learne with rare delight
   to sing your name and prayses over all,
That it hereafter may you not repent,
   him lodging in your bosome to have lent.

Sonnet 74

Most happy letters fram'd by skilfull trade,
   with which that happy name was first desynd,
   the which three times thrise happy hath me made,
   with guifts of body, fortune and of mind.
The first my being to me gave by kind,
   from mother's womb deriv'd by dew descent:
   the second is my sovereigne Queene most kind,
   that honour and large richesse to me lent.
The third my love, my live's last ornament,
   by whom my spirit out of dust was raysed,
   to speake her prayse and glory excellent,
   of all alive most worthy to be praysed.
Ye three Elizabeths for ever live,
   that three such graces did unto me give.

Sonnet 75

One day I wrote her name upon the strand,
   but came the waves and washed it away:
   agayne I wrote it with a second hand,
   but came the tyde, and made my paynes his pray.
'Vayne man', sayd she, 'that doest in vaine assay
   a mortall thing so to immortalize,
   for I my selve shall lyke to this decay,
   and eek my name bee wyped out lykewize.'

'Not so,' (quod I) 'let baser things devize
   to dy in dust, but you shall live by fame:
   my verse your vertues rare shall eternize,
   and in the hevens wryte your glorious name:
Where, whenas death shall all the world subdew,
   our love shall live, and later life renew.

Sonnet 76

Fayre bosome fraught with vertue's richest tresure,
   the neast of love, the lodging of delight,
   the bowre of blisse, the paradice of pleasure,
   the sacred harbour of that hevenly spright;
How was I ravisht with your lovely sight,
   and my frayle thoughts too rashly led astray,
   whiles diving deepe through amorous insight,
   on the sweet spoyle of beautie they did pray:
And twixt her paps like early fruit in May,
   whose harvest seemd to hasten now apace,
   they loosely did theyr wanton winges display,
   and here to rest themselves did boldly place.
Sweet thoughts I envy your so happy rest,
   which oft I wisht, yet never was so blest.

Sonnet 77

Was it a dreame, or did I see it playne,
   a goodly table of pure yvory,
   all spred with juncats, fit to entertayne
   the greatest Prince with pompous roialty?
Mongst which there in a silver dish did ly
   twoo golden apples of unvalewd price,
   far passing those which *Hercules* came by,
   or those which *Atalanta* did entice:
Exceeding sweet, yet voyd of sinfull vice,
   That many sought yet none could ever taste;
   sweet fruit of pleasure brought from paradice
   by Love himselfe and in his garden plaste.
Her brest that table was so richly spredd,
   my thoughts the guests, which would thereon have fedd.

Sonnet 78
Lackyng my love I go from place to place,
 lyke a young fawne that late hath lost the hynd;
 and seeke each where, where last I sawe her face,
 whose ymage yet I carry fresh in mynd.
I seeke the fields with her late footing synd,
 I seeke her bowre with her late presence deckt,
 yet nor in field nor bowre I her can fynd;
 yet field and bowre are full of her aspect.
But when myne eyes I thereunto direct,
 they ydly back returne to me agayne,
 and when I hope to see theyr trew object,
 I fynd my selfe but fed with fancies vayne.
Ceasse then, myne eyes, to seeke her selfe to see,
 and let my thoughts behold her selfe in mee.

Sonnet 79
Men call you fayre, and you doe credit it,
 for that your selfe ye dayly such doe see:
 but the trew fayre, that is the gentle wit
 and vertuous mind, is much more praysd of me.
For all the rest, how ever fayre it be,
 shall turne to nought and loose that glorious hew:
 but onely that is permanent and free
 from frayle corruption, that doth flesh ensew.
That is true beautie: that doth argue you
 to be divine and borne of heavenly seed,
 deriv'd from that fayre Spirit, from whom al true
 and perfect beauty did at first proceed.
He onely fayre, and what he fayre hath made:
 all other fayre lyke flowres untymely fade.

Sonnet 80
After so long a race as I have run
 through Faery land, which those six books compile,
 give leave to rest me being halfe fordonne,
 and gather to my selfe new breath awhile.
Then as a steed refreshed after toyle,
 out of my prison I will breake anew,
 and stoutly will that second worke assoyle,
 with strong endevour and attention dew.

Till then, give leave to me in pleasant mew
 to sport my muse and sing my love's sweet praise,
 the contemplation of whose heavenly hew
 my spirit to an higher pitch will rayse.
But let her prayses yet be low and meane,
 fit for the handmayd of the Faery Queene.

Sonnet 81

Fayre is my love, when her fayre golden heares
 with the loose wynd ye waving chance to marke:
 fayre when the rose in her red cheekes appeares,
 or in her eyes the fyre of love does sparke.
Fayre when her brest lyke a rich laden barke,
 with pretious merchandize she forth doth lay:
 fayre when that cloud of pryde, which oft doth dark
 her goodly light, with smiles she drives away.
But fayrest she, when so she doth display
 the gate with pearles and rubyes richly dight,
 throgh which her words so wise do make their way
 to beare the message of her gentle spright.
The rest be works of nature's wonderment,
 but this the worke of hart's astonishment.

Sonnet 82

Joy of my life, full oft for loving you
 I blesse my lot, that was so lucky placed:
 but then the more your owne mishap I rew,
 that are so much by so meane love embased.
For had the equall hevens so much you graced
 in this as in the rest, ye mote invent
 som hevenly wit, whose verse could have enchased
 your glorious name in golden moniment.
But since ye deigned so goodly to relent
 to me your thrall, in whom is little worth,
 that little that I am shall all be spent
 in setting your immortall prayses forth:
Whose lofty argument, uplifting me,
 shall lift you up unto an high degree.

Sonnet 83

My hungry eyes, through greedy covetize
   still to behold the object of theyr payne,
   with no contentment can themselves suffize,
   but having pine, and having not, complayne.
For lacking it, they cannot lyfe sustayne,
   and seeing it, they gaze on it the more:
   in theyr amazement lyke *Narcissus* vayne
   whose eyes him starv'd: so plenty makes me pore.
Yet are myne eyes so filled with the store
   of that fayre sight, that nothing else they brooke,
   but loath the things which they did like before,
   and can no more endure on them to looke.
All this world's glory seemeth vayne to me,
   and all theyr shewes but shadowes, saving she.

Sonnet 84

Let not one sparke of filthy lustfull fyre
   breake out, that may her sacred peace molest,
   ne one light glance of sensuall desyre
   Attempt to work her gentle minde's unrest.
But pure affections bred in spotlesse brest,
   and modest thoughts breathd from wel-tempred sprites,
   goe visit her in her chast bowre of rest,
   accompanyde with angelick delightes.
There fill your selfe with those most joyous sights,
   the which my selfe could never yet attayne:
   but speake no word to her of these sad plights,
   which her too constant stiffenesse doth constrayn.
Onely behold her rare perfection,
   and blesse your fortune's fayre election.

Sonnet 85

The world that cannot deeme of worthy things,
   when I doe praise her, say I doe but flatter:
   so does the Cuckow, when the Mavis sings,
   begin his witlesse note apace to clatter.
But they that skill not of so heavenly matter,
   all that they know not, envy or admyre,
   rather then envy let them wonder at her,
   but not to deeme of her desert aspyre.

Deepe in the closet of my parts entyre,
   her worth is written with a golden quill:
   that me with heavenly fury doth inspire,
   and my glad mouth with her sweet prayses fill.
Which when as fame in her shrill trump shal thunder,
   let the world chose to envy or to wonder.

Sonnet 86

Venemous toung tipt with vile adder's sting,
   of that selfe kynd with which the Furies fell
   theyr snaky heads doe combe, from which a spring
   of poysoned words and spitefull speeches well:
Let all the plagues and horrid paines of hell
   upon thee fall for thine accursed hyre,
   that with false forged lyes, which thou didst tel,
   in my true love did stirre up coles of yre:
The sparkes whereof let kindle thine own fyre,
   and catching hold on thine owne wicked hed
   consume thee quite, that didst with guile conspire
   in my sweet peace such breaches to have bred.
Shame be thy meed, and mischiefe thy reward,
   dew to thy selfe that it for me prepard.

Sonnet 87

Since I did leave the presence of my love,
   many long weary dayes I have outworne,
   and many nights, that slowly seemd to move
   theyr sad protract from evening untill morne.
For when as day the heaven doth adorne,
   I wish that night the noyous day would end:
   and when as night hath us of light forlorne,
   I wish that day would shortly reascend.
Thus I the time with expectation spend,
   and faine my griefe with chaunges to beguile,
   that further seemes his terme still to extend,
   and maketh every minute seeme a myle.
So sorrow still doth seeme too long to last,
   but joyous houres doo fly away too fast.

Sonnet 88
Since I have lackt the comfort of that light,
   the which was wont to lead my thoughts astray,
   I wander as in darknesse of the night,
   affrayd of every danger's least dismay.
Ne ought I see, though in the clearest day,
   when others gaze upon theyr shadowes vayne,
   but th'onely image of that heavenly ray,
   whereof some glance doth in mine eie remayne:
Of which beholding th'Idæa playne,
   through contemplation of my purest part,
   with light thereof I doe my selfe sustayne,
   and thereon feed my love-affamisht hart.
But with such brightnesse whylest I fill my mind,
   I starve my body and mine eyes doe blynd.

Sonnet 89
Lyke as the Culver on the bared bough
   sits mourning for the absence of her mate,
   and in her songs sends many a wishfull vow
   for his returne that seemes to linger late;
So I alone now left disconsolate
   mourne to my selfe the absence of my love;
   and wandring here and there all desolate,
   seek with my playnts to match that mournful dove:
Ne joy of ought that under heaven doth hove
   can comfort me, but her owne joyous sight,
   whose sweet aspect both God and man can move
   in her unspotted pleasauns to delight.
Dark is my day, whyles her fayre light I mis,
   and dead my life that wants such lively blis.

Epithalamion

Ye learned sisters which haue oftentimes
Beene to me ayding, others to adorne:
Whom ye thought worthy of your gracefull rymes,
That euen the greatest did not greatly scorne
To heare theyr names sung in your simple layes,
But ioyed in theyr prayse.
And when ye list your owne mishaps to mourne,
Which death, or loue, or fortunes wreck did rayse,
Your string could soone to sadder tenor turne,
And teach the woods and waters to lament
Your dolefull dreriment.
Now lay those sorrowfull complaints aside,
And hauing all your heads with girland crownd,
Helpe me mine owne loues prayses to resound,
Ne let the same of any be enuide:
So Orpheus did for his owne bride,
So I vnto my selfe alone will sing,
The woods shall to me answer and my Eccho ring.

Early before the worlds light giuing lampe,
His golden beame vpon the hils doth spred,
Hauing disperst the nights vnchearefull dampe,
Doe ye awake and with fresh lusty hed,
Go to the bowre of my beloued loue,
My truest turtle doue,
Bid her awake; for Hymen is awake,
And long since ready forth his maske to moue,
With his bright Tead that flames with many a flake,
And many a bachelor to waite on him,
In theyr fresh garments trim.
Bid her awake therefore and soone her dight,
For lo the wished day is come at last,
That shall for al the paynes and sorrowes past,
Pay to her vsury of long delight:

And whylest she doth her dight,
Doe ye to her of ioy and solace sing,
That all the woods may answer and your eccho ring.

Bring with you all the Nymphes that you can heare
Both of the riuers and the forrests greene:
And of the sea that neighbours to her neare,
40   Al with gay girlands goodly wel beseene.
And let them also with them bring in hand
Another gay girland
For my fayre loue of lillyes and of roses,
Bound trueloue wize with a blew silke riband.
And let them make great store of bridale poses,
And let them eeke bring store of other flowers
To deck the bridale bowers.
And let the ground whereas her foot shall tread,
For feare the stones her tender foot should wrong
50   Be strewed with fragrant flowers all along,
And diapred lyke the discolored mead.
Which done, doe at her chamber dore awayt,
For she will waken strayt,
The whiles doe ye this song vnto her sing,
The woods shall to you answer and your Eccho ring.

Ye Nymphes of Mulla which with carefull heed,
The siluer scaly trouts doe tend full well,
And greedy pikes which vse therein to feed,
(Those trouts and pikes all others doo excell)
60   And ye likewise which keepe the rushy lake,
Where none doo fishes take,
Bynd vp the locks the which hang scatterd light,
And in his waters which your mirror make,
Behold your faces as the christall bright,
That when you come whereas my loue doth lie,
No blemish she may spie.
And eke ye lightfoot mayds which keepe the deere,
That on the hoary mountayne vse to towre,
And the wylde wolues which seeke them to deuoure,
70   With your steele darts doo chace from comming neer,
Be also present heere,
To helpe to decke her and to help to sing,
That all the woods may answer and your eccho ring.

Wake, now my loue, awake; for it is time,
The Rosy Morne long since left Tithones bed,
All ready to her siluer coche to clyme,
And Phœbus gins to shew his glorious hed.
Hark how the cheerefull birds do chaunt theyr laies
And carroll of loues praise.
80   The merry Larke hir mattins sings aloft,
The thrush replyes, the Mauis descant playes,
The Ouzell shrills, the Ruddock warbles soft,
So goodly all agree with sweet consent,
To this dayes merriment.
Ah my deere loue why doe ye sleepe thus long,
When meeter were that ye should now awake,
T'awayt the comming of your ioyous make,
And hearken to the birds louelearned song,
The deawy leaues among.
90   For they of ioy and pleasance to you sing,
That all the woods them answer and theyr eccho ring.

My loue is now awake out of her dreames,
And her fayre eyes like stars that dimmed were
With darksome cloud, now shew theyr goodly beames
More bright then Hesperus his head doth rere.
Come now ye damzels, daughters of delight,
Helpe quickly her to dight,
But first come ye fayre houres which were begot
In Ioues sweet paradice, of Day and Night,
100   Which doe the seasons of the yeare allot,
And al that euer in this world is fayre
Doe make and still repayre.
And ye three handmayds of the Cyprian Queene,
The which doe still adorne her beauties pride,
Helpe to addorne my beautifullest bride:
And as ye her array, still throw betweene
Some graces to be seene,
And as ye vse to Venus, to her sing,
The whiles the woods shal answer and your eccho ring.

110   Now is my loue all ready forth to come,
Let all the virgins therefore well awayt,
And ye fresh boyes that tend vpon her groome

Prepare your selues; for he is comming strayt.
Set all your things in seemely good aray
Fit for so ioyfull day,
The ioyfulst day that euer sunne did see.
Faire Sun, shew forth thy fauourable ray,
And let thy lifull heat not feruent be
For feare of burning her sunshyny face,
120   Her beauty to disgrace.
O fayrest Phœbus, father of the Muse,
If euer I did honour thee aright,
Or sing the thing, that mote thy mind delight,
Doe not thy seruants simple boone refuse,
But let this day let this one day be myne,
Let all the rest be thine.
Then I thy souerayne prayses loud wil sing,
That all the woods shal answer and theyr eccho ring.

Harke how the Minstrels gin to shrill aloud
130   Their merry Musick that resounds from far,
The pipe, the tabor, and the trembling Croud,
That well agree withouten breach or iar.
But most of all the Damzels doe delite,
When they their tymbrels smyte,
And thereunto doe daunce and carrol sweet,
That all the sences they doe rauish quite,
The whyles the boyes run vp and downe the street,
Crying aloud with strong confused noyce,
As if it were one voyce.
140   Hymen io Hymen, Hymen they do shout,
That euen to the heauens theyr shouting shrill
Doth reach, and all the firmament doth fill,
To which the people standing all about,
As in approuance doe thereto applaud
And loud aduaunce her laud,
And euermore they Hymen Hymen sing,
That al the woods them answer and theyr eccho ring.

Loe where she comes along with portly pace,
Lyke Phœbe from her chamber of the East,
150   Arysing forth to run her mighty race,
Clad all in white, that seemes a virgin best.

So well it her beseemes that ye would weene
Some angell she had beene.
Her long loose yellow locks lyke golden wyre,
Sprinckled with perle, and perling flowres a tweene,
Doe lyke a golden mantle her attyre,
And being crowned with a girland greene,
Seeme lyke some mayden Queene.
Her modest eyes abashed to behold
160   So many gazers, as on her do stare,
Vpon the lowly ground affixed are.
Ne dare lift vp her countenance too bold,
But blush to heare her prayses sung so loud,
So farre from being proud.
Nathlesse doe ye still loud her prayses sing,
That all the woods may answer and your eccho ring.

Tell me ye merchants daughters did ye see
So fayre a creature in your towne before?
So sweet, so louely, and so mild as she,
170   Adornd with beautyes grace and vertues store,
Her goodly eyes lyke Saphyres shining bright,
Her forehead yuory white,
Her cheekes lyke apples which the sun hath rudded,
Her lips lyke cherryes charming men to byte,
Her brest like to a bowle of creame vncrudded,
Her paps lyke lyllies budded,
Her snowie necke lyke to a marble towre,
And all her body like a pallace fayre,
Ascending vppe with many a stately stayre,
180   To honors seat and chastities sweet bowre.
Why stand ye still ye virgins in amaze,
Vpon her so to gaze,
Whiles ye forget your former lay to sing,
To which the woods did answer and your eccho ring?

Bvt if ye saw that which no eyes can see,
The inward beauty of her liuely spright,
Garnisht with heauenly guifts of high degree,
Much more then would ye wonder at that sight,
And stand astonisht lyke to those which red
190   Medusaes mazeful hed.

There dwels sweet loue and constant chastity,
Vnspotted fayth and comely womanhed,
Regard of honour and mild modesty,
There Vertue raynes as Queene in royal throne,
And giueth lawes alone.
The which the base affections doe obay,
And yeeld theyr seruices vnto her will,
Ne thought of thing vncomely euer may
Thereto approch to tempt her mind to ill.
200 Had ye once seene these her celestial threasures,
And vnreuealed pleasures,
Then would ye wonder and her prayses sing,
That al the woods should answer and your echo ring.

Open the temple gates vnto my loue,
Open them wide that she may enter in,
And all the postes adorne as doth behoue,
And all the pillours deck with girlands trim,
For to recyue this Saynt with honour dew,
That commeth in to you.
210 With trembling steps and humble reuerence,
She commeth in, before th'almighties vew:
Of her ye virgins learne obedience,
When so ye come into those holy placcs,
To humble your proud faces;
Bring her vp to th'high altar that she may,
The sacred ceremonies there partake,
The which do endlesse matrimony make,
And let the roring Organs loudly play
The praises of the Lord in liuely notes,
220 The whiles with hollow throates
The Choristers the ioyous Antheme sing,
That al the woods may answere and their eccho ring.

Behold whiles she before the altar stands
Hearing the holy priest that to her speakes
And blesseth her with his two happy hands,
How the red roses flush vp in her cheekes,
And the pure snow with goodly vermill stayne,
Like crimsin dyde in grayne,
That euen th' Angels which continually,

230   About the sacred Altare doe remaine,
Forget their seruice and about her fly,
Ofte peeping in her face that seemes more fayre,
The more they on it stare.
But her sad eyes still fastened on the ground,
Are gouerned with goodly modesty,
That suffers not one looke to glaunce awry,
Which may let in a little thought vnsownd.
Why blush ye loue to giue to me your hand,
The pledge of all our band?
240   Sing ye sweet Angels, Alleluya sing,
That all the woods may answere and your eccho ring.

Now al is done; bring home the bride againe,
Bring home the triumph of our victory,
Bring home with you the glory of her gaine,
With ioyance bring her and with iollity.
Neuer had man more ioyfull day then this,
Whom heauen would heape with blis.
Make feast therefore now all this liue long day,
This day for euer to me holy is,
250   Poure out the wine without restraint or stay,
Poure not by cups, but by the belly full,
Poure out to all that wull,
And sprinkle all the postes and wals with wine,
That they may sweat, and drunken be withall.
Crowne ye God Bacchus with a coronall,
And Hymen also crowne with wreathes of vine,
And let the Graces daunce vnto the rest;
For they can doo it best:
The whiles the maydens doe theyr carroll sing,
260   To which the woods shal answer and theyr eccho ring.

Ring ye the bels, ye yong men of the towne,
And leaue your wonted labors for this day:
This day is holy; doe ye write it downe,
That ye for euer it remember may.
This day the sunne is in his chiefest hight,
With Barnaby the bright,
From whence declining daily by degrees,
He somewhat loseth of his heat and light,

When once the Crab behind his back he sees.
270 But for this time it ill ordained was,
To chose the longest day in all the yeare,
And shortest night, when longest fitter weare:
Yet neuer day so long, but late would passe.
Ring ye the bels, to make it weare away,
And bonefiers make all day,
And daunce about them, and about them sing:
That all the woods may answer, and your eccho ring.

Ah when will this long weary day haue end,
And lende me leaue to come vnto my loue?
280 How slowly do the houres theyr numbers spend?
How slowly does sad Time his feathers moue?
Hast thee O fayrest Planet to thy home
Within the Westerne fome:
Thy tyred steedes long since haue need of rest.
Long though it be, at last I see it gloome,
And the bright euening star with golden creast
Appeare out of the East.
Fayre childe of beauty, glorious lampe of loue
That all the host of heauen in rankes doost lead,
290 And guydest louers through the nights dread,
How chearefully thou lookest from aboue,
And seemst to laugh atweene thy twinkling light
As ioying in the sight
Of these glad many which for ioy doe sing,
That all the woods them answer and their echo ring.

Now ceasse ye damsels your delights forepast;
Enough is it, that all the day was youres:
Now day is doen, and night is nighing fast:
Now bring the Bryde into the brydall boures.
300 Now night is come, now soone her disaray,
And in her bed her lay;
Lay her in lillies and in violets,
And silken courteins ouer her display,
And odourd sheetes, and Arras couerlets.
Behold how goodly my faire loue does ly
In proud humility;
Like vnto Maia, when as Ioue her tooke,

In Tempe, lying on the flowry gras,
Twixt sleepe and wake, after she weary was,
With bathing in the Acidalian brooke.
Now it is night, ye damsels may be gon,
And leaue my loue alone,
And leaue likewise your former lay to sing:
The woods no more shal answere, nor your echo ring.

Now welcome night, thou night so long expected,
That long daies labour doest at last defray,
And all my cares, which cruell loue collected,
Hast sumd in one, and cancelled for aye:
Spread thy broad wing ouer my loue and me,
That no man may vs see,
And in thy sable mantle vs enwrap,
From feare of perrill and foule horror free.
Let no false treason seeke vs to entrap,
Nor any dread disquiet once annoy
That safety of our ioy:
But let the night be calme and quietsome,
Without tempestuous storms or sad afray:
Lyke as when Ioue with fayre Alcmena lay,
When he begot the great Tirynthian groome:
Or lyke as when he with thy selfe did lie,
And begot Maiesty.
And let the mayds and yongmen cease to sing:
Ne let the woods them answer, nor theyr eccho ring.

Let no lamenting cryes, nor dolefull teares,
Be heard all night within nor yet without:
Ne let false whispers breeding hidden feares,
Breake gentle sleepe with misconceiued dout.
Let no deluding dreames, nor dreadful sights
Make sudden sad affrights;
Ne let housefyres, nor lightnings helpelesse harmes,
Ne let the Pouke, nor other euill sprights,
Ne let mischiuous witches with theyr charmes,
Ne let hob Goblins, names whose sence we see not,
Fray vs with things that be not.
Let not the shriech Oule, nor the Storke be heard:
Nor the night Rauen that still deadly yels,

310

320

330

340

Nor damned ghosts cald vp with mighty spels,
Nor griesly vultures make vs once affeard:
Ne let th' unpleasant Quyre of Frogs still croking
350   Make vs to wish theyr choking.
Let none of these theyr drery accents sing;
Ne let the woods them answer, nor theyr eccho ring.

Bvt let stil Silence trew night watches keepe,
That sacred peace may in assurance rayne,
And tymely sleep, when it is tyme to sleepe,
May poure his limbs forth on your pleasant playne,
The whiles an hundred little winged loues,
Like diuers fethered doues,
Shall fly and flutter round about your bed,
360   And in the secret darke, that none reproues,
Their prety stealthes shal worke, and snares shal spread
To filch away sweet snatches of delight,
Conceald through couert night.
Ye sonnes of Venus, play your sports at will,
For greedy pleasure, carelesse of your toyes,
Thinks more vpon her paradise of ioyes,
Then what ye do, albe it good or ill.
All night therefore attend your merry play,
For it will soone be day:
370   Now none doth hinder you, that say or sing,
Ne will the woods now answer, nor your Eccho ring.

Who is the same, which at my window peepes?
Or whose is that faire face, that shines so bright?
Is it not Cinthia, she that neuer sleepes,
But walkes about high heauen al the night?
O fayrest goddesse, do thou not enuy
My loue with me to spy:
For thou likewise didst loue, though now vnthought,
And for a fleece of woll, which priuily,
380   The Latmian shephard once vnto thee brought,
His pleasures with thee wrought.
Therefore to vs be fauorable now;
And sith of wemens labours thou hast charge,
And generation goodly dost enlarge,

Encline thy will t'effect our wishfull vow,
And the chast wombe informe with timely seed,
That may our comfort breed:
Till which we cease our hopefull hap to sing,
Ne let the woods vs answere, nor our Eccho ring.

390   And thou great Iuno, which with awful might
The lawes of wedlock still dost patronize,
And the religion of the faith first plight
With sacred rites hast taught to solemnize:
And eeke for comfort often called art
Of women in their smart,
Eternally bind thou this louely band,
And all thy blessings vnto vs impart.
And thou glad Genius, in whose gentle hand,
The bridale bowre and geniall bed remaine,
400   Without blemish or staine,
And the sweet pleasures of theyr loues delight
With secret ayde doest succour and supply,
Till they bring forth the fruitfull progeny,
Send vs the timely fruit of this same night.
And thou fayre Hebe, and thou Hymen free,
Grant that it may so be.
Til which we cease your further prayse to sing,
Ne any woods shal answer, nor your Eccho ring.

And ye high heauens, the temple of the gods,
410   In which a thousand torches flaming bright
Doe burne, that to vs wretched earthly clods,
In dreadful darknesse lend desired light;
And all ye powers which in the same remayne,
More then we men can fayne,
Poure out your blessing on vs plentiously,
And happy influence vpon vs raine,
That we may raise a large posterity,
Which from the earth, which they may long possesse,
With lasting happinesse,
420   Vp to your haughty pallaces may mount,
And for the guerdon of theyr glorious merit
May heauenly tabernacles there inherit,
Of blessed Saints for to increase the count.

So let vs rest, sweet loue, in hope of this,
And cease till then our tymely ioyes to sing,
The woods no more vs answer, nor our eccho ring.

Song made in lieu of many ornaments,
With which my loue should duly haue bene dect,
Which cutting off through hasty accidents,
430   Ye would not stay your dew time to expect,
But promist both to recompens,
Be vnto her a goodly ornament,
And for short time an endlesse moniment.

FINIS

HENRY CONSTABLE

Diana. *The praises of his Mistress in certaine sweete Sonnets by H. C.*

To his absent Diana

Sever'd from sweete Content, my live's sole light,
   banisht by over-weening wit from my desire,
   this poore acceptance onely I require,
   that though my fault have forc'd me from thy sight,
Yet that thou wouldst (my sorrowes to requite)
   review these Sonnets, pictures of thy praise,
   wherein each woe thy wondrous worth doth raise,
   though first thy worth bereft me of delight.
See them forsaken: for I them forsooke,
   forsaken first of thee, next of my sence;
   and when thou deignst on their blacke teares to looke,
   shed not one teare my teares to recompence:
     But joy in this (though Fates gainst mee repine)
     my verse still lives, to witnes thee divine.

1   Resolv'd to love, unworthie to obtaine,
   I doo no favor crave: but humble wise
   to thee my sighes in verse I sacrifice,
   only some pitie, and no helpe to gaine.
Heare then, and as my heart shall aye remaine
   a patient object to thy lightning eies,
   a patient eare bring thou to thundring cries:
   feare not the cracke, when I the blow sustaine:
So, as thyne eye bred mine ambitious thought,
   so shall thine eare make proud my voyce for joy:
   lo (Deare) what wonders great by thee are wrought,
   when I but little favours doo enjoy.
     The voyce is made the eare for to rejoyce,
     and thyne eare giveth pleasure to my voyce.

2   It maie be, Love my death doth not pretend,
        although he shootes at mee, but thinkes it fit
        thus to bewitch thee for my benefit,
        causing thy will to my wish condiscend:
   For witches, which some murther doo intend,
        doo make a picture, and doo shoote at it;
        and in that part where they the picture hit,
        the partie's selfe doth languish to his end.
   So Love, too weake by force thy hart to taint,
        within my hart thy heavenly shape doth paint;
        suffring therein his arrowes to abide,
        onelie to th' end he might by witches' art
           Within my hart pierce through thy picture's side,
        and through thy picture's side might wound thy hart.

3   Blame not my hart for flieng up too hie,
        sith thou art cause that it this flight begunne;
        for earthlie vapors drawne up by the Sunne
        Comets begin, and night-sunnes in the skie.
   Mine humble hart, so with thy heavenlie eie
        drawne up aloft, all low desires doth shunne:
        raise then me up, as thou my hart hast done,
        so during night, in heaven remaine maie I.
   I saie againe, blame not my high desire,
        sith of us both the cause thereof depends.
        In thee doth shine, in mee doth burne a fire;
        fire drawes up other, and it selfe ascends:
           Thine eie a fier, and so drawes up my love:
           My love a fier, and so ascends above.

4   The Sonne his journey ending in the West,
        taking his lodging up in Thetis' bed,
        though from our eyes his beames be banished,
        yet with his light th' Antipodes be blest.
   Now when the Sunne time brings my Sunne to rest,
        (which mee too oft of rest hath hindered)
        and whiter skinne with white sheete covered,
        and softer cheeke doth on softe pillow rest:
   Then I (O Sunne of Sunnes and Light of Lights)
        wish me with those Antipodes to bee,
        which see and feele thy beames and heate by nights.

Well, though the night both cold and darksome is,
    yet halfe the daye's delight the night graunts mee:
    I feele my Sunne's heate, though his light I misse.

5   Flie lowe deare Love, thy Sunne dost thou not see?
    Take heed, doo not so neere his rayes aspire,
    least (for thy pride, inflam'd with wreakfull ire)
    it burne thy wings, as it hath burned mee.
Thou (haply) saist, thy wings immortall bee,
    and so cannot consumed be with fire:
    the one is Hope, the other is Desire,
    and that the heavens bestow'd them both on thee.
A Muse's words made thee with Hope to flye;
    and Angel's face Desier hath begot;
    thy selfe engendred by a Goddesse' eye:
    yet for all this, immortall thou art not.
        Of heavenly eye though thou begotten art,
        Yet art thou borne but of a mortall hart.

6   Uncivill sickness, hast thou no regard,
    but dost presume my dearest to molest,
    and without leave dar'st enter in that brest
    wheretoo sweete Love approach yet never dar'd?
Spare thow her health, which my life hath not spar'd;
    too bitter such revenge of my unrest:
    although with wrongs my thought she hath opprest,
    my wrongs seeke not revenge, they crave rewarde.
Cease Sicknesse, cease in her then to remaine,
    and come and welcome, harbour thou in mee,
    whom Love long since hath taught to suffer paine.
So she which hath so oft my paines increast,
        (O god, that I might so rewarded bee)
    by my more paine, might have her paine releast.

7   A frend of mine, pitieng my helplesse love,
    hoping (by killing hope) my love to slaie;
    'Let not' (quoth hee) 'thy hope thy hart betraie;
    impossible it is hir hart to move.'
But sith resolved love cannot remove,
    as long as thy divine perfections staie,
    thy Godhead then he sought to take awaie.

Deare, seeke revenge, and him a liar prove.
Gods onelie doo impossibilities:
'Impossible' (saith he) 'thy grace to gaine'.
show then the power of thy devinities,
by graunting me thy favor to obtaine.
So shall thy foe give to himselfe the lie:
a Goddesse thou shalt prove, and happie I.

8   If true love might true love's reward obtaine,
dumbe wonder onely might speake of my joy:
but too much woorth hath made thee too much coy,
and told me long agoe, I sigh'd in vaine.
Not then vaine hope of undeserved gaine
hath made me paint in verses mine annoy;
but for thy pleasure, that thou mightst enjoy
thy beautie's sight, in glasses of my paine.
See then thy selfe (though mee thou wilt not heare)
by looking on my verse; for paine in verse,
love doth in paine, beautie in love appeare.
So, if thou would'st my verses' meaning see,
Expound them thus, when I my love rehearse:
'None loves like him, that is, None faire like mee.'

9   Thine eye the glasse where I behold my hart,
mine eye the window, through the which thine eye
may see my hart, and there thy selfe espye
in bloudie colours how thou painted art.
Thine eye the pyle is of a murdring dart,
mine eye the sight thou tak'st thy levell by
to hit my hart, and never shootes awry;
mine eye thus helpes thine eye to worke my smart.
Thine eye a fier is both in heate and light,
mine eye of teares a river doth become:
Oh that the water of mine eye had might
to quench the flames that from thine eyes doo come,
Or that the fier kindled by thine eye
the flowing streames of mine eyes could make drie.

10   Ladie in beautie and in favor rare,
of favor (not of due) I favor crave:
Nature to thee Beautie and Favor gave;

faire then thou art, and Favor thou maist spare.
When on poore me bestow'd your favors are,
   lesse Favor in your face you shall not have:
   If favor then a wounded soule may save,
   of murther's guilte (deare Ladie) then beware.
My losse of life a million fold were lesse
   than the least losse should unto you befall:
   yet graunt this gift, which gift when I possesse,
   both I have life, and you no losse at all.
      For by your Favour onelie I doo live,
      and Favour you may well both keepe and give.

11   Mine eye with all the deadlie sinnes is fraught,
     1. First *proud*, sith it presum'd to looke so hie:
   a watchman being made, stood gazing by,
     2. and *idle*, tooke no heede till I was caught:
  3. And *envious*, beares envie that my thought
   should in his absence be to her so nie:
   to kill my hart, mine eie let in her eie,
     4. and so consent gave to a *murther* wrought:
  5. And *covetous*, it never would remoove
   from her faire haire, gold so doth please his sight:
     6. *Unchast*, a baud betweene my hart and love:
     7. a *glutton* eie, with teares drunke everie night.
     These sinnes procured have a Goddesse'ire:
     Wherefore my hart is damnd in Love's sweete fire.

12   My *Reason* absent did mine eyes require
   to watch and ward, and such foes to descrie
   as they should neere my hart approching spie:
   but traitor eies my hart's death did conspire;
  (Corrupted with *Hope's* giftes) let in *Desire*
   to burne my hart; and sought no remedie,
   though store of water were in either eie,
   which well imploid, might well have quencht the fire.
Reason returned, *Love* and *Fortune* made
   judges, to judge mine eies to punishment:
   Fortune, sith they by sight my hart betraid,
   from wished sight adjudgd them banishment:
     Love, sith by fire murdred my hart was found,
     adjudged them in teares for to be drownd.

13   Falslie doth envie of your praises blame
      my tongue, my pen, my hart of flatterie:
      because I said there was no sunne but thee,
      it calld my tongue the partiall trumpe of fame;
    And saith my pen hath flattered thy name,
      because my pen did to my tongue agree;
      and that my hart must needs a flattrer bee,
      which taught both tongue and pen to say the same.
    No, no, I flatter not, when I thee call
      the sunne, sith that the sunne was never such:
      but when the sunne thee I compar'd withall,
      doubtles the sunne I flattered too much.
        Witnes mine eies I saie the truth in this:
        they have seene thee and know that so it is.

14   Wonder it is, and pitie ist, that shee,
      in whom all beautie's treasure we may finde
      that may inrich the bodie or the minde,
      towards the poore should use no charitie.
    My Love is gone a begging unto thee,
      and if that Beautie had not been more kinde
      than Pitie, long ere this he had been pinde;
      but Beautie is content his food to bee.
    Oh pitie have, when such poore Orphans beg;
      Love (naked boy) hath nothing on his backe:
      and though he wanteth neither arme nor leg,
      yet maym'd he is, sith he his sight doth lacke.
        And yet (though blinde) he beautie can behold:
        And yet (though nak'd) he feeles more heat than cold.

15   Much sorrow in it selfe my love doth move,
      more my dispaire, to love a hopelesse blisse:
      my follie most, to love whom sure to misse:
      oh helpe me but this last griefe to remove.
    All paines if you commaund it, joy shall prove,
      and wisdome to seeke joy: then say but this:
      'Because my pleasure in thy torment is,
      I doo commaund thee without hope to love.'
    So, when this thought my sorrow shall augment,
      that my owne follie did procure my paine,
      then shall I say, to give my selfe content,

obedience onely made me love in vaine.
　　It was your will, and not my want of wit:
　　I have the paine, beare you the blame of it.

16　　Pitie refusing my poore Love to feed,
　　　a beggar starv'd for want of helpe he lies,
　　　and at your mouth (the doore of Beautie) cries
　　　that thence some almes of sweete grants may proceed.
　　But as he waiteth for some almes-deed,
　　　a cherrie-tree before the door he spies;
　　　'Oh deare,' (quoth he) 'two cherries may suffice,
　　　two onely may save life in this my need.'
　　But beggars, can they naught but cherries eate?
　　　Pardon my Love, he is a Goddesse' sonne,
　　　and never feedeth but on daintie meate,
　　　els need he not to pine as he hath done:
　　　　For onely the sweete frute of this sweete tree
　　　　can give food to my Love, and life to me.

17　　My Ladie's presence makes the Roses red,
　　　because to see her lips, they blush for shame:
　　　the Lillie's leaves (for envie) pale became,
　　　and her white hands in them this envie bred.
　　The Marigold the leaves abroad doth spred,
　　　because the sunne's; and her power is the same:
　　　the Violet of purple colour came,
　　　di'd in the bloud she made my hart to shed.
　　In briefe, all flowers from her theire vertue take;
　　　from her sweete breath theire sweet smells doo proceed;
　　　the living heate which her eie beames doth make,
　　　warmeth the ground, and quickeneth the seed:
　　　　The raine wherewith she watereth these flowers
　　　　falls from mine eyes, which she dissolves in showers.

18　　The Fouler hides (as closelie as he may)
　　　the net, where caught the sillie bird should bee,
　　　least he the threatning prison should but see,
　　　and so for feare be forc'd to flie away.
　　My Ladie so, the while she doth assay
　　　in curled knots fast to entangle mee,
　　　puts on her vayle, to th' end I should not flee

the golden net, wherein I am a pray.
Alas (most sweete) what need is of a net,
    to catch a bird that is alreadie tame,
    sith with your hand alone you maie it get,
    for it desires to flie into the same?
        What neede such art my thoughts then to intrap,
        When (of themselves) they flie into your lap?

19   When your perfections to my thoughts appeare,
        they say among themselves, 'O happie wee,
        which ever shall so rare an object see':
        but happie hart, if thoughts lesse happie were;
    For their delights have cost my hart full deare,
        in whom of love a thousand causes bee,
        and each cause breedes a thousand loves in mee,
        and each love more than thousand harts can beare.
    How can my hart so manie loves then hold,
        which yet (by heapes) encrease from day to day?
        but like a ship that's over-charg'd with golde,
        must either sinke, or hurle the golde away.
            But hurle out love thou canst not, feeble hart:
            In thine owne blood thou therefore drowned arte.

20   Sweete hand, the sweet but cruell bowe thou art,
        from whence at mee five yvorie arrowes flie:
        so with five wounds at once I wounded lie,
        bearing in breast the print of everie dart.
    Saint Frances had the like, yet felt no smart,
        where I in living torments never die:
        his wounds were in his hands and feete, where I
        all these five helplesse wounds feele in my hart.
    Now (as Saint Frances) if a Saint am I,
        the bowe that shot these shafts a relique is:
        I meane the hand, which is the reason whie
        so manie for devotion thee would kisse:
            And some thy glove kisse, as a thing divine,
            this arrowes' quiver, and this relique's shrine.

Last sonnet

Faire Sunne, if you would have me praise your light,
    when night approacheth, wherefore doe you flie?

Time is so short, Beauties so manie bee,
as I have need to see them day and night,
That by continuall view my verses might
tell all the beames of your divinitie;
which praise to you, and joy should be to mee,
you living by my verse, I by your sight.
I by youre sight, but not you by my vearse:
neede mortall skill immortall praise rehearse?
no, no, though eies were blinde, and verse were dumb,
Your beautie should be seene, and your fame knowne.
For by the winde which from my sighes doo come,
Your praises round about the world be blowne.

From *Parthenophil and Parthenophe. Sonnettes, Madrigals, Elegies and Odes*

36   And thus continuing with outrageous fier,
      My Sunne proceeding forward to my sorrow
      Looke up his court, but willing to retier
      Within the Lyon's denne, his rage did borrow:
But whiles within that mansion he remayned,
      How cruell was Parthenophe to me,
      And when of my great sorrowes I complained,
      She Lyon-like wish't they might tenfold be.
Then did I rage and in unkindly passions
      I rent mine heare, and rac'd my tender skinne,
      And raving in such frantique fashions
      That with such crueltie she did beginne
To feede the fier which I was burned in.
      Can women brooke to deale so sore with men?
      She manne's woe learn'd it in the Lyon's denne.

37   But pitie which sometimes doth Lyons move,
      Remov'd my sunne from moodie Lyon's cave,
      And into Virgoe's boure did next remove
      His fierie wheeles: but then she answere gave
That she was all vow'd to virginitie,
      Yet said bove all men she would most affect me.
      Fye, Delian goddesse, in thy companie
      She learn'd with honest colour to neglect me;
And underneath chast vayles of single life
      She shrowdes her craftie clawes, and Lyon's hart,
      Which with my sences now do mingle strife
      Twixt loves, and vertues, which provoke my smart:
Yet from these passions can I never part,
      But still I make my suites importunate
      To thee, which makes my case infortunate.

54 When I was yong, indewd'd with nature's graces,
  I stoule blind love's strong bow and golden arrowes,
  To shoote at redbrestes, goldfinches and sparrowes.
  At shrew'd gyrles, and at boyes in other places
I shot when I was vexed with disgraces:
  I perc't no skinne, but melted up their marrowes.
  How many boyes and gyrles wish't mine embraces?
  How many prayz'd my favour 'bove all faces?
But once (Parthenophe) by thy sweet side sitting,
  Love had espyed me in a place most fitting,
  Betray'd by thine eyes' beames, which makes blind see:
He shot at me, and said 'For thine eyes' light,
  This daring boy that durst usurpe my right,
  Take him, a wounded slave to love, and thee.'

60 Whilst some the Troiane warres in verse recount,
  And all the Grecian Conquerours in fight,
Some valiant Romaine warres 'bove starres do mount,
  With all their warlike leaders, men of might:
Whilst some of Bryttish Arthure's valure sing,
  And register the prayse of Charlemayne;
And some of doughtie Godfrey tydinges bring,
  And some of Germaine broyles, and warres of Spayne:
In none of those myselfe I wounded finde,
  Neither with horseman, nor with man on foote:
But from a cleare bright eye, one captaine blinde
  (Whose puisance to resist did nothing boote)
With men in golden armes, and dartes of golde,
  Wounded my hart, and all which did beholde.

63 Jove for Europae's love tooke shape of Bull,
  And for Calisto playde Dianae's parte,
  And in a golden shower he filled full
  The lappe of Danae with coelestiall arte.
Would I were chang'd but to my mistresse' gloves,
  That those white lovely fingers I might hide;
  That I might kisse those hands, which mine hart loves,
  Or else that cheane of pearle, her necke's vaine pride,
Made proude with her necke's vaines; that I might folde
  About that lovely necke, and her pappes tickle,
  Or her to compasse like a belt of golde;

Or that sweet wine, which downe her throate doth trickle,
　　To kisse her lippes, and lye next at her hart,
　　Runne through her vaynes, and passe by pleasure's part.

65　Oh that I had no hart, as I have none,
　　　(For thou mine harte's full spirite hast possessed)
　　　Then should myne argument be not of mone,
　　　Then under love's yoke should I not be pressed:
　　Oh that without myne eyes I had been borne,
　　　Then had I not my mistresse' bewtie vewed,
　　　Then had I never been so farre forlorne,
　　　Then had I never wep't, then never rewed:
　　Oh that I never had been borne at all,
　　　Or beeing, had been borne of shephearde's broode;
　　　Then should I not in such mischances fall,
　　Quyet my water and content my foode:
　　　But now disquieted, and still tormented,
　　　With adverse fate, perforce must rest contented

66　Ah sweet content, where is thy mylde abode?
　　　Is it with shepheardes and light-harted swaynes,
　　　Which sing upon the downes and pype abroade,
　　　Tending their flockes and cattell on the playnes?
　　Ah sweet content, where doest thou safely rest?
　　　In heaven, with Angels which the prayses sing
　　　Of him that made and rules at his behest
　　　The mindes, and harts of every living thing?
　　Ah sweet content, where doth thine harbour hold?
　　　Is it in Churches, with Religious men,
　　　Which please the goddes with prayers manifold,
　　　And in their studies meditate it then?
　　Whether thou doest in heaven, or earth appeare,
　　　Be where thou wilt, thou will not harbour here

84　My sweet Parthenophe, within thy face
　　　My passion's Calender may plaine be red:
　　　The golden number told upon thine hed;
　　　The sunne dayes (which in carde I holy place
　　And which divinely blesse me with their grace)
　　　Thy chearefull smiles which can recall the dedde:
　　　My working dayes, thy frownes from favours fledde,

Which set a-worke the furies in my brest,
These dayes are six to one more then the rest:
   My leape year is (oh when is that leape yeare?)
   When all my cares I overleape, and feast
With her fruition whom I hould most deare.
   And if some Calenders the truth tell mee,
   Once in fewe yeares that happie leape shall bee.

GILES FLETCHER THE ELDER

From *Licia or Poemes of Love*

Sonnet 1

Sadde all alone, not long I musing satte,
But that my thoughtes compell'd me to aspire:
A Laurell garland in my hande I gatte,
So the Muses I approch'd the nyer.
My sute was this, a Poet to become,
To drinke with them, and from the heavens be fedde.
Phaebus denyed, and sware there was no roome,
Such to be Poets as fonde fancie ledde.
With that I mourn'd, and sat me downe to weepe:
Venus she smil'd, and smyling to me saide,
'Come drinke with me, and sitt thee still and sleepe.'
This voyce I heard, and Venus I obayde.
   That poyson (sweete), hath done me all this wrong,
   For nowe of love must needes be all my song.

Sonnet 17

As are the sandes (faire Licia) on the shore,
Or coloured floures, garlands of the spring,
Or as the frosts not seene, nor felt before,
Or as the fruites that Autume foorth doth bring;
As twinckling starres, the tinsell of the night,
Or as the fish that gallope in the seas,
As aires, each part that still escapes our sight,
So are my sighes, controllers of my ease.
Yet these are such, as needes must have an end,
For things finite, none els hath nature done:
Onlie the sighes, which from my heart I send,
Will never cease, but where they first begunne.
   Accept them (sweete) as incense due to thee:
   For you immortall made them so to be.

Sonnet 26

I live (sweete love) whereas the gentle winde
Murmures with sport, in midst of thickest bowes,
Where loving Wood-bine doth the Harbour binde,
And chirping birdes doe eccho foorth my vowes;
Where strongest elme can scarce support the vine,
And sweetest flowres enameld have the ground,
Where Muses dwell: and yet hereat repine
That on the earth so rare a place was found.
But windes delight: I wish to be content.
I praise the Wood-bine, but I take no joye:
I moane the birdes that musicke thus have spent:
As for the rest, they breede but mine annoye.
  Live thou (fayre Licia) in this place alone:
  Then shall I joye, though all of these were gone.

Sonnet 27

The Chrystal streames, wherein my love did swimme,
Melted in teares, as partners of my woe;
Her shine was such as did the fountaine dimme,
The pearlike fountaine, whiter than the snowe.
Then lyke perfume, resolved with the heate,
The fountaine smoak'd, as if it thought to burne:
A woonder strange, to see the colde so great,
And yet the fountaine into smoake to turne.
I searcht the cause, and found it to be this:
She toucht the water, and it burnt with love.
Now by her meanes, it purchast hath that blisse
Which all diseases quicklie can remoove.
  Then if by you, these streames thus blessed be:
  (Sweet) graunt me love, and be not woorse to me.

Sonnet 28

In tyme the strong and statelie turrets fall,
In tyme the Rose, and silver Lillies die,
In tyme the Monarchs captives are and thrall,
In tyme the sea, and rivers are made drie:
The hardest flint in tyme doth melt asunder,
Still-living fame in tyme doth fade away,
The mountaines proud, we see in tyme come under,
And earth for age, we see in tyme decay:

The sunne in tyme forgets for to retire
From out the east, where he was woont to rise:
The basest thoughtes, we see in time aspire,
And greedie minds in tyme do wealth dispise.
   Thus all (sweet faire) in tyme must have an end,
   Except thy beautie, vertues, and thy friend.

Sonnet 31

When as her lute is tuned to her voyce,
The aire growes proude, for honour of that sound;
And rockes doe leape, to shewe howe they rejoyce,
That in the earth such Musicke should be found.
When as her haire, more worth, more pale, then golde,
Like silver threed, lies waffting in the ayre,
Diana-like she lookes, but yet more bolde:
Cruell in chase, more chaste, and yet more fayre.
When as she smyles, the cloudes for envie breakes;
She Jove in pride encounters with a checke:
The Sunne doeth shine for joye when as she speakes:
Thus heaven, and earth doe homage at her becke
   Yet all these graces blottes, not graces are,
   Yf you my love, of love doe take no care.

Sonnet 41

If (aged Charon), when my life shall end,
I passe thy ferrye, and my wafftage pay,
Thy oares shall fayle thy boate, and maste shall rend,
And through the deepe shall be a drye-foote-way.
For why? My heart with sighs doth breath such flame,
That ayre and water both incensed be:
The boundless Ocean from whose mouth they came,
For from my heate not heaven it selfe is free.
Then since to me thy losse can be no gaine,
Avoyd thy harme and flye what I foretell.
Make thou my love with me for to be slaine,
That I with her, and both with thee may dwel.
   Thy fact thus (Charon) both of us shall blesse:
   Thou save thy boat, and I my love possesse.

Sonnet 42

For if alone thou thinke to waft my love,
Her cold is such as can the sea commaund:
And frosen Ice shall let thy boate to move,
Nor can thy forces rowe it from the land.
But if thou friendly both at once shalt take,
Thy selfe mayst rest. For why? My sighes will blowe.
Our colde and heate so sweete a thawe shall make,
As that thy boate without thy helpe shall rowe.
Then will I sitte and glut me on those eyes,
Wherewith my life, my eyes could never fill.
Thus from thy boate that comfort shall arise,
The want whereof my life and hope did kill.
    Together plac'd so thou her skorne shalt crosse,
    Where if we part, thy boate must suffer losse.

THOMAS LODGE

From *Phillis: Honoured with Pastorall Sonnets, Elegies and amorous delights*

4   Long hath my sufferance labored so inforce
One pearle of pittie from hir prettie eyes,
Whilest I with restlesse rivers of remorse,
Hath bathde the bankes where my faire Phillis lies.
    The moning lines which weeping I have written,
And writing red unto my ruthfull sheepe,
And reading sent with teares that never fitten,
To my love's Queene, that hath my heart in keepe,
    Have made my Lambkins lay them downe and sigh:
But Phillis sittes, and reades, and cals them trifles:
Oh heavens why clime not happie lines so high,
To rent that ruthlesse heart, that all hearts rifles?
      None wrightes with truer faith, or greater love,
      Yet out, alas, I have no power to move.

22   Faire art thou Phillis, I, so faire (sweet mayd)
As nor the sunne, nor I have seene more faire,
For in thy cheekes sweet roses are embayde,
And golde more pure then gold doth guilde thy haire.
    Sweet Bees have hiv'd their hony on thy tongue,
And Hebe spic't hir Necter with thy breath:
About thy necke do all the graces thronge,
And lay such baites as might entangle death.
    In such a breast what heart would not be thrall?
From such sweet armes who would not wish embraces?
At thy faire handes who wonders not at all,
Wounder itselfe through ignorance embases?
      Yet naithelesse tho wonderous giftes you call these,
      My faith is farre more wonderfull then all these.

34   I would in rich and golden coloured raine,
With tempting showers in pleasant sort discend,
Into faire Phillis' lappe (my lovely friend)

When sleepe hir sence with slomber doth restraine.
   I would be chaunged to a milk-white Bull,
When midst the gladsome fieldes she should appeare,
By pleasant finenes to surprise my deere,
Whilest from their stalkes, she pleasant flowers did pull:
   I were content to wearie out my paine,
To bee Narsissus so she were a spring
To drowne in hir those woes my heart do wring:
And more I wish transformed to remaine;
     That whilest I thus in pleasure's lappe did lye,
     I might refresh desire, which else would die.

35   I hope and feare, I pray and hould my peace,
Now freeze my thoughtes and straight they frie againe;
I now admire and straight my wounders cease,
I loose my bondes and yet my selfe restraine:
   This likes me most that leaves me discontent,
My courage serves and yet my heart doth faile;
My will doth clime whereas my hopes are spent,
I laugh at love, yet when he comes I quaile.
   The more I strive, the duller bide I still,
I would be thrald, and yet I freedome love;
I would redresse, yet hourly feede myne ill,
I would repine, and dare not once reprove;
     And for my love I am bereft of power,
     And strengthlesse strive my weaknes to devoure.

(ANONYMOUS)

From *Zepheria*

8   Illuminating Lamps, ye Orbs christallite,
Transparant mirrolds, globes devining beautie,
How have I joyd to wanton in your light?
(Though was I slayne by your artillerie.)
    Ye blithsome starres, (like Leda's lovely twins,
When cleare they twinckle in the firmament,
Promise esperance to the Sea-men's wandrings)
So have your shine made ripe mine heart's content:
   Or as the light which Sestyan Hero show'd
Arme-finnd Leander to direct in waves,
When through the raging Hellespont he row'd,
Steering to Love's port: so by thine eyes' cleere rayes
    Blest were my wayes: but since no light was found,
    Thy poore Leander in the deepe is drownd.

17   How shall I deck my love in love's habiliment,
And her embellish in a right depaint?
Sith now is left nor Rose, nor Hyacint,
Each one their beauties with their hue acquaint.
    The golden seeling of thy browe's rich frame
Designes the proud pomp of thy face's architure:
Chrystall transparant casements to the same
Are thine eyes' sunne, which doe the world depure,
    Whose silverie canopie gold wier fringes:
Thy brow the bowling place for Cupid's eye:
Love's true-love knots, and lilly-lozenges
Thy cheekes depaynten in an immortall dye.
    If well thou limn'd art now by face immagerie,
    Judge how by life I then should pencill thee.

20   How often hath my pen, mine heart's solicitour,
Instructed thee in breviat of my case?
While fancie-pleading eyes (thy beautie's visitour)
Have patternd to my quill an angel's face.

How have my Sonnets (faithfull counsellers)
Thee without ceasing mov'd for day of hearing?
While they my plaintive cause (my faith's revealers)
Thy long delay, my patience, in thine eare ring.
    How have I stood at barre of thine owne conscience,
When in requesting court my suite I brought?
How have thy long adjournments slow'd the sentence,
Which I through much expence of teares besought?
        Through many difficulties have I run:
        Ah sooner wert thou lost (I wis) then wonne.

21   And is it by immutable decree
(Immutable, yet cruell ordenance)
Ordayn'd (still forst I cry, 'Oh strange impietie')
On true-love to impose such tyrant penance,
    That we unto each other shall surrender
The seal'd indentures of our love compacted,
And that thereof we make such loyall tender,
As best shall seeme to them that so enacted?
    Then list while I advertize once againe:
Though we yeeld up our charters so ensealed,
Yet see that thou safe-guard my counterpane,
And I in heart shall keepe thy bond uncanceled:
        And so hereafter (if at least you please)
        Weele plead this redeliverie was by duresse.

37   When last mine eyes dislodged from thy beautie,
Though serv'd with proces of a parents' writ,
A Supersedeas countermanding dutie
Even then I saw upon thy smiles to sit.
    Those smiles which me invited to a partie,
Disperpling clowdes of faint respecting feare
Agaynst the summons which was serv'd on me,
A larger priviledge of dispence did beare.
    Thine eyes' edict, the statute of repeale,
Doth other duties wholly abrogate,
Save such as thee endeere in heartie zeale:
Then be it farre from me that I should derogate
        From nature's law enregistred in thee:
        So might my love encur a premunire.

38 From the revenew of thine eyes' exchequer,
My faith his subsidie did neare detract:
Though in thy favour's booke I rest thy debter,
Yet 'mongst accomptants who their faith have crackt,
 My name thou findest not irrotulat.
I list not stand indebted to infame;
Fowle them befall who pay in counterfaite;
Be they recogniz'd in black booke of shame.
 But if the rent which wont was of assise
Thou shalt enhance, through pride and coy disdayne,
Exacting double tribute to thine eyes,
And yet encrochest on my heart's demaync,
 Needs must I wish, though gaynst my foyaltie,
 That thou unsceptred be of nature's royaltie.

RICHARD BARNFIELD

Certaine Sonnets from *Cynthia.*
With Certaine Sonnets (1595)

Sonnet 1
Sporting at fancie, setting light by love,
   There came a theefe and stole away my heart,
   (And therefore robd me of my chiefest part)
Yet cannot Reason him a felon prove.
For why his beauty (my hearts thiefe) affirmeth,
   Piercing no skin (the bodies fensive wall)
   And having leave, and free consent withall,
Himselfe not guilty, from love guilty tearmeth,
Conscience the Iudge, twelve Reasons are the Iurie,
   They finde mine eies the beutie t'have let in,
   And on this verdict given, agreed they bin,
Wherefore, because his beauty did allure yee,
   Your Doome is this: in teares still to be drowned,
   When his faire forehead with disdain is frowned.

Sonnet 2
Beuty and Maiesty are falne at ods,
   Th'one claimes his cheeke, the other claimes his chin;
   Then Vertue comes, and puts her title in.
(Quoth she) I make him like th'immortall Gods.
(Quoth Maiestie) I owne his lookes, his Brow,
   His lips, (quoth Love) his eies, his faire is mine.
   And yet (quoth Maiesty) he is not thine,
I mixe Disdaine with Loves congealed Snow.
I, but (quoth Love) his lockes are mine (by right)
   His stately gate is mine (quoth Maiestie,)
   And mine (quoth Vertue) is his Modestie.
Thus as they strive about this heavenly wight,
   At last the other two to Vertue yeeld,
   The lists of Love, fought in faire Beauties field.

Sonnet 3

The Stoicks thinke, (and they come neere the truth.)
   That vertue is the chiefest good of all,
   The Academicks on *Idea* call.
The Epicures in pleasure spend their youth,
The Perrepatetickes iudge felicitie,
   To be the chiefest good above all other,
   One man, thinks this: and that conceaves another:
So that in one thing very few agree.
Let Stoicks have their Vertue if they will,
   And all the rest their chiefe-supposed good,
   Let cruell Martialists delight in blood,
And Mysers ioy their bags with gold to fill:
   My chiefest good, my chiefe felicity,
   Is to be gazing on my loves faire eie.

Sonnet 4

Two stars there are in one faire firmament,
   (Of some intitled *Ganymedes* sweet face),
   Which other stars in brightnes doe disgrace,
As much as *Po* in clearnes passeth *Trent*.
Nor are they common natur'd stars: for why,
   These stars when other shine vaile their pure light,
   And when all other vanish out of sight,
They adde a glory to the worlds great eie.
By these two stars my life is onely led,
   In them I place my ioy, in them my pleasure,
   Love's piercing Darts, and Natures precious treasure
With their sweet foode my fainting soule is fed:
   Then when my sunne is absent from my sight
   How can it chuse (with me) but be dark night?

Sonnet 5

It is reported of faire *Thetis* Sonne,
   (*Achilles* famous for his chivalry,
   His noble minde and magnanimity,)
That when the Troian wars were new begun,
Whos'ever was deepe-wounded with his speare,
   Could never be recured of his maime,

Nor ever after be made whole againe:
Except with that speares rust he holpen were.
Even so it fareth with my fortune now,
   Who being wounded with his piercing eie,
   Must either thereby finde a remedy,
Or els to be releev'd I know not how,
   Then if thou hast a minde still to annoy me,
   Kill me with kisses, if thou wilt destroy me.

Sonnet 6

Sweet Corrall lips, where Nature's treasure lies,
   The balme of blisse, the soveraigne salve of sorrow,
   The secret touch of loves heart-burning arrow,
Come quench my thirst or els poor *Daphnis* dies.
One night I dream'd (alas twas but a Dreame)
   That I did feele the sweetnes of the same,
   Where-with inspir'd, I young againe became,
And from my heart a spring of blood did streame,
But when I wak't, I found it nothing so,
   Save that my limbs (me thought) did waxe more strong
   And I more lusty far, and far more yong.
This gift on him rich Nature did bestow.
   Then if in dreaming so, I so did speede,
   What should I doe, if I did so indeede?

Sonnet 7

Sweet *Thames* I honour thee, not for thou art
   The chiefest River of the fairest Ile,
   Nor for thou dost admirers eies beguile,
But for thou hold'st the keeper of my heart,
For on thy waves, (thy Christal-billow'd waves,)
   My fairest faire, my silver Swan is swimming:
   Against the sunne his pruned feathers trimming:
Whilst *Neptune* his faire feete with water laves,
Neptune, I feare not thee, not yet thine eie,
   And yet (alas) *Apollo* lov'd a boy,
   And *Cyparissus* was *Silvanus* ioy.
No, no, I feare none but faire *Thetis*, I,
   For if she spie my Love, (alas) aie me,
   My mirth is turn'd to extreame miserie.

Sonnet 8
Sometimes I wish that I his pillow were,
  So might I steale a kisse, and yet not seene,
  So might I gaze upon his sleeping eine,
Although I did it with a panting feare:
But when I well consider how vaine my wish is,
  Ah foolish Bees (thinke I) that doe not sucke
  His lips for hony; but poore flowers doe plucke
Which have no sweet in them: when his sole kisses,
Are able to revive a dying soule.
  Kisse him, but sting him not, for if you doe,
  His angry voice your flying will pursue:
But when they heare his tongue, what can controule,
  Their back-returne? for then they plaine may see,
  How hony-combs from his lips dropping bee.

Sonnet 9
Diana (on a time) walking the wood,
  To sport herselfe, of her faire traine forlorne,
  Chaunc't for to pricke her foote against a thorne,
And from thence issu'd out a streame of blood.
No sooner shee was vanisht out of sight,
  But loves faire Queen came there away by chance,
  And having of this hap a glym'ring glance,
She put the blood into a christall bright,
When being now come unto mount *Rhodope*,
  With her faire hands she formes a shape of Snow,
  And blends it with this blood; from whence doth grow
A lovely creature, brighter than the Dey.
  And being christned in faire *Paphos* shrine,
  She call'd him *Ganymede*: as all divine.

Sonnet 10
Thus was my love, thus was my *Ganymed*,
  (Heavens joy, worlds wonder, natures fairest work,
  In whose aspect Hope and Dispaire doe lurke)
Made of pure blood in whitest snow yshed,
And for sweete *Venus* only form'd his face,
  And his each member delicately framed,

And last of all faire *Ganymede* him named,
His limbs (as their Creatrix) her imbrace.
But as for his pure, spotles, vertuous minde,
    Because it sprung of chaste *Dianaes* blood,
    (Goddess of Maides, directresse of all good,)
Hit wholy is to chastity inclinde.
    And thus it is: as far as I can prove,
    He loves to be belov'd, but not to love.

Sonnet 11

Sighing, and sadly sitting by my Love,
    He ask't the cause of my hearts sorrowing,
    Coniuring me by heavens eternall King
To tell the cause which me so much did move.
Compell'd: (quoth I) to thee will I confesse,
    Love is the cause; and only love it is
    That doth deprive me of my heavenly blisse.
Love is the paine that doth my heart oppresse.
And what is she (quoth he) whom thou do'st love?
    Looke in this glasse (quoth I) there shalt thou see
    The perfect forme of my faelicitie.
When, thinking that it would strange Magique prove,
    He open'd it: and taking off the cover,
    He straight perceav'd himselfe to be my Lover.

Sonnet 12

Some talke of *Ganymede* th'*Idalian* Boy,
    And some of faire *Adonis* make their boast,
    Some talke of him whom lovely *Laeda* lost,
And some of *Ecchoes* love that was so coy.
They speake of heere-say, I of perfect truth,
    They partially commend the persons named,
    And for them, sweet Encomions have framed:
I onely t'him have sacrifiz'd my youth.
As for those wonders of antiquitie,
    And those whom later ages have inioy'd,
    (But ah what hath not cruell death destroide?
Death, that envies this worlds felicitie),
    They were (perhaps) lesse faire then Poets write,
    But he is fairer then I can indite.

Sonnet 13

Speake Eccho, tell; how may I call my love?   *Love.*
  But how his Lamps that are so christaline?   *Eyne.*
  Oh happy starrs that make your heavens divine:
And happy Iems that admiration move.
How tearm'st his golden tresses wav'd with aire?   *Haire.*
  Oh lovely haire of your more-lovely Maister,
  Image of love, faire shape of Alablaster,
Why do'st thou drive thy Lover to dispaire?
How do'st thou cal the bed wher beuty grows?   *Rose.*
  Faire virgine-Rose, whose mayden blossoms cover
  The milke-white Lilly, thy imbracing Lover:
Whose kisses makes thee oft thy red to lose
  And blushing oft for shame, when he hath kist thee,
  He vades away, and thou raing'st where it list thee.

Sonnet 14

Here; hold this glove (this milk-white cheveril glove)
  Not quaintly over-wrought with curious knots,
  Not deckt with golden spangs, nor silver spots,
Yet wholsome for thy hand as thou shalt prove.
Ah no: (sweet boy) place this glove neere thy heart,
  Weare it, and lodge it still within thy brest,
  So shalt thou make me (most unhappy,) blest.
So shalt thou rid my paine, and ease my smart:
How can that be (perhaps) thou wilt reply,
  A glove is for the hand not for the heart,
  Nor can it well be prov'd by common art,
Nor reasons rule. To this, thus answere I:
  If thou from glove do'st take away the g,
  Then glove is love: and so I send it thee.

Sonnet 15

Ah fairest *Ganymede*, disdaine me not,
  Though silly Sheepeheard I, presume to love thee,
  Though my harsh songs and Sonnets cannot move thee,
Yet to thy beauty is my love no blot.
Apollo, *Iove*, and many Gods beside,
  S'daind not the name of cuntry shepheards swains,

Nor want we pleasure, though we take some pains,
We live contentedly: a thing call'd pride,
Which so corrupts the Court and every place,
    (Each place I meane where learning is neglected,
    And yet of late, even learnings selfe's infected)
I know not what it meanes, in any case:
    Wee onely (when *Molorchus* gins to peepe)
    Learne for to folde, and to unfold our sheepe.

Sonnet 16

Long have I long'd to see my Love againe,
    Still have I wisht, but never could obtaine it;
    Rather than all the world (if I might gaine it)
Would I desire my loves sweet precious gaine.
Yet in my soule I see him everie day,
    See him, and see his still sterne countenaunce,
    But (ah) what is of long continuance,
Where Maiestie and Beautie beares the sway?
Sometimes, when I imagine that I see him,
    (As love is full of foolish fantasies)
    Weening to kisse his lips, as my loves fee's,
I feele but Aire: nothing but Aire to bee him.
    Thus with *Ixion*, kisse I clouds in vaine:
    Thus with *Ixion*, feele I endles paine.

Sonnet 17

Cherry-lipt *Adonis* in his snowie shape,
    Might not compare with his pure Ivorie white,
    On whose faire front a Poets pen may write,
Whose rosiate red excels the crimson grape,
His love-enticing delicate soft limbs,
    Are rarely fram'd t'intrap poore gazing eies:
    His cheekes, the Lillie and Carnation dies,
With lovely tincture which *Apolloes* dims.
His lips ripe strawberries in Nectar wet,
    His mouth a Hive, his tongue a hony-combe,
    Where Muses (like Bees) make their mansion.
His teeth pure Pearle in blushing Correll set.
    Oh how can such a body sinne-procuring,
    Be slow to love, and quicke to hate, enduring?

Sonnet 18

Not *Megabaetes* nor *Cleonymus*,
  (Of whom great *Plutarck* makes such mention,
  Praysing their faire with rare invention)
As *Ganymede* were halfe so beauteous.
They onely pleas'd the eies of two great Kings,
  But all the worlde at my love stands amazed,
  Nor one that on his Angels face hath gazed,
But (ravisht with delight) him Presents brings.
Some weaning Lambs, and some a suckling Kyd,
  Some Nuts, and fil-beards, others Peares and Plums,
  Another with a milk-white Heyfar comes;
As lately *Aegons* man (*Damoetas*) did:
  But neither he, nor all the Nymphs beside,
  Can win my *Ganymede;* with them t'abide.

Sonnet 19

Ah no; nor I my selfe: though my pure love
  (Sweete *Ganymede*) to thee hath still beene pure,
  And even till my last gaspe shall aie endure,
Could ever thy obdurate beuty move:
Then cease oh Goddesse sonne (for sure thou art,
  A Goddesse sonne that canst resist desire)
  Cease thy hard heart, and entertaine loves fire,
Within thy sacred breast: by Natures art.
And as I love thee more than any Creature,
  (Love thee, because thy beautie is divine;
  Love thee, because my selfe, my soule is thine,
Wholie devoted to thy lovelie feature)
  Even so of all the vowels, I and U,
  Are dearest unto me, as doth ensue.

Sonnet 20

But now my Muse toyld with continuall care,
  Begins to faint, and slacke her former pace,
  Expecting favour from that heavenly grace,
That maie (in time) her feeble strength repaire.
Till when (sweete youth) th'essence of my soule,
  (Thou that dost sit and sing at my hearts griefe.

Thou that dost send thy shepheard no reliefe)
Beholde, these lines; the sonnes of Teares and Dole.
Ah had great *Colin* chiefe of shepheards all,
   Or gentle *Rowland*, my professed friend,
   Had they thy beautie, or my pennance pend,
Greater had beene thy fame, and lesse my fall:
   But since that everie one cannot be wittie,
   Pardon I crave of them, and of thee, pitty.

To his Friend Maister R. L. In Praise of Musique and Poetrie

If Musique and sweet Poetrie agree,
As they must needes (the Sister and the Brother)
Then must the Love be great, twixt thee and mee,
   Because thou lov'st the one, and I the other.
   Dowland to thee is deare; whose heavenly tuch
Upon the Lute, doeth ravish humaine sense:
Spenser to mee; whose deepe Conceit is such,
   As passing all Conceit, needs no defence.
   Thou lov'st to heare the sweete melodious sound,
That *Phoebus* Lute (the Queene of Musique) makes:
And I in deepe Delight am chiefly drownd,
   When as himselfe to singing he betakes.
     One God is God of Both (as Poets faigne)
     One Knight loves Both, and Both in thee remaine.

SIR ROBERT SIDNEY

From *An Untitled Sonnet Sequence* (c. 1596)

Sonnet 1

You purest stars, whose never dying fires
   Deck heavenly spheres, and rule the world below,
   Grudge not if I in your clear beauties know
The fair maid's eyes, the stars of my desires.
To earthly hearts your light, which not expires,
   Makes known the matchless place wherein you go;
   And they the mind which through them shines do show,
Whose clearest beams, my soul as heaven admires.
   You shine still one, and alter not your race
At suit of those which most your lights adore,
For well you know, you shine for heaven's grace:
   And they, in whom all eyes on earth are blest,
Though than the heavenly lights I love them more,
Shine to the world, and me but with the rest.

Sonnet 6

When rest locks up the treasures of delight,
   That face, those eyes, that voice, those hands, that breast,
   Not in them nor the sun sad earth now blest,
And no power left, that comfort may the night;
Cares which in darkness shine, finding her sight
   Eclipsed, which from them is my safeguard best,
   Revive my secret flames, and without rest
Show me unto myself in a true light.
   They are not flames of love, but fires of pain
That burn so fair; love far from me is fled,
Who all love give and no love have again.
   Repulses and the thousand-formed head
Of scorn I see, while unjust night from me
Her beauty hides, and shows her cruelty.

Sonnet 7

The hardy Captain, unused to retire,
 Turns and returns to the too-well-kept place
 Where wound to wound, disgrace upon disgrace
He takes, while will and power 'gainst him conspire:
Scorn of repulse, of loss the stinging fire,
 His heart with grief doth fill, with shame his face;
 But no force finding way, with heavy pace
Forsake he doth his ill-blest fair desire.
 With equal care, but with an end more high,
I sought to win the kingdom seat of love,
Beauty's best treasure, praise of victory:
 But scorned, repulsed, heartbroken I remove,
Reaping loss for desert, for love contempt,
And grief and shame for so dear foiled attempt.

Sonnet 9

Oft had I passed the joys and griefs in love
 And weary of them both, was laid to rest,
 And now desire, as an unworthy guest
Which did oppress his friend, I did remove:
No woman's force, I thought, should ever move
 My soul come home again to new unrest,
 When you, or in your shape an Angel dressed,
Called out my quiet thoughts once more to love:
 Straight my proud will did unto prayers turn,
For who in you, not cause of love doth find,
Or blind he is of eyes, or blind of mind.
 I yield, I love: to you, than erst, I burn
More hot, more pure; like wood oft warm before,
But to you burnt to dust, can burn no more.

Sonnet 16

Most fair, when first with pleased but cursed eyes
 I did behold that piece of heaven in you,
 O that I had, as to divinesse due,
Only to vows and prayers done sacrifice;
And blessed so, in so contented wise,
 From passions free enjoyed pleasures true;

When you yourself (I would I said untrue)
Kindled the sparks whence love and rage did rise.
    Yet on those hopes, though false, would I had stayed,
But I in searching out your truth did prove
My true mishaps in your betraying love.
    Cruel, I love you still, though thus betrayed,
Nor dare lay blame on you; but my fond mind
Do curse, which made such haste your faults to find.

Sonnet 17

The endless Alchemist, with blinded will,
    That feeds his thoughts with hopes, his hopes on shows,
    And more his work proves vain, more eager grows
While dreams of gold his head with shadows fill,
Feels not more sure the scourge of flatt'ring skill
    When in false trust of wealth true need he knows,
    Than I, on whom a storm of losses blows,
And tides of errors run: yet sail on still
    While my corrupted sense doth think it sees
The long sought land of rest, and while to bliss
I think there is a way, though yet I miss.
    Thus shunning to have lost, I still do leese,
And hope and want: and strive and fail: and prove
Nor end with joys, nor end from cares in love.

Sonnet 19

When other creatures all, each in their kind,
    Comfort of light, quiet from darkness fetch,
    Of wretched monsters, I most monstrous wretch
Nor day from pains, nor night with rest can find;
But as the slave, whom storm, or Sun or wind
    All day doth beat, in whose side bloody breach
    The scourge doth leave, who on the oar doth stretch
His limbs all day, all night his wounds doth bind,
    Chained to those beauties whence I cannot fly
I know no day so long, wherein each hour
Shows not new labours lost, and wherein I
Take not new wounds from their unsparing power:
    Nor longest night is long enough for me
    To tell my wounds, which restless bleeding be.

Sonnet 23

Absence, what floods of plaints 'gainst thee would rise,
   Which even the hellish wants dost make me taste
   If perished bark on shore by tempest cast
Which late prayed for the land, now on it dies,
Did not paint out my life, which fettered lies
   And famished, dark, in prison, cold, doth waste
   Till, when my life's Queen present shines at last,
A medicine worse than grief itself it tries.
   For as the condemned man from dungeon led
Who with first light he sees, ends his last breath,
When I see her, I see scorn's banner spread,
Each word refuses, each refuse gives death.
   Then thee sad absence I no longer curse,
   As present pain, than absent joy, is worse.

Sonnet 26

'Ah dearest limbs, my life's best joy and stay,
   How must I thus let you be cut from me,
   And losing you, myself unuseful see,
And keeping you, cast life and all away'
Full of dead Gangrenes doth the sick man say
   Whose death of part, health of the rest must be;
   Alas, my love, from no infections free,
Like law doth give, of it or my decay.
   My love, more dear to me than hands or eyes,
Dearer to me than what with me was born,
Delayed, betrayed, cast under change and scorn,
   Sick past all help or hope, or kills or dies;
While all the blood it sheds my heart doth bleed
And with my bowels I his cankers feed.

Sonnet 27

Falsehood: how long did I your stings endure
   And lazar-like, no sense had of your blows,
   While you not feared wrought my close overthrows
And I deaf to all doubts, did sleep secure.
Thorough the shadows of my love, a sure
   Standing you took, to guide your poisoned blows;

My love, which made his ends one with his shows
And sure in his own course, like did assure.
　　Tell how you could draw beauties pure and true
To shroud you with their wings? or so fair mind
Itself in league with your foul ways to bind?
　　Religious vows are broken, labours new
Reap of long faith the hire: and all too late
I learn, when help is past, my sickness' state.

Sonnet 31
Forsaken woods, trees with sharp storms oppressed,
　　Whose leaves once hid the sun, now strew the ground,
　　Once bred delight, now scorn, late used to sound
Of sweetest birds, now of hoarse crows the nest;
Gardens, which once in thousand colours dressed
　　Showed nature's pride, now in dead sticks abound,
　　In whom proud summer's treasure late was found
Now but the rags of winter's torn coat rest;
　　Meadows whose sides late fair brooks kissed, now slime
Embraced holds; fields whose youth green and brave
Promised long life, now frosts lay in the grave:
　　Say all, and I with them, 'What doth not time!'
But they who knew time, time will find again:
I that fair times lost, on time call in vain.

Sonnet 35
Time, cruel time, how fast pass you away
　　And in my case from your own custom fly,
　　While I unknown in blackest shadows lie
And dumb with fear, not that I love dare say:
Alas, your wings do to the light display
　　What choicest care in darkest bands doth tie;
　　But thus forsaking me, you make me try
That who to time trusts doth himself betray.
Speak time, and time's child truth: since first I saw
　　That bodied Angel, did my faith e'er quail,
　　Or was not spurred love held with reins of awe?
But you hear not: pack on then your best sail,
　　Leave me behind! Time, you shall nowhere move
　　Where, while you are, you shall not see my love.

B. GRIFFIN

From *Fidessa, more chaste then kinde*

3   Venus, and yong Adonis sitting by her,
         Under a Myrtle Shade began to woe him:
      She told the yong-ling how god Mars did trie her,
         And as he fell to her, so fell she to him.
      'Even thus' (quoth she) 'the wanton god embrac'd me,'
         (And then she clasp'd Adonis in her armes)
      'Even thus' (quoth she) 'the warlike god unlac'd me,'
         As if the boy should use like loving charmes.
      But he a wayward boy refusde her offer,
         And ran away, the beautious queene neglecting;
      Shewing both folly to abuse her proffer,
         And all his sex of cowardise detecting.
      Oh that I had my mistris at that bay,
      To kisse and clippe me till I ranne away!

13   Compare me to the child that plaies with fire,
         Or to the flye that dyeth in the flame:
      Or to the foolish boy that did aspire,
         To touch the glorie of high heaven's frame.
      Compare me to Leander struggling in the waves,
         Not able to attaine his safetie's shore:
      Or to the sicke that doe expect their graves,
         Or to the captive crying ever more.
      Compare me to the weeping wounded Hart,
         Moning with teares the period of his life;
      Or to the Bore that will not feele his smart,
         When he is stricken with the butcher's knife.
      No man to these can fitly me compare:
      These live to dye: I dye to live in care.

15   Care-charmer sleepe, sweet ease in restles miserie,
         The captive's libertie, and his freedome's song:
      Balme of the brused heart, man's chiefe felicitie,
         Brother of quiet death, when life is too too long.

A Comedie it is, and now an Historie:
　　What is not sleepe unto the feeble minde?
It easeth him that toyles, and him that's sorrie;
　　It makes the deaffe to heare, to see the blinde.
Ungentle sleepe, thou helpest all but me,
　　For when I sleepe my soule is vexed most:
It is Fidessa that doth master thee;
　　If she approach (alas) thy power is lost.
But here she is: see how he runnes amaine,
I feare at night he will not come againe.

16　For I have loved long, I crave rewarde;
　　Rewarde me not unkindlie: thinke on kindnes:
Kindnes becommeth those of high regarde:
　　Regard with clemencie a poore man's blindnes.
Blindnes provokes to pittie when it crieth:
　　It crieth 'Give'. Deere Lady shew some pittie;
Pittie, or let him die that daylie dieth:
　　Dieth he not oft, who often sings this dittie?
This dittie pleaseth me although it choke me;
　　Me thinkes dame Eccho weepeth at my moning,
Moning the woes, that to complaine provoke me.
　　Provoke me now no more, but heare my groning:
Groning both night and day doth teare my hart;
My hart doth know the cause, and triumphs in his smart.

31　Tongue, never cease to sing Fidessae's praise;
　　Heart (how ever she deserve) conceave the best;
Eyes, stand amaz'd to see her beautie's raies;
　　Lippes, steale one kisse and be for ever blest.
Hands, touch that hand wherein your life is closed;
　　Brest, locke up fast in thee thy live's sole treasure;
Armes, still imbrace and never be disclosed;
　　Feete, runne to her without or pace or measure:
Tongue, hart, eyes, lipps, hands, brest, armes, feete,
　　Consent to doe true homage to your Queene;
Lovelie, faire, gentle, wise, vertuous, sober, sweete,
　　Whose like shall never be; hath never beene.
Oh that I were all tongue her praise to show:
Then surelie my poore hart were freed from woe.

39   My Ladies haire is threads of beaten gold,
      Her front the purest Christall eye hath seene;
    Her eyes the brightest starres the heavens hold,
      Her cheekes red Roses, such as seld have been;
    Her pretie lips of red vermilion dye,
      Her hand of yvorie the purest white;
    Her blush Aurora or the morning skye,
      Her breast displaies two silver fountaines bright;
    The Spheares her voyce, her grace the Graces three,
      Her bodie is the Saint that I adore;
    Her smiles and favours sweet as honey bee,
      Her feete faire Thetis praiseth evermore.
    But ah the worst and last is yet behind,
    For of a Gryphon she doth beare the mind.

WILLIAM SMITH

From *Chloris or the Complaint of the passionate despised shepheard*

5   You Fawnes and Silvans, when my Chloris brings
    Hir flocks to water on your pleasant plaines,
    Sollicite hir to pitie Corin's stings,
    The smart whereof for hir he still sustaines,
    For she is ruthlesse of my wofull song.
    My oaten reede she not delights to heare.
    O Chloris, Chloris, Corine thou dost wrong,
    Who loves thee better than his owne hart deere.
    The flames of Aetna are not halfe so hot,
    As is the fire which thy disdaine hath bred.
    Ah cruell fates, why do you then besot
    Poore Corin's soule with love when love is fled?
      Either cause cruell Chloris to relent,
      Or let me die upon the wound she sent.

18   My Love, I cannot thy rare beauties place
    Under those formes which many writers use.
    Some like to stones compare their mistres' face;
    Some in the name of flowers do love abuse;
    Some makes their love a goldsmith's shop to be,
    Where orient pearles and pretious stones abounde.
    In my conceite these farre do disagree,
    The perfect praise of beautie foorth to sounde.
    O Chloris thou dost imitate thy selfe;
    Self's imitating passeth pretious stones,
    Or all the Easterne Indian golden pelfe:
    Thy red and white with purest faire attones:
      Matchlesse for beautie nature hath thee framed,
      Onely unkinde, and cruell thou art named.

20   Yee wastefull woods beare witnes of my woe,
        Wherein my plaints did oftentimes abound:
        Ye carelesse birds my sorrowes well do knoe,
        They in your songs were wont to make a sound.
        Thou pleasant spring canst record like wise beare
        Of my designes and sad disparagment,
        When thy transparent billowes mingled weare
        With those downfals which from mine eies were sent.
        The eccho of my still-lamenting cries
        From hollow vaults in treble voice resoundeth,
        And then into the emptie aire it flies,
        And backe againe from whence it came reboundeth.
            That Nimphe unto my clamors doth replie,
            Being likewise scorned in love as well as I.

26   Though you be faire and beautiful withall,
        And I am blacke for which you me despise,
        Know that your beauty subject is to fall
        Though you esteeme it at so high a prise.
        And time may come when that whereof you boast,
        (which is your youth's chief wealth and ornament)
        Shall withered be by winter's raging froast,
        When beautie's pride and flowring yeeres are spent.
        Then wilt thou morne when none shall thee respect:
        Then wilt thou think how thou hast scornd my tears:
        Then pitilesse ech one will thee neglect,
        When hoary gray shall die thy yellow hears.
            Then wilt thou thinke upon poore Corin's case,
            Who lov'd thee deere yet liv'd in thy disgrace.

SIR JOHN DAVIES

Gullinge Sonnets

[*Dedication*]
To his good freinde Sir Anthony Cooke

Here my Camelion Muse her selfe doth chaunge
To divers shapes of gross absurdities,
And like an Antick mocks with fashion straunge
The fond admirers of lewde gulleries.
Your judgement sees with pitty and with scorne
The bastard Sonnetts of these Rymers bace,
Which in this whiskinge age are daily borne
To theire owne shames, and Poetrie's disgrace.
Yet some praise those, and some perhappes will praise
Even these of myne: and therefore thes I send
To you that pass in Courte your glorious dayes,
That if some rich, rash gull these Rimes commend,
Thus you may sett his formall witt to schoole,
Use your owne grace, and begg him for a foole.

J.D.

Gullinge Sonnets

1 The Lover under burthen of his Mistress' love,
   Which lyke to *Aetna* did his harte oppresse,
   Did give such piteous grones that he did move
   The heav'nes at length to pitty his distresse.
   But for the fates in theire highe Courte above
   Forbad to make the grevous burthen lesse,
   The gracious powers did all conspire to prove
   Yf miracle this mischeife mighte redresse.
   Therefore regardinge that the loade was such
   As noe man mighte with one man's mighte sustayne,
   And that mylde patience imported much
   To him that shold indure an endles payne,

By their decree he soone transformed was
Into a patiente burden-bearinge Asse.

2 As when the brighte Cerulian firmament
Hathe not his glory with black cloudes defas'te,
Soe were my thoughts voyde of all discontent
And with noe myste of passions overcast;
They all were pure and cleare, till at the last
An ydle, carles thoughte forthe the wandringe wente,
And of that poysonous beauty tooke a taste
Which doe the harts of lovers so torment.
Then as it chauncethe in a flock of sheepe
When some contagious yll breedes first in one,
Daylie it spreedes, and secretly doth creepe
Till all the silly troupe be overgone;
So by close neighbourhood within my brest,
One scurvy thoughte infecteth all the rest.

3 What Eagle can behould her sunbrighte eye,
Her sunbrighte eye that lights the world with love,
The world of Love wherein I live and dye,
I live and dye and divers chaunges prove,
I chaunges prove, yet still the same am I,
The same am I and never will remove,
Never remove untill my soule dothe flye,
My soule dothe fly and I surcease to move,
I cease to move which now am mov'd by you,
Am mov'd by you that move all mortall hartes,
All mortall hartes whose eyes your eyes doth veiwe,
Your eyes doth veiwe whence Cupid shoots his darts,
Whence Cupid shootes his dartes and woundeth those
That honor you, and never weare his foes.

4 The hardnes of her harte and truth of myne
When the all seeinge eyes of heaven did see,
They streight concluded that by powre devine
To other formes our hartes should turned be.
Then hers as hard as flynte, a Flynte became,
And myne as true as steele, to steele was turned,
And then betwene our hartes sprange forthe the flame
Of kindest love which unextinguish'd burned.

And longe the sacred lampe of mutuall love
Incessantlie did burne in glory brighte,
Untill my folly did her fury move
To recompence my service with despighte,
And to put out, with snuffers of her pride,
The lampe of love which els had never dyed.

5   Mine Eye, myne eare, my will, my witt, my harte,
Did see, did heare, did like, discerne, did love,
Her face, her speche, her fashion, judgement, arte,
Which did charme, please, delighte, confounde and move.
Then fancie, humor, love, conceipte, and thoughte
Did soe drawe, force, intyse, perswade, devise,
That she was wonne, mov'd, caryed, compast, wrought,
To thinck me kinde, true, comelie, valyant, wise.
That heaven, earth, hell, my folly and her pride
Did worke, contrive, labor, conspire and sweare
To make me scorn'd, vile, cast of, bace, defyed
With her my love, my lighte, my life, my deare;
So that my harte, my witt, will, eare, and eye
Doth greive, lament, sorrowe, dispaire and dye.

6   The sacred Muse that firste made love devine
Hath made him naked and without attyre;
But I will cloth him with this penn of myne
That all the world his fashion shall admyre:
His hatt of hope, his bande of beautye fine,
His cloake of crafte, his doblett of desyre;
Greife for a girdell shall aboute him twyne;
His pointes of pride, his Iletholes of yre,
His hose of hate, his Codpeece of conceite,
His stockings of sterne strife, his shirte of shame;
His garters of vaine glorie, gaye and slyte,
His pantofels of passions I will frame;
Pumpes of presumption shall adorne his feete,
And Socks of sullennes excedinge sweete.

7   Into the Midle Temple of my harte
The wanton Cupid did himselfe admitt,
And gave for pledge your Eagle-sighted witt
That he wold play noe rude uncivill parte.

Longe tyme he cloak'te his nature with his arte,
And sadd and grave and sober he did sitt;
But at the last he gan to revell it,
To breake good rules, and orders to perverte.
Then love and his younge pledge were both convented
Before sadd Reason, that old Bencher grave,
Who this sadd sentence unto him presented
By Dilligence, that slye and secreate knave:
That love and witt for ever shold departe
Out of the Midle Temple of my harte.

8   My case is this: I love Zepheria brighte.
Of her I hold my harte by fealtye
Which I discharge to her perpetuallye,
Yet she thereof will never me accquite.
For now supposinge I withold her righte,
She hathe distreinde my harte to satisfie
The duty which I never did denye,
And far away impounds it with despite.
I labor therefore justlie to repleave
My harte which she unjustly doth impounde,
But quick conceite which nowe is love's highe Shreife
Retornes it as esloynde, not to be founde:
Then, which the lawe afords, I onely crave
Her harte for myne in withername to have.

9   To Love, my lord, I doe knighte's service owe,
And therefore nowe he hath my witt in warde;
But while it is in his tuition soe,
Me thincks he doth intreate it passinge hard.
For thoughe he hathe it marryed longe agoe
To Vanytie, a wench of noe regarde,
And nowe to full, and perfect age doth growe,
Yet nowe of freedome it is most debarde.
But why should love, after minoritye,
When I am past the one and twentith yeare,
Perclude my witt of his sweete libertye
And make it still the yoake of wardshippe beare?
I feare he hath an other Title gott,
And holds my witt now for an Ideott.

LADY MARY WROTH

Pamphilia to Amphilanthus (1621)

1   When night's blacke Mantle could most darknesse prove,
     And sleepe (deaths Image) did my senses hyre
     From Knowledge of my selfe, then thoughts did move
     Swifter then those, most swiftnesse neede require:

    In sleepe, a Chariot drawne by wing'd Desire
     I saw, where sate bright *Venus* Queene of Love,
     And at her feete her Sonne, still adding Fire
     To burning hearts, which she did hold above,

    But one heart flaming more then all the rest
     The Goddesse held, and put it to my breast,
     Dear Sonne, now shut said she: thus must we winne;

    He her obeyd, and martyr'd my poore heart,
     I waking hop'd as dreames it would depart,
     Yet since, O me, a Lover I have beene.

2   Deare eyes how well indeed you doe adorne
     That blessed Sphere, which gazing soules hold deare:
     The loved place oft sought for triumphs neere:
     The Court of Glory, where Loves force was borne:

    How may they terme you *Aprills* sweetest morne
     When pleasing lookes, from those bright lights appeare:
     A Sunne-shine day, from clowdes, and mists still cleare
     Kinde nursing fires for wishes yet unborne!

    Two Starres of Heaven, sent downe to grace the Earth,
     Plac'd in that Throne which gives all joyes their birth;
     Shining, and burning; pleasing yet their Charmes;

Which wounding, even in hurts are deem'd delights,
   So pleasant is their force! So great their mights
   As, happy, they can tryumph in their harmes.

3   Yet is there hope, then Love but play thy part,
   Remember well thy selfe, and thinke on me;
   Shine in those eyes which conquer'd have my heart,
   And see if mine be slacke to answer thee:

Lodge in that breast, and pitty mooving see
   For flames which in mine burne in truest smart
   Exciling thoughts that touch Inconstancy,
   Or those which waste not in the constant Art.

Watch but my sleepe, if I take any rest
   For thought of you, my spirit so distrest
   As, pale and famished, I for mercy cry;

Will you your servant leave? thinke but on this,
   Who wears Love's Crowne, must not doe so amisse,
   But seeke their good, who on thy force doe lye.

4   Forbeare darke night, my joyes now budd againe,
   Lately grown dead, while cold aspects did chill
   The roote at heart, and my chiefe hope quite kill,
   And thunders strooke me in my pleasures waine.

Then I alas with bitter sobs, and paine,
   Privately groan'd, my Fortunes present ill;
   All light of comfort dimb'd, woes in prides fill,
   With strange encrease of griefe, I griev'd in vaine,

And most, when as a memory to good
   Molested me, which still as witness stood
   Of those best dayes, in former time I knew:

Late gone as wonders past, like the great Snow,
   Melted and wasted, with what, change must know:
   Now backe the life comes where as once it grew.

5   Can pleasing sight, misfortune ever bring?
            Can firme desire a painefull torment trye?
            Can winning eyes prove to the heart a sting?
            Or can sweet lips in Treason hidden lye?

        The Sunne most pleasing, blindes the strongest eye,
            If too much look'd on, breaking the sights string;
            Desires still crost must unto mischiefe hie,
            And as Despaire, a lucklesse chance may fling.

        Eyes having wunn, rejecting prooves a sting,
            Killing the budd before the tree doth spring;
            Sweet lipps, not loving, do as poyson prove:

        Desire, sight, eyes, lipps; seeke, see, prove, and finde,
            You love may winn, but curses if unkind;
            Then shew you harmes dislike, and joy in love.

6   O strive not still to heape disdaine on me,
            Nor pleasure take, your cruelty to show
            On haplesse me, on whom all sorrowes flow,
            And byding make, as given, and lost by thee,

        Alas, even griefe is growne to pitty me,
            Scorne cryes out 'gainst it selfe such ill to show,
            And would give place for joyes delights to flow;
            Yet wretched I, all tortures bear from thee.

        Long have I suffer'd, and esteem'd it deare,
            Since such thy will, yet grew my paine more neere:
            Wish you my ende, say so, you shall it have;

        For all the deapth of my heart-held despaire
            Is that for you, I feele not Death for care;
            But now I'le seeke it, since you will not save.

        Song 1

        The Spring now come at last
            To Trees, Fields, to Flowres,
        And Meadowes makes to taste
            His pride, while sad showres

Which from mine eyes doe flow
   Makes knowne with cruell paines
   Cold Winter yet remaines
No sign of Spring wee knowe.

The Sunne which to the Earth
   Gives heate, light, and pleasure,
Joys in Spring, hateth Dearth,
   Plenty makes his Treasure.
His heate to me is colde,
   His light all darknesse is
   Since I am barr'd of blisse
I heate, nor light behold.

A Shepherdesse thus said
   Who was with griefe opprest
For truest Love betrayd
   Barr'd her from quiet rest
And weeping thus, said shee
   My end approacheth neere
   Now Willow must I weare
My Fortune so will be.

With Branches of this tree
   I'le dresse my haplesse head
Which shall my witnesse bee
   My hopes in Love are dead;
My cloathes imbroder'd all
   Shall be with Garlands round
   Some scatter'd, others bound
Some tyde, some like to fall.

The Barke my Booke shall bee
   Where dayly I will write
This tale of haples mee
   True slave to Fortunes spite;
The roote shall be my bedd
   Where nightly I will lye,
   Wailing in constancy
Since all true love is dead.

And these Lines I will leave
  If some such Lover come
Who may them right conceive,
  And place them on my Tombe:
She who still constant lov'd
  Now dead with cruel care
  Kill'd with unkind Dispaire,
And change, her end heere prov'd.

7   Love leave to urge, thou knowest thou hast the hand
    Tis Cowardize to strive where none resist,
    Pray thee leave off, I yeeld unto thy band,
    Do not thus still in thine owne power persist,

Behold, I yeeld, let forces be dismist,
  I am thy subject, conquer'd, bound to stand,
  Never thy foe, but did thy claime assist
  Seeking thy due of those who did withstand.

But now it seemes thou would'st I should thee love,
  I doe confesse, 'twas thy will made me choose,
  And thy faire shewes made me a lover prove
  When I my freedome did for paine refuse.

Yet this, Sir God, your Boy-ship I despise,
Your charmes I obey, but love not want of eyes.

8   Ledd by the power of griefe, to wailings brought
    By false conceit of change fallen on my part,
    I seeke for some small ease by lines, which bought
    Increase the paine; griefe is not cur'd by Art:

Ah! how unkindnesse moves within the heart
  Which still is true, and free from changing thought:
  What unknowne woe it breeds, what endlesse smart,
  With ceaselesse teares which causelessly are wrought.

It makes me now to shun all shining light,
  And seeke for blackest clouds me light to give:
  Which to all others onely darknesse drive;
  They on me shine, for Sunne disdaines my sight.

Yet though I darke doe live, I triumph may;
Unkindnes, nor this wrong shall love allay.

9   Bee you all pleas'd? your pleasures grieve not me:
         Doe you delight? I envy not your joy:
         Have you content? contentment with you be:
         Hope you for blisse? hope still, and still enjoy:

      Let sad misfortune, haplesse me destroy,
         Leave crosses to rule me, and still rule free,
         While all delights their contraries imploy
         To keepe good backe, and I but torments see,

      Joyes are bereav'd me, harmes doe only tarry;
         Despaire takes place, disdaine hath got the hand;
         Yet firme love holds my senses in such band
         As (since despised) I with sorrow marry;

      Then if with griefe I now must coupled bee
      Sorrow I'le wed; Despaire thus governes mee.

10   The weary Traveller who tired sought
         In places distant farre, yet found no end
         Of paine or labour, nor his state to mend,
         At last with joy is to his home backe brought;

      Findes not more ease though he with joy be fraught,
         When past his feare, content like soules ascend
         Then I, on whom new pleasures doe descend,
         Which now as high as first-borne blisse is wrought;

      He tyred with his paines, I, with my mind;
         He all content receives by ease of lymbs;
         I, greatest happinesse that I doe finde
         Beliefe for faith, while hope in pleasure swimmes;

      Truth saith 'twas wrong conceit bred my despight,
      Which once acknowledg'd, brings my hearts delight.

11   You endlesse torments that my rest oppresse
      How long will you delight in my sad paine?
      Will never Love your favour more expresse?
      Shall I still live, and ever feele disdaine?

    Alasse now stay, and let my griefe obtaine
      Some end; feede not my heart with sharpe distresse:
      Let me once see my cruell fortunes gaine
      At last release, and long-felt woes redress;

    Let not the blame of cruelty disgrace
      The honor'd title of your god-head, Love.
      Give not just cause for me to say, a place
      Is found for rage alone on me to move;

    O quickly end, and do not long debate
    My needfull ayd, lest helpe doe come too late.

12   Cloy'd with the torments of a tedious night
      I wish for day; which come, I hope for joy:
      When crosse I finde new tortures to destroy
      My woe-kild heart, first hurt by mischiefes might,

    Then crye for night, and once more day takes flight
      And brightnesse gone, what rest should heere injoy
      Usurped is; Hate will her force imploy
      Night cannot Griefe intombe though black as spite.

    My thoughts are sad, her face as sad doth seeme;
      My paines are long, her howers tedious are;
      My griefe is great, and endlesse is my care;
      Her face, her force, and all of woes esteeme:

    Then welcome Night, and farewell flattering day
    Which all hopes breed, and yet our joyes delay.

Song 2

All Night I weepe, all Day I cry, Ay me
I still do wish, though yet deny, ay me

I sigh, I mourne, I say that still
I only am the store for ill, ay me;

In coldest flames I freeze, yet burne, ay me
From flames I strive to flye, yet turne, ay me
From griefe I hast, but sorrowes hye
And on my heart all woes doe lye, ay me;

From contraries I seeke to run, ay me
But contraries I cannot shun, ay me
For they delight their force to trye
And to Despaire my thoughts doe tye, ay me;

Whither alasse then shall I goe, ay me
When as Despaire all hopes outgoe, ay me
If to the Forrest, Cupid hies
And my poore soule to his law tyes, ay me;

To the Court? O no, he cryes fye, ay me
There no true love you shall espye, ay me
Leave that place to falsest Lovers
Your true love all truth discovers, ay me;

Then quiet rest, and no more prove, ay me
All places are alike to Love, ay me
And constant be in this begun
Yet say, till Life with Love be done, Ay me.

13   Deare famish not what you your selfe gave foode,
          Destroy not what your glory is to save;
          Kill not that soule to which you spirit gave,
          In pitty, not disdaine, your triumph stood;

      An easie thing it is to shed the bloud
          Of one, who at your will, yields to the grave;
          But more you may true worth by mercy crave,
          When you preserve, not spoyle, but nourish good;

      Your sight is all the food I doe desire,
          Then sacrifice me not in hidden fire,
          Or stop the breath which did your praises move:

Thinke but how easie 'tis a sight to give,
   Nay, even desert; since I by it doe live,
   I but Camelion-like would live, and love.

14   Am I thus conquer'd? have I lost the powers
      That to withstand, which joyes to ruine me?
      Must I bee still while it my strength devoures
      And captive leads me prisoner bound, unfree?

Love first shall leave mens fant'sies to them free,
   Desire shall quench loves flames, Spring hate sweet
      showres,
   Love shall loose all his Darts, have sight, and see
   His shame, and wishings hinder happy houres;

Why should we not Loves purblinde charmes resist?
   Must we be servile, doing what he list?
   No, seeke some host to harbour thee: I flye

Thy Babish tricks, and freedome doe professe;
   But O, my hurt makes my lost heart confesse
   I love, and must, so farewell liberty.

15   Truely (poore night) thou welcome art to me:
      I love thee better in this sad attire
      Then that which rayseth some mens fant'sies higher
      Like painted outsides, which foule inward be;

I love thy grave and saddest lookes to see,
   Which seemes my soule and dying heart entire,
   Like to the ashes of some happy fire
   That flam'd in joy, but quench'd in misery:

I love thy count'nance, and thy sober pace
   Which evenly goes, and as of loving grace
   To us, and mee among the rest opprest

Gives quiet, peace to my poore selfe alone,
   And freely grants day leave when thou art gone
   To give cleare light, to see all ill redrest.

16   Sleepe fye possesse me not, nor doe not fright
            Me with thy heavy, and thy deathlike might
            For counterfetting's vilder then death's sight,
            And such deluding more my thoughts doe spight.

        Thou suffer'st falsest shapes my soule t'affright
            Sometimes in likenesse of a hopefull spright,
            And oft times like my Love, as in despight,
            Joying, thou canst with malice kill delight,

        When I (a poore foole made by thee) thinke joy
            Doth flow, when thy fond shadows doe destroy
            My that while sencelesse selfe, left free to thee,

        But now doe well, let me for ever sleepe,
            And so for ever that deere Image keepe,
            Or still wake, that my senses may be free.

17   Sweet shades, why doe you seeke to give delight
            To me, who deeme delight in this vilde place
            But torment, sorrow, and mine owne disgrace
            To taste of joy, or your vaine pleasing sight?

        Shew them your pleasures who saw never night
            Of griefe, where joyings fawning, smiling face
            Appeares as day, where griefe found never space
            Yet for a sigh, a groane, or envies spite;

        But O on me a world of woes doe lye,
            Or els on me all harmes strive to relye,
            And to attend like servants bound to me,

        Heate in desire, while frosts of care I prove,
            Wanting my love, yet surfet doe with love
            Burne, and yet freeze, better in Hell to be.

18   Which should I better like of, day, or night
            Since all the day I live in bitter woe
            Injoying light more cleere my wrongs to know,
            And yet most sad, feeling in it all spite;

In night, when darknesse doth forbid all light
   Yet I see griefe apparent to the show
   Follow'd by jealousie whose fond tricks flow,
   And on unconstant waves of doubt alight,

I can behold rage cowardly to feede
   Upon foule error, which these humors breede
   Shame, doubt, and feare, yet boldly will thinke ill,

All these in both I feele, then which is best
   Darke to joy by day, light in night opprest?
   Leave both, and end, these but each other spill.

Song 3

Stay, my thoughts, doe not aspire
To vaine hopes of high desire:
See you not all meanes bereft
To injoy? no joy is left;
Yet still me thinks my thoughts doe say
Some hopes doe live amid dismay;

Hope then once more, hope for joy,
Bury feare which joyes destroy,
Thought hath yet some comfort given
Which despaire hath from us driven;
Therefore deerely my thoughts cherish
Never let such thinking perish;

'Tis an idle thing to plaine
Odder farre to dye for paine,
Thinke, and see how thoughts doe rise
Winning where there no hope lies:
Which alone is lovers treasure
For by thoughts we love doe measure;

Then kinde thought my fant'sie guide
Let me never haplesse slide;
Still maintaine thy force in me,
Let me thinking still be free:
Nor leave thy might untill my death
But let me thinking yeeld up breath.

19   Come darkest Night, becoming sorrow best;
         Light, leave thy light, fit for a lightsome soule,
         Darknesse doth truely sute with me opprest
         Whom absence' power doth from mirth controule:

     The very trees with hanging heads condole
         Sweet Summers parting, and of leaves distrest
         In dying colours make a grief-full role;
         So much (alas) to sorrow are they prest.

     Thus of dead leaves, her farewell carpets made:
         Their fall, their branches, all their mournings prove;
         With leavelesse, naked bodies, whose hues vade
         From hopeful greene, to wither in their love,

     If trees, and leaves for absence mourners be
     No marvell that I grieve, who like want see.

20   The Sunne which glads the earth at his bright sight
         When in the morne he showes his golden face,
         And takes the place from tedious drowsie Night
         Making the world still happy in his grace;

     Shewes happinesse remaines not in one place,
         Nor may the Heavens alone to us give light,
         But hide that cheerefull face, though no long space,
         Yet long enough for tryall of their might;

     But never Sun-set could be so obscure
         No Desart ever had a shade so sad,
         Nor could black darknesse ever prove so bad
         As paines which absence makes me now indure;

     The missing of the Sunne a while makes Night
     But absence of my joy sees never light.

21   When last I saw thee, I did not thee see,
         It was thine Image, which in my thoughts lay
         So lively figur'd, as no times delay
         Could suffer me in heart to parted be;

And sleep so favourable is to me,
   As not to let thy lov'd remembrance stray,
   Lest that I waking might have cause to say
   There was one minute found to forget thee;

Then since my faith is such, so kinde my sleepe
   That gladly thee presents into my thought:
   And still true Lover-like thy face doth keepe
   So as some pleasure shadow-like is wrought,

Pitty my loving, nay of conscience give
Reward to me in whom thy selfe doth live.

22   Like to the Indians scorched with the Sunne,
      The Sunne which they doe as their God adore
      So am I us'd by Love, for evermore
      I worship him, lesse favours have I wonne,

   Better are they who thus to blacknesse run,
      And so can onely whitenesse' want deplore
      Then I who pale and white am with griefes store,
      Nor can have hope, but to see hopes undone;

   Besides their sacrifice receav'd in sight
      Of their chose Saint: mine hid as worthlesse rite;
      Grant me to see where I my offerings give,

   Then let me weare the marke of *Cupids* might
      In heart, as they in skin of *Phoebus* light,
      Not ceasing offerings to Love while I live.

23   When every one to pleasing pastime hies,
      Some hunt, some hauke, some play, while some delight
      In sweet discourse, and musicke shewes joyes might
      Yet I my thoughts doe farre above these prize.

   The joy which I take is that free from eyes
      I sit, and wonder at this day-like night
      So to dispose themselves as void of right,
      And leave true pleasure for poore vanities;

When others hunt, my thoughts I have in chase;
   If hauke, my minde at wished end doth flye,
   Discourse, I with my spirit talke, and cry
   While others musicke choose as greatest grace:

O God, say I, can these fond pleasures move
Or musicke be but in sweet thoughts of Love?

24   Once did I heare an aged father say
   Unto his sonne, who with attention heares
   What Age, and wise experience ever cleares
   From doubts of feare, or reason to betray,

My Sonne (said hee) behold thy father gray,
   I once had as thou hast, fresh tender yeares
   And like thee sported, destitute of feares
   But my young faults made mee too soone decay,

Love once I did, and like thee fear'd my Love,
   Led by the hatefull threed of Jealousie,
   Striving to keepe, I lost my liberty,
   And gain'd my griefe, which still my sorrowes move,

In time shun this; to love is no offence
But doubt in Youth, in Age breeds penitence.

Song 4

Sweetest Love returne againe
   Make not too long stay:
Killing mirth and forcing paine
   Sorrow leading way:
Let us not thus parted be
Love, and absence ne're agree;

But since you must needs depart,
   And me haplesse leave,
In your journey take my heart
   Which will not deceive
Yours it is, to you it flies
Joying in those loved eyes,

So in part, we shall not part
   Though we absent be;
Tyme, nor place, nor greatest smart
   Shall my bands make free
Ty'd I am, yet thinke it gaine;
In such knots I feele no paine.

But can I live, having lost
   Chiefest part of me
Heart is fled, and sight is crost
   These my fortunes be
Yet deare heart goe, soone returne
As good there, as heere to burne.

25   Poore eyes be blinde, the light behold no more
     Since that is gone which is your deare delight
     Ravish'd from you by greater power and might
     Making your loss a gaine to others store,

Oreflow, and drowne, till sight to you restore
     That blessed Starre, and as in hatefull spight
     Send forth your teares in flouds, to kill all sight
     And lookes, that lost, wherein you joy'd before.

Bury these beames, which in some kindled fires,
     And conquer'd have their love-burnt hearts desires
     Losing, and yet no gaine by you esteem'd,

Till that bright Starre doe once againe appeare
     Brighter than *Mars* when hee doth shine most cleare
     See not: then by his might be you redeem'd.

26   Deare cherish this, and with it my soules will,
     Nor for it ran away doe it abuse,
     Alas it left poore me your brest to choose
     As the blest shrine, where it would harbour still;

Then favour shew, and not unkindly kill
     The heart which fled to you, but doe excuse

That which for better, did the worse refuse,
And pleas'd I'le be, though heartlesse my life spill,

But if you will bee kinde, and just indeed,
Send me your heart, which in mine's place shall feede
On faithfull love to your devotion bound;

There shall it see the sacrifices made
Of pure and spotlesse Love, which shall not vade
While soule and body are together found.

27   Fie tedious Hope, why doe you still rebell?
Is it not yet enough you flatter'd me?
But cunningly you seeke to use a Spell
How to betray; must these thy Trophees bee?

I look'd from you farre sweeter fruite to see
But blasted were your blossomes when they fell,
And those delights expected from hands free
Wither'd and dead, and what seemd blisse proves hell.

No Towne was won by a more plotted slight
Then I by you, who may my fortune write
In embers of that fire which ruin'd me,

Thus Hope, your falshood calls you to be tryde
You'r loth, I see, the tryall to abide;
Prove true at last, and gaine your liberty.

28   Griefe, killing griefe, have not my torments beene
Already great, and strong enough? but still
Thou dost increase, nay glory in mine il,
And woes new past, afresh new woes begin!

Am I the onely purchase thou canst win?
Was I ordain'd to give despaire her fill
Or fittest I should mount misfortunes hill
Who in the plaine of joy cannot live in?

If it be so, Griefe come as welcome guest
   Since I must suffer for anothers rest:
   Yet this good, Griefe, let me intreat of thee,

Use still thy force, but not from those I love
   Let me all paines, and lasting torments prove
   So I misse these, lay all thy waights on me.

29   Flye hence, O Joy, no longer heere abide
   Too great thy pleasures are for my despaire
   To looke on, losses now must prove my fare
   Who not long since, on better foode relide;

But foole, how oft had I Heav'ns changing spi'de
   Before of mine owne fate I could have care,
   Yet now past time I can too late beware
   When nothings left but sorrowes faster ty'de;

While I enjoyd that Sunne, whose sight did lend
   Me joy, I thought that day could have no end,
   But soone a night came cloath'd in absence darke,

Absence more sad, more bitter then is gall
   Or death, when on true Lovers it doth fall
   Whose fires of love, disdaine rests poorer sparke.

30   You blessed shades, which give me silent rest,
   Witnes but this when death hath clos'd mine eyes,
   And separated me from earthly tyes,
   Being from hence to higher place adrest;

How oft in you I have laine heere opprest,
   And have my miseries in wofull cryes
   Deliver'd forth, mounting up to the Skyes
   Yet helplesse, backe return'd to wound my brest,

Which wounds did but strive how to breed more harm
   To me, who can be cur'd by no one harm
   But that of Love, which yet may me releeve;

If not, let Death my former paines redeeme,
　　My trusty friends, my faith untouch'd, esteeme
　　And witnesse I could love, who so could grieve.

Song 5

Time onely cause of my unrest
By whom I hop'd once to be blest
　　How cruell art thou turn'd?
That first gav'st life unto my love,
And still a pleasure not to move
　　Or change, though ever burn'd;

Have I thee slack'd, or left undone
One loving rite, and so have wonne
　　Thy rage, or bitter changing?
That now no minutes I shall see,
Wherein I may least happy be
　　Thy favours so estranging.

Blame thy selfe, and not my folly,
Time gave time but to be holy;
　　True Love such ends best loveth,
Unworthy love doth seeke for ends
　　A worthy Love, but worth pretends
Nor other thoughts it proveth:

Then stay thy swiftnes cruell Time,
And let me once more blessed clime
　　To joy, that I may praise thee:
Let me pleasure sweetly tasting
　　Joy in Love, and faith not wasting
And on Fames wings I'le raise thee:

Never shall thy glory dying
Bee untill thine owne untying
　　That Tyme no longer liveth;
　　'Tis a gaine such time to lend:
Since so thy fame shall never end
　　But joy for what she giveth.

31 After long trouble in a tedious way
    Of Loves unrest, laid down to ease my paine
    Hoping for rest, new torments I did gaine
    Possessing me, as if I ought t'obey:

When Fortune came, though blinded, yet did stay,
    And in her blessed armes did me inchaine;
    I, cold with griefe, thought no warmth to obtaine
    Or to dissolve that yce of joyes decay;

Till rise (said she) Reward to thee doth send
    By me the servant of true Lovers, joy;
    Bannish all clouds of doubt, all feares destroy,
    And now on Fortune, and on Love depend.

I her obey'd, and rising felt that Love
Indeed was best, when I did least it move.

32 How fast thou fliest, O Time, on Loves swift wings
    To hopes of joy, that flatters our desire
    Which to a Lover still contentment brings!
    Yet, when we should injoy, thou dost retire,

Thou stay'st thy pace (false Time) from our desire,
    When to our ill thou hast'st with Eagles wings,
    Slow only to make us see thy retire
    Was for Despaire, and harme, which sorrow brings;

O! slake thy pace, and milder passe to Love;
    Be like the Bee, whose wings she doth but use
    To bring home profit, masters good to prove
    Laden, and weary, yet againe pursues,

So lade thy selfe with hony of sweet joy,
And do not me, the Hive of Love, destroy.

33 How many eyes (poore Love) hast thou to guard
    Thee from thy most desired wish, and end?
    Is it because some say th'art blinde, that barr'd
    From sight, thou should'st no happinesse attend?

Who blame thee so, small Justice can pretend
   Since twixt thee, and the Sunne, no question hard
   Can be; his sight but outward, thou can'st bend
   The heart, and guide it freely, thus unbar'd

Art thou, while we both blinde, and bold, oft dare
   Accuse thee of the harmes our selves should finde
   Who led with folly, and by rashness blinde
   Thy sacred power, doe with a child's compare.

Yet Love, this boldnesse pardon, for admire
Thee sure we must, or be borne without fire.

34   Take heed mine eyes, how you your looks doe cast
   Lest they betray my hearts most secret thought;
   Be true unto your selves, for nothing's bought
   More deare then Doubt, which brings a Lovers fast.

Catch you alwatching eyes, ere they be past,
   Or take yours fix't, where your best Love hast sought
   The pride of your desires, then let them be taught
   Their faults for shame they could no truer last;

Then looke, and looke with joy, for conquest won
   Of those that search'd your hurt in double kinde;
   So you kept safe, let them themselves looke blinde
   Watch, gaze, and marke till they to madnesse run,

While you, mine eyes, enjoy full sight of Love
Contented that such happinesses move.

35   False Hope which feeds but to destroy, and spill
   What it first breeds; unnaturall to the birth
   Of thine owne wombe; conceiving but to kill,
   And plenty gives to make the greater dearth,

So Tyrants doe, who falsly ruling Earth
   Outwardly grace them, and with profits fill
   Advance those who appointed are to death
   To make their greater fall to please their will.

Thus shadow they their wicked vile intent
 Colouring evill with a show of good
 While in faire showes their malice so is spent;
 Hope kills the heart, and Tyrants shed the blood.

For Hope deluding brings us to the pride
Of our desires the farther downe to slide.

36 How well (poore heart) thou witnesse canst I love,
 How oft my grief hath made thee shed forth teares
 Drops of thy dearest blood, and how oft feares
 Borne testimony of the paines I prove,

What torments hast thou suffer'd, while above
 Joy, thou tortur'd wert with racks, which longing bears
 Pinch'd with desires, which yet but wishing reares
 Firme in my faith, in constancie to move,

Yet it is said that sure love cannot be
 Where so small shew of passion is descri'd,
 When thy chiefe paine is, that I must it hide
 From all, save onely one, who should it see.

For knowe, more passion in my heart doth move
Then in a million that make shew of love.

Song 6

You happy blessed eyes,
 Which in that ruling place
 Have force both to delight, and to disgrace,
Whose light allures, and tyes
 All hearts to your command
 O! looke on me who doe at mercy stand:

'Tis you that rule my life
 'Tis you my comforts give;
 Then let not scorne to me my ending drive,
Nor let the frownes of strife

Have might to hurt those lights
Which while they shine they are true loves delights;

See but, when Night appeares,
And Sunne hath lost his force
How his losse doth all joy from us divorce;
And when he shines, and cleares
The Heavens from clowdes of Night
How happy then is made our gazing sight,

But more then Sun's faire light
Your beames doe seeme to me,
Whose sweetest lookes doe tye, and yet make free;
Why should you then so spight
Poore me as to destroy
The only pleasure that I taste of joy?

Shine then, O dearest lights
With favour, and with love,
And let no cause, your cause of frowning move
But as the soules delights
So blesse my then blest eyes
Which unto you their true affection tyes.

Then shall the Sunne give place
As to your greater might,
Yeelding that you doe show more perfect light,
O, then, but grant this grace
Unto your Love-tide slave
To shine on me, who to you all faith gave;

And when you please to frowne
Use your most killing eyes
On them, who in untruth and falshood lies;
But (Deare) on me cast downe
Sweet lookes, for true desire
That banish doe all thoughts of faigned fire.

37   Night, welcome art thou to my minde distrest
       Darke, heavy, sad, yet not more sad then I
       Never could'st thou finde fitter company
       For thine owne humour, then I thus opprest.

If thou beest darke, my wrongs still unredrest
 Saw never light, nor smallest blisse can spye;
 If heavy, joy from mee too fast doth hie
 And care out-goes my hope of quiet rest,

Then in friendship joyne with haplesse me,
 Who am as sad, and darke as thou canst be
 Hating all pleasure, or delight of life;

Silence, and griefe, with thee I best doe love
 And from you three, I know I cannot move,
 Then let us live companions without strife.

38 What pleasure can a banish'd creature have
  In all the pastimes that invented are
  By wit or learning, Absence making warre
  Against all peace that may a biding crave?

 Can wee delight but in a welcome grave
  Where we may bury paines? and so be farre
  From loathed company, who alwaies jarre
  Upon the string of mirth that pastime gave;

 The knowing part of joy is deem'd the heart;
  If that be gone, what joy can joy impart
  When senslesse is the feeler of our mirth;

 No, I am banish'd, and no good shall finde
  But all my fortunes must with mischiefe binde
  Who but for misery did gaine a birth.

39 If I were given to mirth, 'twould be more crosse
  Thus to be robbed of my chiefest joy;
  But silently I beare my greatest losse
  Who's us'd to sorrow, griefe will not destroy;

 Nor can I as those pleasant wits injoy
  My owne fram'd wordes, which I account the drosse
  Of purer thoughts, or reckon them as mosse
  While they (wit-sick) themselves to breath imploy,

Alas, thinke I, your plenty shewes your want,
   For where most feeling is, wordes are more scant,
   Yet pardon me, live, and your pleasure take,

Grudge not, if I neglected, envy show
   'Tis not to you that I dislike doe owe
   But crost my selfe wish some like me to make.

40   It is not Love which you poore fooles doe deeme,
   That doth appeare by fond, and outward showes
   Of kissing, toying, or by swearings gloze
   O no, these are farre off from loves esteeme;

Alas, they are not such that can redeeme
   Love lost, or winning keepe those chosen blowes
   Though oft with face and lookes love overthrowes
   Yet so slight conquest doth not him beseeme,

'Tis not a shew of sighes or teares can prove
   Who loves indeed, which blasts of faigned love
   Increase or dye, as favours from them slide;

But in the soule true love in safety lies
   Guarded by faith, which to desert still hies,
   And yet kinde lookes do many blessings hide.

41   You blessed Starres, which doe Heaven's glory show,
   And at your brightnesse make our eyes admire
   Yet envy not, though I on earth below
   Injoy a sight which moves in me more fire;

I doe confesse such beauty breeds desire,
   You shine, and clearest light on us bestow,
   Yet doth a sight on Earth more warmth inspire
   Into my loving soule his grace to know;

Cleare, bright, and shining as you are, is this
   Light of my joy: fix'd stedfast, nor will move
   His light from me, nor I change from his love,
   But still increase as th'eith of all my blisse.

His sight gives life unto my love-rulde eyes
My love content, because in his, love lies.

42 If ever love had force in humane brest,
  If ever he could move in pensive heart
  Or if that he such powre could but impart
  To breed those flames, whose heat brings joyes unrest

Then looke on me; I am to these adrest,
 I, am the soule that feeles the greatest smart;
 I, am that heartlesse Trunck of hearts depart
And I, that One, by love and griefe opprest;

None ever felt the truth of loves great misse
 Of eyes, till I deprived was of blisse;
 For had he seene, he must have pitty show'd;

I should not have beene made this Stage of woe
 Where sad Disasters have their open show
 O no, more pitty he had sure bestow'd.

Song 7

Sorrow, I yeeld, and grieve that I did misse:
Will not thy rage be satisfied with this?
   As sad a Divell as thee,
   Made me unhappy be.
Wilt thou not yet consent to leave, but still
Strive how to show thy cursed, divelish skill;

I mourne, and dying am; what would you more?
My soule attends, to leave this cursed shoare
    Where harmes doe onely flow
    Which teach me but to know
The saddest houres of my lifes unrest,
And tyred minutes with griefes hand opprest:

Yet all this will not pacifie thy spight;
No, nothing can bring ease but my last night.

Then quickely let it be
While I unhappy see
That time, so sparing to grant Lovers blisse
Will see for time lost, there shall no griefe misse,

Nor let me ever cease from lasting griefe,
But endlesse let it be without reliefe:
To winn againe of Love,
The favour I did proove;
And with my end please him; since dying, I
Have him offended, yet unwillingly.

43   O Dearest eyes, the lights, and guides of Love,
The joyes of *Cupid*, who himselfe borne blinde
To your bright shining doth his tryumphs binde,
For in your seeing doth his glory move;

How happy are those places where you proove
Your heavenly beames, which makes the Sun to find
Envy, and grudging, he so long hath shin'd
For your cleare lights, to match his beames above.

But now, alas, your sight is heere forbid
And darkenes must these poore lost roomes possesse
So be all blessed lights from henceforth hid
That this blacke deede of darkenesse have excesse,

For why should Heaven affoord least light to those
Who for my misery such darkenesse chose.

44   How fast thou hastst (O Spring) with sweetest speed
To catch thy waters which before are runne,
And of the greater Rivers welcome woone,
Ere these thy new-borne streames these places feede,

Yet you doe well, lest staying here might breede
Dangerous flouds, your sweetest bankes t'orerunn,
And yet much better my distresse to shun
Which makes my tears your swiftest course succeed,

But best you doe when with so hasty flight,
   You fly my ills, which now my selfe outgoe,
   Whose broken heart can testifie such woe,
   That so orecharg'd, my life-bloud wasteth quite.

Sweet Spring then keepe your way, be never spent
And my ill dayes, or griefes, assunder rent.

45   Good now be still, and doe not me torment
           With multitude of questions, be at rest,
           And onely let me quarrell with my breast
           Which stil lets in new stormes my soule to rent;

        Fye, will you still my mischiefes more augment?
           You say, I answere crosse, I that confest
           Long since, yet must I ever be opprest
           With your tongue torture which wil ne're be spent?

        Well then I see no way but this will fright
           That Devill speech; alas, I am possest,
           And madd folkes senseles are of wisdomes right,

        The hellish spirit, Absence, doth arrest
           All my poore senses to his cruell might,
           Spare me then till I am myselfe, and blest.

46   Love, thou hast all, for now thou hast me made
           So thine, as if for thee I were ordain'd;
           Then take thy conquest, nor let me be pain'd
           More in thy Sunne, when I doe seeke thy shade,

        No place for helpe have I left to invade,
           That shew'd a face where least ease might be gain'd;
           Yet found I paine increase, and but obtain'd
           That this no way was to have love allay'd,

        When hott, and thirsty, to a Well I came
           Trusting by that to quench part of my flame,
           But there I was by Love afresh imbrac'd;

Drinke I could not, but in it I did see
My selfe a living glasse as well as shee
For love to see himselfe in, truely plac'd.

47   O Stay mine eyes, shed not these fruitlesse teares
Since hope is past to win you back againe
That treasure which, being lost, breeds all your paine,
Cease from this poore betraying of your feares,

Thinke this too childish is, for where griefe reares
So high a powre, for such a wretched gaine;
Sighes, nor laments should thus be spent in vaine:
True sorrow, never outward wailing beares;

Be rul'd by me, keepe all the rest in store,
Till no roome is that may containe one more,
Then in that Sea of teares, drowne haplesse me,

And I'le provide such store of sighes, as part
Shall be enough to breake the strongest heart,
This done, we shall from torments freed be.

48   How like a fire doth Love increase in me,
The longer that it lasts, the stronger still,
The greater, purer, brighter; and doth fill
No eye with wonder more, then hopes still bee

Bred in my breast, when fires of Love are free
To use that part to their best pleasing will,
And now unpossible it is to kill
The heate so great where Love his strength doth see.

Mine eyes can scarce sustaine the flames, my heart
Doth trust in them my passions to impart,
And languishingly strive to shew my love;

My breath not able is to breathe least part
Of that increasing fuell of my smart;
Yet love I will, till I but ashes prove.
                    Pamphilia

MARK ALEXANDER BOYD

Sonet

Fra banc to banc, fra wod to wod, I rin
   Owrhailit with my feble fantasie,
   Lyc til a leif that fallis from a trie
   Or til a reid owrblawin with the win'.
Twa gods gyds me: the ane of tham is blin',
   Ye, and a bairn brocht up in vanitie;
   The nixt a wyf ingenrit of the se,
   And lichter nor a dauphin with hir fin.
Unhappie is the man for evirmaire
   That teils the sand and sawis in the aire,
   Bot twyse unhappier is he, I lairn,
That feidis in his hairt a mad desyre,
   And follows on a woman throu the fyre,
   Led be a blind and teichit be a bairn.

NOTES

Sir Philip Sidney Astrophel and Stella (c. 1582)

MODERN EDITIONS
Astrophel and Stella ed. Mona Wilson (Nonesuch) 1931.
The Poems of Sir Philip Sidney ed. William A. Ringler Jr
(Oxford) 1962.
Sir Philip Sidney. Selected Poems ed. Katherine Duncan-Jones
(Oxford Paperback English Texts) 1973.

The sonnet cycle first appeared in print in 1591 in two incomplete and
unauthorised quartos (Q1, Q2). The complete text was printed at the end
of the 1598 Folio of the *Arcadia*, apparently under the supervision of the
Countess of Pembroke herself. I have used the 1598 Folio (F) as my text,
with minor emendations from the Quartos and from Ringler (R). All
substantial variations from 1598 are indicated below. Where these agree
with Ringler, as most of them inevitably do, I have acknowledged the
debt, and where I have retained the 1598 or quarto reading in preference
to Ringler, the fact is also noted. I have followed Ringler and the Quartos
in replacing the rigid sonnet pattern used by the printers of 1598 by a
variety of forms designed to draw attention to the variations in Sidney's
rhyme schemes. I have retained the spelling of 1598, but have modernised
the punctuation where necessary. I have kept the spelling 'Astrophel' of
1598, although Ringler's 'Astrophil' — 'star-lover' — with its play on
Sidney's christian name, is more apt.

1 2. *she (deare she)* (F). R, 'the deare She'. 10. *Invention*: See general
    introduction pp. xxiv–xxv. 13. *Trewand*: truant.
2 1. *dribbed*: random. 3. *mine*: tunnel dug under the walls in a siege —
    cf. 'undermine'.
3 1–8. An ironic and very concentrated description of those poets
    who invoke the nine Muses to help them dress up their fancies in fine
    words (1–2); or who become servile imitators of the Greek
    rhapsodic poet, Pindar, in overlaying their commonplace thoughts
    with the various colours of rhetoric (3–4); or who use new-fangled
    figures of speech (Tropes) which are so inept that even the most
    hackneyed themes expressed through them serve to improve them

(5–6); or who embellish their poems with extravagant similes from natural history (as in Lyly's *Euphues*). By *Pindare's Apes*, Sidney may be alluding to Ronsard's claim 'Le premier de France/J'ai Pindarisé', or more likely to the claim of the hack sonneteer, Soowthern in the Ode prefacing his *Sonnets to Diana* (c. 1584) that 'never man before/Now in England, knewe Pindar's string'.

4 2. *bate*: debate. 5. *Catoe*: Roman moralist and ascetic. 11. *prove*: test.

6 1–4. A list of the commonest clichés of the Petrarchan sonnet. 2. *wot*: know. 5–6. *Jove's strange tales*: reference to Jove's metamorphoses when wooing Europa, Leda and Danae. 6. *Brodered*: embroidered. R, 'Broadred'. F, 'Bordred'. *powdred*: dusted over. 7–8. A hackneyed theme of the pastoral romance. 8. *vaine*: vein.

7 7. *vaile*: veil. 8. *then*: than. 13. *weed*: garment.

8 1. *his native place*: Cyprus, home of Cupid's mother, Venus, captured by the Turks in 1573. 6. *clips*: embraces.

9 2. *choisest* (F). R, 'chiefest'. 12. *touch*: multiple wordplay on 'touch' which, in addition to its primary meaning, signified a jet-like substance able, when rubbed, to attract straws etc. by static electricity. Also 'touchstone', used for testing gold, and 'touch', tinder for lighting fires. 13. *mine* (R). F, 'mind'.

10 2. *brabling*: disputing. 11. *fence*: use of the sword.

11 6. *Velume*: vellum. 10. *lookst babies*: looked at your own reflection. 11. *pitfould*: trap. 12. *bopeepe or couching*: nursery game involving hiding and peeping out unexpectedly.

12 2. *day-nets* (R). F, 'daunces'. Nets of hair in which small birds were caught after being attracted by mirrors – in this case, Stella's eyes. 3. *swell* (R). F, 'sweld'.

13 2. *armes*: coat-of-arms. That of Jove includes the eagle in which form he carried off the boy, Ganymede. Mars's coat-of-arms represents love's war and the triumph of Venus over him. Cupid's shield proclaims (blazes) the red and white of Stella's cheeks, but also alludes to the Devereux arms, three scarlet circles on a silver ground. 11. *'sables'*, *'Vert'*, and *'gueuls'*, heraldic colours; black, green and scarlet respectively. 14. *scantly* (F). R, 'scarcely'.

14 2. *Upon whose breast*: Prometheus, whose punishment for stealing fire from heaven was to be chained to a rock and have his liver devoured by Jove's vulture each day. *tire*: tear. 5. *Rubarb*: purgative. 10. *staid*: unchanging.

15 2. *Parnassus*: mountain in Greece sacred to Apollo and the Muses. 8. *denisend*: naturalised in a foreign country. 9. *far-fet*: far-fetched. 10. *inward tuch*: judgement and inspiration.

16 2. *Carrets*: carat, as of gold. 8. *soule* (F). R, 'love'. 9. *young* (Qs, R), omitted F.

17 3. *pricking*: a typical Sidneian *double entendre*. *he*: i.e. Cupid.
6. *prove*: make trial of. 7. *chafe*: anger. 13. *wags*: mischievous boys.

18 1. *shent*: disgraced. 4. *hath* (R). F, 'have'. 5–6. *Nature's rent . . .
birthright*: unable to perform the duties he owes to nature, including
even that of begetting children.

19 2. *wracke*: wreck. 8. *Avise*: apprise. 12. *prop*: find a support for.

20 5. *Tyran*: tyrant. 6. *levell*: level place from which to take aim. *stay*:
resting-place. 9. *passenger*: passer-by.

21 1. *caustiks*: corrosives. 2. *windlas*: go round about to intercept the
game in hunting. 5. *but if*: unless. 6. *coltish gyres* (R). 'youthfull
running around'. F, 'yeeres'.

22 2. *faire twinnes*: Gemini, the zodiacal sign governing May/June
when the sun is at its highest. 11. *the wealth*: her beauty which owed
nothing to cosmetics. 12. *where*: F, 'were'.

23 2. *Bewray*: make visible.

24 1. *Riche*: for this play on Stella's married name, see also sonnets 35,
37, & 79. 2. *hatching*: a play on the double meaning of the word; to
hatch out, i.e. breed more, and to close up, shut in; cf. sonnet 38.
3. *Tantal*: Tantalus, whose punishment in hell was to suffer the
torments of hunger and thirst whilst standing in water which never
rose as high as his lips, and in sight of fruit always out of reach.
4. *blist*: blessed.

25 1. *The wisest scholler*: Plato, whose teacher, Socrates, was judged the
wisest of mankind by Apollo's oracle at Delphi. 5. *But for that*: But
because. 6. *wayes*: weighs. 8. *inward sunne*: the Right Reason in
man which kindles an instinctive love of virtue so long as it is not
obscured by the passions. 9. *ster*: stir, arouse.

26 3. *wayes* (R). F, 'weighs'. 7. *brawle*: a French dance. 11. *those Bodies
high raigne on the low*: Sidney is playing with the traditional
conception of the power of the stars, but it is likely that he believed in
it himself. He had his horoscope cast; he was a friend of Dr Dee, the
queen's astrologer; and Giordano Bruno, the noted Italian Hermeti-
cist, dedicated two books to him. The relationship between eyes and
stars is more than merely a conceit. It is a commonplace of the
Renaissance neo-Platonic belief in the real affinities between
different levels of the universe – eyes at the material level embodying
the same 'Platonic Idea' as stars at the celestial.

27 5. *doome*: judgement, cf. 25, 2.

28 7. *raines*: reins. *slake*: slack. 9. *I beg no subject*: I don't appropriate
any subject simply as an excuse to show off my eloquence.
11. *quintessence*: inner truth and meaning.

30 A series of references to contemporary affairs which might be
expected to preoccupy the mind of a young statesman such as
Astrophel/Sidney in 1582. For a full analysis see Ringler, pp. 470–1.
1. *the Turkish new-moone*: the Crescent, standard of the Turks who

were expected to attack Spain in 1582. 3. *Poles' right king*: the elected king of Poland, Stephen Bathory, who invaded Russia in 1580–1. 5. *three parts*: the three French factions before Henry of Navarre gained the throne; Catholics, Huguenots and the moderate Politiques. 6. *Dutch*: Germans (Deutsch). *full diets*: the Diet of the Holy Roman Empire at Augsburg, July–September, 1582. 8. *Orange*: William of Orange lost a number of towns to the Spaniards in 1581–2. 9. *golden bit*: Sir Henry Sidney, three times governor of Ireland, subdued Ulster in 1576–8, in part by imposing a land tax on the great landowners to pay for the maintenance of his troops there. 11. *weltring*: the conflict of factions in the Scottish Court. Changed in F to 'If in the *Scotch* Court be no weltring yet', perhaps as a tactful move towards James VI of Scotland, soon to become James I of England.

31 7. *thy languisht grace*: presumably a waning moon. 8. *descries*: proclaims. 14. *Do they call Vertue there ungratefulnesse?* An ambiguous line. Ringler suggests a simple inversion, 'Do the ladies there consider ungratefulness a virtue?' There is no need, however, to change Sidney's order. From the male point of view, Stella's virtue could in this case be considered a form of ungratefulness since the traditional courtly lover expects by right a reward for his constant love, a reward which Stella's virtue denies him. Astrophel is making this point but ruefully showing, at the same time, that he is fully aware of the sophistry of his plea.

32 1. *Morpheus*: son of Somnus, the god of sleep. He was responsible for bringing dreams which appear in human form to sleepers, '*them that living die*'. Such dreams were either prophetic (3), out of memory (3), or out of fantasy (4), depending on which bodily humour was predominant. 7. *descrie*: discover by observation. 9. *of all acquaintance*: cf. 'auld acquaintance', long-standing fellowship.

34 3. *glasses*: mirrors. 7. *fond*: foolish. 8. *close*: unpublished. 9. *hard*: heard. 12. *wreake*: revenge.

35 5. *Nestor*: oldest and wisest of the Greeks at the siege of Troy, hence the prototype of the wise counsellor. 6. *blow the cole*: blow up the fire.

36 2. yelden (R). F, 'golden'. Qs, 'yeelding'. 8. *now* (F). R, 'new'. 14. *By Sence's priviledge*: even though they lack feeling.

37 5. *Aurora's Court*: Aurora, goddess of the dawn; hence the east, where Lord Rich had his family seat in Essex. 13. *make the patents*: entitle one to the possession of.

38 2. *hatch*: close. *unbitted*: without a bit, uncontrolled. 4. *leave the scepter*: give up the rule of. 7. *curious drought*: skilful draftsmanship. 14. *him, her host*: sleep, destroyed by Stella's image, 'that unkind guest'.

39 2. *baiting place*: inn where travellers rest and horses are fed and watered. 4. *indifferent*: impartial. 5. *prease*: attack.

41 7. *sleight*: skill coming from practice rather than natural ability alone. 12. *shoote* (R). F, 'shot'. 14. *race*: course in a tournament.

42 1. *Spheares*: Stella's eyes are like the angelic 'intelligences' which move the planetary spheres (cf. sonnet 26). 14. *Wrackes*: wrecks, defeats.

43 2. *pray*: prey. 13. *rome*: room.

44 5. R, 'yet I no pitty find'. 7. *overthwart*: adverse. 11. *Those daintie dores*: her ears.

45 3. *cannot skill*: is not able. 7. *gate*: got. 11. *Then*: than. *wracke*: ruin.

46 6. *Rogue*: a vagrant without master or possessions. 11. *misse*: fail to learn. 12. *this* (R). F, 'his'. 13. *myche*: play truant. 13–14. 'Let love be pardoned for playing truant and forsaking your chaste rules to follow desire, until you yourself are able to arouse love without arousing the passion which fuels it.'

47 2. *those blacke beames*: one of the many references to the paradox of the brightness of Stella's dark eyes. 6. *sprite*: spirit. 12. *Let her go* (R). F, 'Let her do'.

· 49 4. *descrie*: perceive. 5. *raines*: reins. 9. *Wand*: whip. *Will*: sexual desire. 14. *Manage*: the training of a horse in its paces.

50 2. *staid*: contained. 6. *behest*: command. 8. *portrait*: portray. 11. *those* (R). F, 'these'. *poor babes*: i.e. his verses.

51 5. *silly*: unsophisticated. 7–8. *Hercules*: Atlas supported the weight of the heavens on his shoulders until Hercules relieved him for a time. 7. *in steed*: instead. 10. *cunningst* (R). F, 'cunning'.

52 2. *pretends*: makes a legal claim. 12. *demurre*: legal objection.

53 1. *cunning*: skill. 2. *stave*: shaft of a lance. 5. *describe*: caught sight of. 6. *presse*: the thick of the fight. 7. *I would no lesse*: 'You must do as well for me as you have for Mars.' 13. *heat the aire*: His opponent gallops up the tilting yard but finds no one there to oppose him, since Astrophel, gazing at the window, has not stirred.

54 2. *set colours*: Stella's colours, as a declaration of his love. 4. *a full point*: a full stop. 9. *And thinke so still*: 'And let them continue to think so, as long as Stella knows my mind.' 13. *Pies*: magpies.

55 2. *choisest flowers*: the 'flowers' or adornments of rhetoric. 4. *in your sweet grace* (F). R, 'in your sweet skill'. 8. *their blacke banner*: how, by the inspiration of the Muses and the embellishments of rhetoric, the words might be made most tragic and moving: cf. Marlowe, *Tamburlaine* I. v, 1.

56 2. *without booke*: by heart. 4. *misse*: begin to ignore. 11. *flegmatike*: Phlegm, the cold and dull humour.

57 1. *fights* (F). Qs, 'sighes'.

58 This sonnet refers to the traditional debate as to whether the orator owes his power of persuasion primarily to his fine language and strength of argument or to his mode of utterance and the impression of his personality. In this case, the latter wins. 6. *tropes*: figures of speech. 12. *maugre*: in spite of.

59 9. *clips*: see sonnet 8. 14. *clog*: hindrance.

61 3. *assayll* (R). F, 'assaid'. Qs, 'assailde'. 8. *Thence* (R). F, 'Then'. 12–13. *Doctor*: teacher, associated especially with the medieval Schoolmen, among whom Thomas Aquinas was called the Angelic doctor. Scholasticism was out of fashion by Sidney's day; hence 'Angel's sophistrie'. 14. *without I leave to love*: unless I leave off loving.

63 2. *So children*: 'let children continue to study you with eyes full of awe so long as . . .' 9. *Io Pean*: paeon of triumph or joy, especially a marriage song. 12. *weigh* (R). Qs, 'waye'. F, 'nay'. 14. *affirme*: make a positive.
First song 5. *state*: dignity and decorum. 10. *deckes and stayneth*: adorns and puts to shame by outshining. 13. *all* (R). F, 'of'. 24. *rueth*: grieves. 28. *the flatterer*: 'flattery can't improve on the truth'. 32. *not miracles*: 'wonders are not miracles but natural'.

64 12. *wishe* (R). F, 'with'.

65 3. *my good turnes*: my good services. 14. *the arrow head*: Sidney's own arms were a blue arrow-head on a gold background.

66 6. *Fortune wheeles . . . slow* (R). F, 'Fortunes'. Q, 'Fortunes windes . . . blowe'.

67 4. *take time*: cf. 'carpe diem'.

68 6. *Amphion's lyre*: Amphion, son of Jupiter and inventor of music, whose lyre had the power to move stones, and build the walls of Thebes. 8. *kindled* (R). F, 'blinded'.

69 11. *I, I, O I*: cf. sonnet 63. In a sonnet vowing chastity, the verse ironically echoes the 'Io' of the traditional marriage song. 14. *covenants*: legal agreements to do or refrain from doing certain acts.

70 5. *annoy*: misery. The traditional Petrarchan sonnet is a lament over the denial of love.

72 3. *descrie*: distinguish. 6. *Dian's wings*: Diana, the patron goddess of chastity. 8. *Vertue's gold*: as opposed to Cupid's golden-headed arrow which kindled passion.
Second song 17. *danger*: the traditional medieval 'daunger', the terrifying power of the mistress's anger.

73 3. *misse*: ignore. 4. *so soft a rod*: typical *double entendre*. 11. *Those scarlet judges*: her lips.

74 1. *Aganippe*: a fountain on Mount Helicon, sacred to the Muses. 2. *Tempe*: a vale in Thessaly much celebrated by poets: more specifically, the place where Daphne, in flight from Apollo, was turned into a laurel, which became henceforth the symbol of poetic

achievement, the poet's 'bays'. Astrophel is dissociating himself from all high-flown pretensions to poetic inspiration, but also denying that he is copying Petrarch, whose verses to his 'Laura' were the source of the sonnet tradition. 6. *wot*: know.

75 Ringler suggests that this is a sonnet written with tongue in cheek, since Edward IV was mainly known in the period for his notorious love affair with Shore's wife and the murder of his brother Clarence, drowned in a butt of malmsey. 4. *impe*: engraft feathers to improve the flight of a falcon. 5–6. *His Sire's revenge*: Edward usurped the throne in 1461, avenging his father, the Duke of York, killed in battle by the Lancastrians. 8. *That Ballance weigh'd*: he ruled with justice the kingdom he had gained by the sword. 9–11. He invaded France (the Floure delice) and was bought off by Louis XI. *bloudy Lyon*: the Red Lion of Scotland, though in this case the 'old alliance' between France and Scotland against England was not in operation. 14. *To lose his Crowne*: Edward was driven into temporary exile by Warwick the Kingmaker because he married Lady Elizabeth Gray while Warwick was, under his orders, negotiating a French marriage for the King.

77 2. *lecture*: reading. 8. *sublime the quintessence*: alchemical terms: 'refine and produce the purest essence'. 11. *consterd*: expressed.

78 11. *as stirre still*: which keep on treading, even though on thorns. 12. *ay*: ever. 14. *wants hornes*: is not cuckolded. Astrophel turns his general statement about jealousy into a specific reference to Lord Rich.

79 3. *consort*: group of musical instruments in harmony. 4. *coupling Doves*: Venus's chariot was drawn by doves. 5. *retrait*: retreat. 9. *meane*: means. 12. *ostage*: hostage.

80 3. *stall*: seat of office and dignity. 8. *graine*: a fast dye. 12. *resty*: indolent, lazy. Feeling such hyperbolic praise must be flattery, his mouth refuses to utter further praise unless another kiss convinces it that even such hyperboles fall short of the truth.

81 6. *only Nature's art*: the art of nature herself. 8. *shade out*: literally, to represent the shadows on an object in painting it; hence to suggest some part of.

82 3. *His*: Narcissus who was drowned through falling in love with his own reflection in the water. 4. *hers*: Venus at the judgement of Paris. 6. *th'Esperian tast*: the golden apples of the Hesperides.

83 1. *Philip*: traditional name for a sparrow: cf. John Skelton's *Philip Sparrowe*. 3. *your cut to keepe*: to know your place. 6. *peepe*: chirp. Third song 4. *Amphyon's lyre*: see sonnet 68. 7–10. Reference to stories in Pliny's *Natural History* of an Arcadian rescued from brigands by a snake which he had fed when he was a child (III, xxii) and of an eagle which flew into the funeral pyre of a maiden of Sestos who had reared it (III, vi) (Loeb). 11. *trow*: believe. 12. *O birds, O*

beasts (R). F, 'O beasts, O birds'. Ringler reverses the order to restore the elaborate pattern of Chiasmus around which the poem is organised: Verse 1: trees, stones, stones, trees. Verse 2: Lyzard, Eagle; birds, beasts. Verse 3: birds, beasts, stones, trees; trees, stones, beasts, birds. *Also*, Verse 1, hearing; Verse 2, sight; Verse 3, eyes, ears.

85   6. *pointing*: appointing. 13. *indentures*: contracts.

Fourth song 9. *Danger*: cf. **Second song**, 17. *hence*: Danger is on guard elsewhere but not here. 15. *flowers*: embroidered on the bedspread, but also like 'flowers', i.e. figures of rhetoric wooing 'in their best language'. 33. *stay*: postponement. 38. *curtaines*: drawn around the four-poster bed. 40. *endite*: a *double entendre* related to the Elizabethan euphemism, 'to have ink in one's pen'. 50. *but*: unless. The tone changes in the last verse from tragic to half humorous. Stella will not grant but neither will she damn.

86   14. *one's* (R). F, 'once'. A pun is probably intended.

Fifth song This rather laboured poem differs from the other songs in its hostile attitude to Stella; and Ringler and earlier critics have argued convincingly that it was not designed for a place in *A. and S.* but belongs to the sequence of Philisides/Mira poems in the *Old Arcadia*. I omit it, therefore.

Sixth song 3. *whether*: which of the two: cf. line 53. 4. *former*: foremost. 5. *bate*: debate. 14. *wage*: plead at the bar. 31. *affected*: inclined towards. 40. *The judgement* (R). F, 'Eye-judgement'. 42. *exceptions*: legal objections. 43. *The common sence*: the faculty by which the soul receives impressions from the senses and transmits them to the reason. 47. *on this* (R). F, 'on this side'.

Seventh song 3. *closde* (F). R, 'cloyed'. I retain 'closde', shut in, in opposition to the 'things past bounds of wit' in line 6. 8. *wodden*: wooden.

Eighth song 40. *to acquaintance*: to the level of human understanding. 71. *such wise*: in such a way. 74. *in these effects*: 'Do not try to test my love by arousing it in this way' – i.e. by his hands 'in their speech'. 94. *try*: undergo. 102. *so* (R). F, 'to'.

Ninth song 30. *sterved*: starved. 40. *But*: unless. 49. *blaying*: bleating.

87   8. *saddest* (F). R, 'sadded'.

88   3. *heere marcheth she*: another mistress who offers immediate rewards. 8. *cates*: delicacies.

90   6. *Lawrell tree*: cf. sonnet 74. He doesn't seek fame as a poet. 9. *Ne*: nor. *could I* (R). F, 'I could'. 11. *Without*: unless.

91   4. *Vaile*: veil. 8. *seeing jets, blacke*: her dark eyes (Ringler's emendation). F, 'seeing gets blacke'. Qs, 'seeming jett blacke'. 11. *wood globes*: wooden globes showing the disposition of the constellations; hence, painted, artificial reproductions.

92 1. *Indian ware*: rare and precious materials as from the Indies. 3. *cutted*: abrupt, brief (cf. George Puttenham, 'Brachiologia or the cutted comma', *Arte of English Poesie*). The Spartans were notoriously men of action rather than of words. 5. *totall*: curt. 9. *did*: omitted F.

Tenth song 6. *thy* (R). F, 'the'. 7. *O if I my selfe* (R). F, 'Or if I me selfe'. 12. *aymes at*: can hope to achieve. 33. *licorous*: sensual, lecherous. 41. *depart*: yield, share. R, 'imparte'. 43. *surcease*: stop.

93 5. *may* (F). R, 'might'. 8. *misse*: fall into error. 11. *quite*: acquit.

94 6. *tries*: undergoes. 8. *harbengers*: Officers who rode ahead of the court when it was travelling, to secure accommodation in advance. 9–10. 'if grief, normally so given to lamenting, refuses to inspire my lament on the grounds that I deserve my punishment'.

95 2. *best*: (Q1). R, 'least'. F, 'left'. All three are tenable, but 'best', besides balancing 'worst', agrees with 'as you with my breast I oft have nurst'. 9. *maine*: strong.

96 2. *kind*: nature. 4. *sunne's* (R). F, 'sun'. 8. *expresse*: as well as the normal meaning, the literal sense, 'press out'. 9. *mazefull*: bewildering. 10. *stur*: go abroad. 12. *fur*: by far.

97 1–4. *Dian . . . mortall wight*: Diana, the huntress goddess of the moon, accompanied by her nymphs, the stars, which shoot their rays at and influence human beings. 4. *standing*: position from which to shoot. *wight*: person. 5. *Phoebus*, who drove the chariot of the sun. 8. *dight*: array herself.

98 4. *lee shores*: sheltered shores. 7. *gald* (R). F, 'gold'. Q1, 'held'. *and shortly raind*: made sore with rubbing of saddle or harness, and with the reins pulled back hard. 11. *marks* (R). F, 'makes'. 12. when dawn comes. 13. *winke*: shut.

99 3. *marke-wanting*: lacking a target. 9. *charme*: tune their voices. 14. light in the world of the senses, in contrast to the 'inward night' 'of the mind'.

100 1. *O teares, no teares*: Kyd may have taken a hint for his famous line in *The Spanish Tragedy* from this, 'O eyes! no eyes but fountain fraught with tears.' 9. *conserv'd*: preserved in sugar. *sugred* (R). F, 'surged'.

101 3. *such fine conclusions tries*: tries out such experiments. 6. *palenesse*: spotlessness. 7–8. *And joy . . . in thee*. There is a compressed syllogism in these lines: joy is inseparable from Stella's eyes: Stella weeps with her eyes: therefore Stella unites joy with weeping. 9. *Love moves thy paine*: as in 31. 14. Ringler suggests an inversion: 'Thy pain moves love who runs up and down . . .' Such a distortion of normal syntax is not characteristic of Sidney. Possibly 'moves' could convey the sense of 'plead', 'utter': 'Love proclaims thy pain.' 10. *sturre*: 'as your fevered glances dart in different directions'. 'runs' (R.) F, 'comes'. 11. *prest*: prompt. 12. *with care*: full of fear.

102   3. *kindly*: natural. *badge of shame*: i.e. blushes. 5. *vade*: fade. 6. *engraind*: dyed with a fast dye. 9. *Gallein's adoptive sonnes*: doctors, followers of the Greek physician, Galen, who stick to the old and out-of-date methods of diagnosis. 11. *feeling proofe*: the evidence of my feelings.

103   4. *those faire planets*: her eyes. 9. *those Aeols' youth*: breezes. Aeolus was the god of the winds.

104   8. *rigour's* (F). Q1, 'rigorous'. R, 'rigrows'. 10. *stars*: they see a reference to Stella. 11. *empty glasse*: linked both with 'thirsty' and with Stella's windows. 12. *Your morall notes*: cf. the medieval *Ovid Moralised*: finding meanings under the surface.
      Eleventh song 2. *playneth*: mourns, sings a lover's complaint. 12. *Leave*: leave off. 23. *theye* (R). F, 'thy'. 27. *minds*: states of mind. 40. *there* (R). F, 'thee'. 42. *Argus*: a beast with a hundred eyes set by the jealous Juno to watch Io. 43. *unjustest* (R). F, 'unjust'.

105   3. *Dead glasse*: his eyes which missed seeing Stella because of the darkness of the night, the speed of the coach and the fact that the page dropped the torch. 6. *dazling race*: dazzled beam. 11. *whome* (R). F, 'whence'.

106   3. *Bare me in hand*: amused yourself by deceiving me. 10. *charme*: cf. sonnet 99 line 9.

107   7. *Lieftenancy*: delegated authority.
      From Certaine Sonnets
      These two sonnets are the last two pieces in the collection of assorted sonnets and songs, *Certaine Sonnets written by Sir Philip Sidney: Never before Printed*, which follow the *Arcadia* and precede *The defence of Poesie* and *Astrophel and Stella* in the 1598 Folio.
         Nineteenth-century editions often included them as the conclusion of *Astrophel and Stella*, but it is generally accepted now that they were composed earlier, perhaps as early as 1577.

1   4. *web*: woven fabric. *never wrought*: never complete.

2   Sidney uses the Shakespearean sonnet form occasionally in *Certaine Sonnets*, but abandons it totally for variations on the Petrarchan form in *Astrophel and Stella*.

Samuel Daniel To Delia (1594 text)

MODERN EDITIONS
The Complete Works in Verse and Prose of Samuel Daniel (5 volumes) ed. Grosart, 1885: reprinted 1963, vol. i.
Poems and a Defence of Ryme ed. A. C. Sprague, London (1930, 1950, 1972).

Daniel, like Constable, is one of the earlier among the Elizabethan sonneteers. Twenty-seven sonnets of Delia were printed together with

Sidney's *Astrophel and Stella* in the pirated edition of 1591, which may
have driven Daniel to print his own edition of fifty sonnets in 1592, *Delia.
Contayning certayne Sonnets: with the complaint of Rosamond.* The
book was not surprisingly dedicated to Sidney's sister, the Countess of
Pembroke, who later became his patron. *Delia* was reprinted thereafter,
with constant revisions and additions, again in 1592, in 1594, 1595,
1598, 1601, 1602, 1611, and in *The Whole Workes of Samuel Daniel*
(1623), by which time it had reached a total of sixty sonnets, many of the
original ones being omitted. I have chosen the text of 1594, *Delia and
Rosamond Augmented*, since this, while published at the height of the
sonnet vogue, indicates in its revisions the direction in which Daniel was
developing.

The identity of Delia cannot be established with any certainty. The
Countess of Pembroke has been suggested, but sonnet 53 indicates that
Delia lived near Daniel's own home at Beckington near the Wiltshire
Avon. In his successive revisions of the sonnets, Daniel eliminated many
of the autobiographical hints in the earlier versions, and Delia is reduced
to the role of the generic Petrarchan mistress. The name Delia is, in any
case, one of the names of Diana, the chaste goddess of the moon. For an
examination of the whole question of identity, see Joan Rees, *Samuel
Daniel. A Critical and Biographical Study* (Liverpool University 1964),
ch. ii.

1 For a similar use of the image from accountancy, cf. Sidney, *A and S*,
   18 and Drayton, *Idea* 3. 12. *crosse*: draw a line under and finish the
   sum.
2 2. *Minerva*: born out of Jupiter's forehead.
3 10. *outcast Eaglets*: cast out of the nest because, unlike true eaglets,
   unable to gaze directly at the sun.
4 1. *Posts*: messengers. 5. *lymned*: painted. 6. *For that*: because.
   10. *cleer-eyde Rector*: Apollo. 14. *steemes*: esteems.
5 The sonnet uses the story of Actaeon who, for spying on Diana
   while she was bathing, was pursued by her hounds.
8 4. *even*: equal. 8. *treate*: entreat. 10. *processe*: the formal pro-
   ceedings in a legal action.
9 2. *Paint on floods* . . . : 'paint on water which holds no lasting
   impression; plough the sea-shore where no crops can grow; cry to
   the empty air.'
10 6. *Laughter-loving goddesse*: Venus. 7. *Intenerat*: make tender.
   11. *Trophey*: memorial of victory. 13. *Once*: at once.
11 3. *convart*: convert.
13 Refers to Pygmalion who fell in love with the statue of a woman
   which he had carved. The gods favoured him by bringing it to life.
   1. *hap*: fortune. 6. *Table*: blank sheet on which a picture is to be
   painted. 8. *proper*: play on double meaning of the word, 'own' and
   'excellent'. 13. *joy'd*: had joy of.

14 1. *snary*: ensnaring. Changed from 'amber' in 1592 text. 11. *salve*: ointment. 13. *least*: lest. *travailes*: labours.

15 8. *Vultur-gnawne*: like that of Prometheus, continually torn by Jupiter's vulture.

16 2. *Imbracing clowdes*: reference to Ixion who thought he was embracing Juno when he was only embracing a cloud in her likeness. 9. *Hydra*: a monster slain by Hercules which grew two new heads for every one which he cut off.

18 11. *innated*: born and established within.

19 2. *Citherea's sonne*: Venus's son, Cupid. *those Arkes*: the arcs of her eyebrows to make him a bow. (cf. Sidney, *A and S*, 17). 7. *Aurora*: goddess of the dawn. 8. *Thetis*: 'silver-footed Thetis' of the *Iliad*. 9. *her resign'd*: by her resigned. 10. *the Spheares*: cf. 'the music of the spheres'. 12. *Hyrcan Tygers*: Hyrcania, an Asian country noted for its wild beasts: cf. *Macbeth*, III, iv, 100.

20 7. *Sith*: since.

21 5. *prospective*: scene.

25 12. *rain'd*: reined, with possibly a pun on 'Raigne' of line 1.

27 1. *trace*: track.

29 6. Reference to Icarus whose wings, fastened on by wax, melted as he approached the sun, so that he fell into the sea and was drowned.

30 3. *venter*: venture. 10. *Meane-observer*: who keeps the middle way.

31 1–5. The reference is to the giants who rebelled against Jupiter and attempted to scale the heavens by heaping Mount Pelion upon Mount Ossa. Jupiter struck them down with his thunderbolts and piled the mountain on top of them. From their rage came volcanoes, 'all this fire'. 13. *spill*: perish.

32 2. *Gazing*: gazing at. 12. *Narcissus*: who fell in love with his own image in a stream, and pining away, was transformed into a flower.

33 1. *wreck*: avenge.

34 1. *steeme*: cf. 4. 14.

35 7. *done*: spelt 'dunne' in 1592 edition, probably involving a pun.

36 2. *carefull*: full of care.

39 2. *Bewray*: reveal.

40 4. *ear'd*: ploughed. 12. *instarre*: set among the stars, make immortal. *Raile*: garment, kerchief or decoration on a gown. The image would seem to refer back to 'the fairest vaile' – her body, and to mean 'Though time destroys her beauty, it makes immortal through poetry those qualities which created that beauty', (the needle which sewed the veil and the garment which decorated it – i.e. that grace, that virtue). 13. *t'in-woman*: to make her a woman.

41 2. *Leander*: drowned while swimming the Hellespont to reach Hero. 11. 1592 has the more aggressive version, 'Ile not revenge olde wrongs, my wrath shall cease'.

42 The metaphor refers to Helen, and the burning of Troy as described

in the *Iliad*.

43 6. *the night's pale Queen*: Cynthia, the moon which governs the tides. 1592 has 'Cynthia' for 'Delia' in the first line. 7. *impost*: tribute. 12. *joy*: have joy of. 13. *I doubt to finde*: I don't think that I should find.

45 3. *but till*: only until. 12. *Kalends*: the first day of the month – in this case, the beginning of the last period of our lives.

47 This sonnet 'At the Author's going into Italie', which first appeared in 1594, forms a marked contrast in tone to the happier sonnet 'made at the Author's being in Italie' (no. 48) published in 1592 and presumably written earlier. Joan Rees (op. cit. pp. 20–1) suggests that both sonnets are autobiographical, referring, in the case of 48, to a visit to Italy which Daniel made in 1590–1, and in 47, to a second visit about which no detail is known. While accepting that 48 is autobiographical, I would suggest that in the 1594 text Daniel was attempting a dramatic development of the sonnet situation. Having written his sonnet from Italy (48), he prefaces it by a conventional sonnet about the pains of parting, very much in the mode of the late sonnets of *Astrophel and Stella*.

48 2. *cost*: coast. 3. *My joyfull North*: because Delia is in England. 4. *levell*: mark aimed at.

49 4. *With darke forgetting*: forgetting in sleep. 13. *imbracing clowdes*: cf. sonnet 16 line 2.

50 1. *Palladines*: heroes. 2. *aged . . . untimely*: perhaps a slighting reference to the archaisms of *The Faerie Queene*, as line 3 may refer to its allegory. 3. *imaginarie*: out of imagination. 6. *Autentique*: authentic, possessing authority.

51 1. *the Roman*: Brutus.

52 1. *joyes or els dislikes*: pleases or displeases. 7. *deskant . . . ground*: variations played around the basic tune.

53 *Avon*: the Wiltshire Avon which runs near Beckington, where Daniel may have been born, and to which he retired in his later years. 11. '*poore in fame, and poore in waters*': an example of Daniel's increasing literalness. 1592 has 'rich in fame, though poore in waters'.

54 5. *unrespecting*: heedless.

55 1. *impost*: cf. 43, 7.

Michael Drayton Idea in Sixtie Three Sonnets (1619 text)

MODERN EDITIONS
The Works of Michael Drayton ed. J. W. Hebel. 4 volumes. Vol. v, Notes and Variant Readings, ed. Kathleen Tillotson and Bernard Newdigate (Oxford, 1931–41). Vol. ii reprints

Drayton's collected works published 1619 and includes *Idea*.
In the same series Bernard H. Newdigate, *Michael Drayton and
His Circle* (Oxford, 1941).
Michael Drayton, *Poems*, 1619 (Scolar Press Facsimile, 1969).
Poems of Michael Drayton ed. John Buxton (London 1963)
2 vols, includes a selection from *Idea* in vol. i.

Drayton's sonnet sequence first appeared in 1594 under the title of *Ideas
Mirrour. Amours in quatorzains* (Hebel, vol. i). It comprises fifty-one
sonnets. The subsequent editions in 1599, 1600, 1602, 1605 and 1619
embody a process of revision in which thirty-two of the more conceited or
plaintive sonnets of the original version were omitted, and forty-four new
sonnets were added. Like Daniel, Drayton was an inveterate reviser and
persevered with the sequence long after the sonnet fashion had passed.
He was also extremely sensitive to criticism and to changes in poetical
fashion (see his prefatory sonnet *To the Reader of these sonnets*, and also
sonnet 31), and his later sonnets contain qualities of irony and
concentration of meaning which have affinities with the drama and the
poetry of the Metaphysicals (e.g. sonnets 6, 8, 15, 21, 61) rather than
with the Elizabethan love sonnet. I have used the edition of 1619,
however, although it is a less typical sonnet sequence than that of 1594,
because it reveals Drayton in his prime and is an immeasurably more
impressive collection. The notes indicate the edition in which each sonnet
first appeared, but I have not commented on Drayton's revisions of
earlier sonnets which he retained.

The name *Idea* suggests the Platonic Idea of a woman; but the sonnets
are also a specific tribute to Anne Goodere, younger daughter of Sir
Henry Goodere, friend of Sidney, and Drayton's early patron. Drayton
knew her all his life from the time that he was a page in her father's
household, and his affection survived her marriage to Henry Rainsford in
1595 and continued after her husband's death in 1622. It is not necessary
to assume, however, as Bernard Newdigate does (op. cit.) that the
sonnets resulted from a passionate attachment on Drayton's part. He
wrote an elegie 'upon the death of his incomparable friend' when Sir
Henry Rainsford died, and he was clearly a valued friend of the family.
Like so many other sonnet sequences of the period, *Idea* is the sort of
compliment which could be paid by a poet to a friend and patron.

To the Reader of these sonnets: first printed 1599. 9. *the true image of
my Mind*: a conventional pose, since the description, 'Ever in
motion, still desiring change', embodies the stock symptoms of the
generic lover whose mind, like that of Orsino in *Twelfth Night*, is a
'changeable opal'. For the type of the lover, see Puttenham, *Arte of
English Poesie*, Bk I, ch. xxii.

1 (1619). 8. *As how the Pole*: according to the direction of the North Pole. 11. *spent*: worn down.

2 (1599). 5. *the view*: inspection by a jury. 6. *quit*: acquit the dead heart of slaying itself. 7. *prov'd by you*: i.e. to be done by you.

3 (1594). 1. *cast*: calculate. 6. *crosse*: draw a line under and complete the sum; cf. *Delia*, sonnet 1. 7. *Substracting*: subtracting his pains from his joys. 8. *arrerage*: deficit.

4 (1600).

5 (1599). A sequence of wordplay on 'I' and 'Aye'. 5. *sleightly*: cunningly.

6 (1619).

7 (1599). 1. *Humor*: whim: see sonnet 19. 10. *Ruffin*: bully.

8 (1619). 13. *thou* (Hebel). Omitted 1619.

9 (1600). 2. *Invention*: see *Astrophel and Stella*, sonnet 1 and note. 9. *Bedlam*: as in a mad-house. 10. *twaine*: divided. 11. *nine yeeres*: suggesting that Drayton's affection for Anne Goodere may have begun around 1591.

10 (1599). 2. *Penny-father*: skin-flint. 5. *chest*: coffer.

11 (1599). 10. *but*: only.

12 (1599). 1. *That learned Father*: Saint Augustine. 3. *Offices*: functions. 4. *Anima*: the vital principle. 7. *Mens*: 'the same in kind', i.e. Mind. 10. *Sensus*: consciousness.

13 (1594). 3. *once*: one day. 6. *of force*: necessarily. 13–14. 'so that everything which has a shadow may find in it a reminder of my love story, since my poem is like the shadow of my love produced by the brightness of Idea, my sun'.

14 (1600). Prometheus stole fire from heaven and with it, animated the clay from which he made men and women. For his punishment, see *Delia*, 15.

15 (1619). 1. *sted*: avail.

16 (1594). The Phoenix, the mythical bird of which only one at a time exists. It dies in a fire of spices and is born anew from its own ashes. 3. *is knowne*: its qualities are best reproduced and made known by yours.

17 (1594). 5. *Tralucent*: clear.

18 (1594). Drayton bases his conceit on the traditional 'Nine Worthies', the nine famous heroes of antiquity, *These with the Gods are ever resident*.

19 (1599). 7. *meane*: middle way. 10. *coyle*: perplexity.

20 (1599). 9–12. Drayton plays on the traditional temptations to suicide with which the devil attacks the man who is in despair. (cf. *The Faerie Queene*, I. ix.)

21 (1619).

22 (1600). 1–2. 'Discretion makes allowances for fools and children, so bear with Cupid, the child and me, the fool. 5. *Gawdes*: trinkets,

toys. 14. 'some who appear wise are in fact more foolish than they are'.

23 (1599).

24 (1600). cf. *Astrophel and Stella*, 54.

25 (1599). 4. *Piren's*: Pyrenees. 5. *to Scotland*: Drayton may have visited Scotland at this period, and possibly had his mind on James VI, shortly to succeed Elizabeth. 6. *Orcades*: the Orkneys. 9. *the Bards*: for Drayton's knowledge of the Irish bards, see his *Ode, To himselfe, and the Harpe* (Hebel, Vol II, Odes). 11. *the stiffe-neck'd Rebels*: Many of the Irish chieftains had fled to the Continent or Spain during the Irish wars of 1595–9. 12. *Galliglasse*: galloglass, Irish soldier.

26 (1594). A complex play of words around the paradox that despair alone makes hope necessary, so that to stop despairing is to stop hoping. Thus love, freed from despair is also removed from hope and is thus, so to speak, imprisoned in nothingness.

27 (1619). 13. *partiall*: biased. *Or . . . Or*: Either . . . or.

28 (1600). 5. *then*: than. 7–8. 'What I invest would yield them nothing, even at the most favourable rates, but gives me back triple interest.

29 (1599).

30 (1599). *Vesta*, the Roman goddess of fire. 4. *Being stedfastly opposed*: Being turned always to face the sun. 11. *Desire* (Hebel). 1619, 'Desires'.

31 (1599). 1. *crooked Mimicke*: for an account of the contemporary criticism of the sonnet and its probable effects on Drayton's revisions, see Hebel, vol. v, pp. 137–8, Introduction and Notes to *Idea*. 4. *Antike*: in grotesque parody. 7. *pack-Horse*: routine, hackneyed. 8. *Dudgen*: mean, ordinary. 9. *imprest*: turned out in print, mass-produced. 10. *satiate*: satiated. 14. *Scarabies*: beetles.

32 (1594). See Drayton's *Poly-Olbion* for a full catalogue of English rivers and their special qualities. 4. *Avon's Fame*: Kathleen Tillotson suggests that this may be a compliment to Daniel: cf. *Delia*, 53. 13–14. *Arden's sweet Ankor*: a reference to the Goodere home at Polesworth on the banks of the Ancor in Warwickshire.

33 (1594). *Imagination*: the image-making faculty which allows the heart to retain an image of Idea when the eyes cannot see her. 7. *These*: the eyes. *the other's*: the heart's. 14. *or*: 1619, 'of'.

34 (1599). 1. *admire*: wonder at. 'Don't marvel, Love, that in spite of the more than human things I attempt under your domination, the only reward I get is refusal. The only thing to marvel at is that I find nothing to marvel at in this.'

35 (1594). 7. *by Kind*: by Nature. 8. *One*: the dumb-borne Muse able to speak through the virtue of Idea's name. *the other*: the cripple

hand able to write by the virtue of her touch. 12. *lyne*: lain.

36 (1619). 1. *purblind*: blind. 3. *Wracke*: destruction. 5. *Styx*: one of the rivers of the underworld by which the gods, including Jupiter the thunderer, swore their most binding oaths. 6. *thy faire Mother*: Venus. *unavoided*: inescapable. 7. *Hecat's Names*: because of her power in earth, heaven and hell she was known as the triform goddess and called Diana on earth, Luna in heaven and Hecat in hell. *Proserpine*: carried off to the underworld by Pluto. 9. *Psyche*: Cupid's Psyche.

37 (1602).

38 (1594). 10. *Despiteth*: shows contempt for. 11. *contemning*: despising. 13. *put back*: repulsed.

39 (1594). cf. *Astrophel and Stella*, 6 and 74 2. *Exordium*: the introductory part of a composition. 5. *Elizium*: the Paradise to which the heroes were transported after death. 6. *Phlegeton*: the burning river of the underworld. 8. *Like they* . . . 'Let those like them who want to: I don't.' 9. *Erinnis*: one of the Eumenides, the Furies. 10. *Ate*: Goddess of Discord. 11. *charming*: having magical powers. Hecate was also the chief goddess of magic arts. 12. *in Apollo's Cell*: in connection with poetry. 13. *I passe not*: I don't care for. *Minerva* . . . *Astrea*: goddesses of wisdom and justice respectively.

40 (1594). 10. *gleed*: ember. 13. *Sisiphus*: punished in Hades by being forever forced to push uphill a huge rock which always rolled down again. 14. *Ixion*: tied to a fiery wheel by Jupiter for trying to seduce Juno.

41 (1594). 3. *prove*: experience.

42 (1594). 1. *Method*: the basic order and arrangement of a discourse according to the rules of logic and rhetoric. 2. *Vaine*: vein. 4. *Humor*: my own particular line of fancy. 6. *As Poets doe*: refers to the common renaissance conception of poetry as 'imitation' or feigning. See Sidney's *Defence of Poesie* where it is so defined. 7. *And in bare words* . . . : 'though using plain words, still give a false colouring to my pain'. 9. *I passe not*: cf. sonnet 39 line 13.

43 (1605). 8. *bent*: limit.

44 (1599). 6. *Medea-like*: by her magic she made Aeson young again.

45 (1599).

46 (1605). 2. *evidently*: plainly. 3. *Schoole-men*: learned man. 7. *happily*: haply, by chance.

47 (1605). 5–6. Drayton worked as a writer of plays for Henslowe, the theatre owner and entrepreneur between 1599–1602. 6. *in the Circuit for the Lawrell*: in pursuit of poetic fame. 10. *the proud Round*: the circular auditorium: cf. 'this wooden O' (Prol., *Henry V*).

48 (1619). 3. *Fascia*: fillet around the head. 6. *preferre*: offer yourself

for employment. **8.** *Practise thy Quiver*: shoot your arrows to scare away the birds. **11.** *blind*: cf. Sidney's reference in the *Defence* to the blind crowder singing the old songs of Percy and Douglas. **13–14.** For the reference to Venus and Mars, cf. *Astrophel and Stella*, 17.

49 (1599). **2.** *move*: stir the reader. **5.** *Packe-Horse*: drudge. **13.** *refines*: purifies.

50 (1605). **7.** *Coarse*: corpse.

51 (1605). **5.** *Lastly*: lately. The references are to the execution of Essex (1601); the surrender and pardon of Tyrone in Ireland, the death of Elizabeth, the arrival of James, whom Drayton welcomed with a *Paean Triumphall* (1603); the Treaty of Hampton Court with Spain (1604) which allowed James to keep his garrison towns in the Low Countries provided they gave no help to the Dutch rebels against Spain.

52 (1619). **6.** *Rebate*: diminish. **7.** *scorse*: exchange.

53 (1594). cf. sonnet 32. **10.** *thy Shepheard*: in 1593, Drayton had published his first collection of pastoral eclogues, *Idea, The Shepheards Garland*, using himself the pseudonym of Rowland, the shepherd poet. **13.** *Tempe*: vale in Thessally sacred to Apollo. **14.** *Helicon*: home of the Muses.

54 (1594).

55 (1594). **3.** *prove*: experience.

56 (1594). **6.** For the ability of eagles to gaze unblinded at the sun, see *Delia* 3. **9.** *summ'd*: fully grown. **10.** *Pynions*: flight feathers of the wing. **11.** *needsly*: of necessity.

57 (1605). **1.** *best discern'd of*: best perceived by.

58 (1605). **9.** *That*: i.e. the guardian spirit.

59 (1600). **1.** *harbour'd*: lodged. **11.** *the By*: the secondary matter.

60 (1594). **10.** *let*: obstruct.

61 (1619).

62 (1594). **3.** *Wan*: won. **4.** *Pined*: starved. **6.** *Conceit*: thought.

63 (1599). cf. *Amoretti*, 14.

Edmund Spenser Amoretti and Epithalamion (1595)

MODERN EDITIONS
The Yale Edition of the Shorter Poems of Edmund Spenser ed. William B. Oram *et al.* (Yale U.P. 1989).

In this edition of *Elizabethan Sonnets*, *Epithalamion* has been added to the *Amoretti*. It is increasingly recognised that a sonnet sequence was often published with a long poem, the male complainant of the sonnets set off by a poem of female complaint: Daniel's *Delia* with *The*

Complaint of Rosamond, Shakespeare's sonnets with *A Lovers Complaint*. Such contrastive works as these are, however, still more easily read as poems in a different genre. But the intricate interdependency between *Amoretti* and *Epithalamion* argues the long poem's inclusion in this volume. The marriage-hymn should be read as the proper festal climax to the courtship cycle, and while it is hard to locate what part the 'silent poetry' of numerology plays in a reader's reaction to a Renaissance poem, what Spenser joined together in an elaborate calendrical and horological re-creation of the period of his courtship and the wedding day itself, no edition should put asunder.

As much recent scholarship on Spenser and on Elizabethan sonnets has explored and speculated upon the significance of number symbolism, it is worth digressing to the topic here. Once these numerological aspects have been pointed out, the changes to our understanding can be pervasive. It has recently been noticed, for instance, that Philip Sidney uses the word 'love' 108 times in his sequence of 108 sonnets and 11 songs totalling 108 stanzas: as Katherine Duncan-Jones says of this in her biography of Sidney (p. 232), it shows the poet creating 'effects of spontaneity and naturalism within a tightly organised framework'. The number is $2^2 \times 3^3$, 2 being the first male and 3 the first female number; though Fowler and Roche endorse a more elaborate explanation.

In his 1595 publication, Spenser was operating through numbers to establish connections of microcosm and macrocosm. Alexander Dunlop has explained a scheme within the sequence whereby sonnets 22–68 correspond to the days from Ash Wednesday to Easter Day in 1594, Fowler relates the 89 sonnets to the days of winter. After A. Kent Hieatt's insights, *Epithalamion*'s 24 stanzas, 365 long lines are understood to re-create the daytime and night-time hours of Barnabus's day, 11 June, 1594. For Spenser, the possibility of robust ('fescennine') comments on having the shortest night of the year as a wedding night was transcended by having the cosmic significance of the day permeate the literary celebration of the wedding.

Full discussion of the numerological discoveries of Hieatt and Dunlop can be found in Alistair Fowler's *Triumphal Forms* (Cambridge U. P. 1970), Chapters 8 and 9; and, more head-spinningly, Thomas P. Roche's *Petrarch and the English Sonnet Sequences* (AMS Press 1987). It should always be borne in mind that numbers do just crop up: Kent Hieatt's study appeared 365 years after its subject, for instance.

The most memorable part of the long poem is its refrain, given 16 variations in its 23 manifestations, and I will confine my comments to the aspect of the poem which is most prominent in our reading experience. It is a doubly resonant refrain: in part, 'That all the woods shall answer and their echo ring', the festal community the poem has invited into existence extends into nature itself, which echoes the rejoicing. But there is also an undertone: that outside the town there is only the threatening forested landscape, from which the sound of a community rejoicing returns as a disembodied echo, the woods in which the dispossessed native Irish hide, from which the kern and gallowglass will emerge in rebellion. In the destruction of the second Munster plantation, Spenser fled from his estates at Kilcolman, four years after the wedding he so elaborately commemorated.

1   2. *dead-doing*: death-dealing. 6. *lamping*: lighting as with a lamp. 8. *close bleeding*: secret inward bleeding. 10–11. *Helicon . . . Angel's*: Spenser has identified the hill of the Muses with the Christian heaven.

2   2. *bale*: misery. *love-pined*: love-starved. 3. *sithens*: since. 6. *viper's brood*: which were thought to be born by gnawing their way out of their mother's belly. (See Pliny, *Natural History* X, lxxxii.) 11. *humblesse*: humility.

4   1. *Janus' gate*: god of entrances, doors, beginnings; (*Janua*: a door). In this case, the opening of the year, hence January. He was normally depicted with two faces, one 'forth looking', the other backwards, 'bidding th' old Adieu'. 4. *dumpish spright*: dejected spirits. 7. *dight*: make ready. 13. *raine*: reign.

5   2. *portly*: stately, magnificent. 4. *envide*: envied. 6. *sdeigne*: disdain. 10. *boldned*: confident.

6   5. *durefull*: long-lasting. 7. *divide*: dispense. 11. *dints*: impresses. 12. *affects*: passions. 13. *thinke not long*: don't think it a long time.

7   1. *the myrrour*: this is either a very difficult or an imprecise image. The eyes could be the mirror in which the heart sees its own bewilderment, or a mirror in the sense of a magic crystal which causes the disturbance; or even a burning glass which concentrates the sun's rays upon an object. The last interpretation is supported by line 3 as well as by the reference to living fire in line 12 and in sonnet 8. The eyes would thus be like a lens transmitting the living fire from the mistress to the heart of the lover. 14. *ensample*: example.

8   One of Spenser's rare attempts at the Shakespearean sonnet form. 2. *unto the maker neere*: near to God himself. 5. *the blinded guest*: Cupid. 6–8. *to base affections' wound . . .* : to wound by arousing lustful passions, 'But the angelic nature of your glances converts them to chaste adoration'. 12. *strong . . . weak*: 'passions strong since caused by your beauty but weak because of your virtue.'

9   7. *for they have purer sight*: they appear brighter. 11. *sever*: cleave, separate.

10 3. *licentious*: unrestrained by law. 10. *comptroll*: control. 11. *bow to a baser make*: either 'bow that high look to a baser mate' or – since so many of the lines end with verbs – 'make that high look bow to someone baser'.

11 5. *rewth*: compassion. 7. *fell*: cruel. 9. *assoyle*: purge, get rid of.

14. *surcease*: bring to an end.

12 7. *eyen*: eyes.

13 1. *port*: bearing. 3. *embaseth*: lowers. 4. *temperature*: combination of opposite humours and qualities. 5. *awfull*: creating awe.

14 4. *peece*: fortress. 6. *wont belay*: accustom to besiege. 7. *enur'd*: inured, used to. 12. *engins*: instruments of war.

15 1. *tradefull*: busy. 3. *both the Indias*: East and West Indies. 10. *weene*: think. 11. *on ground*: in the world. 12. *sheene*: shining.

16 4. *illusion*: deceptive because ultimately causing pain. 5–7. *glauncing sight . . . arrowes*: this very common conceit of Cupid shooting his arrows through the mistress's glances is based on the traditional physiological theory of the animal spirits. These were thought to consist of fine particles which, generated in the heart, flowed out in streams through the eyes, and entering through the eyes of the other person, penetrated to the heart where they set up the disturbance which is love. Many sonnet conceits are variations on this. cf. *Astrophel and Stella*, 17, 20, 42, 48, etc.

17 2. *skil*: reason. 4. *fill*: fullness. 11. *pleasance*: courtesy, desire to give pleasure.

18 3. *redound*: flow. 9. *play my part*: a stage metaphor; 'carry on with my act'.

19 A spring sonnet following the new year of sonnet 4. 4. *girland*: garland. 5. *resounded*: uttered loudly. 10. *of her*: from her. *ought*: play on the double meaning, 'owed' and 'owned'. She ought to honour love and deserved to be honoured by love. 14. *rebell*: 'let her be proclaimed a rebel'.

20 14. *blooded*: stained with blood.

21 2. *tempred*: blended. 9. *inure*: exercise. 11. *recure*: restore. 14. *in bookes*: i.e. an art based on nature not on learning.

22 1. *This holy season*: Lent leading up to Good Friday, 'so holy day'.

23 1–6. *th'importune suit*: to keep her importunate wooers at bay during Ulysses' long absence, Penelope swore not to remarry until her tapestry was finished, but she unravelled each night what she had woven during the day. 4. *unreave*: unwind. 11. *spils*: destroys.

24 3. *complement*: fulfilment. 8. *Pandora*: the beautiful woman endued with all gifts from Jupiter created and sent to earth as a punishment for Prometheus because he had stolen fire from heaven. She brought with her a box full of plagues and disasters which, when opened, flew out among mankind. Spenser moralises the myth by making them a scourge to 'wicked men'. Of all the qualities, only Hope remained in Pandora's box, which may account for the hopeful plea in the last couplet.

25 4. *depending*: hanging. 10. *close*: hidden. 14. *meede*: reward.

26 1. *brere*: briar. 4. *firbloome*: furze-bloom (Renwick). 6. *pill*: peel. 8. *Moly*: a mythical plant with a white flower and a black root

possessing magical properties; mentioned in the *Odyssey*, Bk X.

27 4. *weene*: think; cf. sonnet 15. 5. *beseene*: appearing.

28 1. *The laurell leafe*: the bays. The wreath of laurel bestowed upon poets (hence laureate) and conquerors (see sonnet 29). 8. *whom now those leaves attyre*: Daphne, having broken her faith with Apollo, fled from him and at her entreaty, was turned by the gods into a laurel, which henceforth was sacred to Apollo. Spenser changes the myth at line 11. The gods metamorphosed Daphne out of pity, not revenge (cf. *Astrophel and Stella* 74).

29 5. *The bay*: see sonnet 28. 11. *triumph*: an extension of the metaphor of conquest: the public demonstration and procession awarded to the conqueror. 12. *trump*: trumpet. *blaze*: proclaim.

30 14. *kynd*: nature.

31 9. *scath*: damage. 12. *embrew*: stain.

32 1. *paynefull*: painstaking, labouring with care. 3. *sledge*: hammer. 4. *list*: pleases. 6. *soft awhit*: soften the smallest bit.

33 2. *that most sacred Empresse*: *The Faerie Queene* was dedicated 'to the most mighty and magnificent Empresse Elizabeth'. *dear dred*: both loved and feared. 3. *not finishing*: the first three books of *The Faerie Queene* were published in 1590, the second three in 1596. Spenser's apology implies a date of writing a considerable time later than 1590, e.g. 1594. 5. *Lodwick*: Lodovick Bryskett, friend of Spenser in Ireland. 5. *aread*: counsel.

34 5. *wont*: was accustomed. 10. *Helice*: the Great Bear near the North Pole, or Spenser may be confusing it with the Little Bear in which the Pole Star lies (*Variorum*). 13. *carefull*: full of care.

35 This sonnet is printed again with minor variations as sonnet 83. 2. *still*: ever. 7. *Narcissus*: see *Delia*, 32. 10. *brooke*: enjoy.

36 6. *thrilling*: piercing. 12. *mote*: might.

37 4. *heare*: hair (cf. False Florimel, *F.Q.* Bks III and IV). 13. *Fondnesse*: foolishness.

38 1. *Arion*: the lyric poet of Lesbos whose myth forms the basis of this sonnet, although Spenser alters it considerably. Arion was about to be murdered by the crew for his riches and he asked, therefore, to be allowed to sing one last song before he died, which charmed the dolphins and brought them to his rescue. Spenser replaces the crew by the tempest, and turns both it and the dolphin into attributes of the lady.

39 3. *temper*: moderate, assuage.

41 9. *ydle boast*: promising much but performing nothing.

42 7. *thrall*: slave. 9. *start*: break away. 11. *pervart*: pervert. 14. *doe*: make.

43 14. *construe*: interpret.

44 1. *those renoumed noble Peres*: the Argonauts who under the command of Jason gained the Golden Fleece. Orpheus was among them. 7. *of passions warreid arre*: ravaged by warring passions.

8. *aslake*: abate, control.

45 4. *semblant*: resemblance. 7. *Idea*: the Platonic Idea, the essential being. 11. *visnomy*: physiognomy; features as they indicate inner qualities.

47 2. *traynes*: deceits. 12. *beguyle*: distract by pleasure.

49 3. *the mightie's*: the Almighty's. 10. *Cockatrice*: basilisk; a mythical serpent hatched from a cock's egg, having the power to kill with its glance.

50 3. *leach*: doctor. 5. *quod*: quoth. *priefe*: experience. 9. *cordialls*: medicines designed to cure heart trouble.

51 4. *moniments*: records of something to be commemorated. 7. *assayde*: attempted. 9. *attend*: to apply oneself long enough.

53 1. *The Panther*: a common myth derived from Pliny's *Natural History*. 2. *fray*: frighten. 11. *embrew*: stain with blood.

54 3. *pageants*: scenes on a stage. 4. *disguysing*: dressing up, covering as with a mask. cf. 'guisers'. 9. *constant*: unchanging.

55 10. *the skye*: the immaterial element, purer than fire, the highest of the terrestrial elements.

56 4. *felly*: cruelly. 11. *desolate*: destitute.

57 3. *lenger*: longer. *sue*: follow. 7. *through-launched*: shot through. 10. *stoures*: combats.

58 5. *unstayd*: unsteady. 7. *prayd*: preyed upon.

59 A complementary sonnet to the previous one, in praise of self-assurance. 4. *feard*: frightened. *to any chaunce to start*: to change to any unconsidered course. 11. *stay*: support.

60 2. *his sundry yeare*: the planetary year, in the Ptolemaic system of astronomy, was the length of time that a planet and the sun, moving on their separate courses, took to return to the position relative to each other from which they started. Ptolemy calculated the period for Mars as 79 years (see Dodge, *Variorum*). Spenser's conceit extends the principle to Cupid, 'the winged God', although he was not a planetary deity. 8. *al those fourty*: this reference has led to much speculation, both about the dates of composition of the *Amoretti*, and of Spenser's birth, which would seem to be between 1550–4. The 'fourty', however, could simply be a round figure. *outwent*: preceded it and exceeded it in number. 13. *short*: shorten.

61 3. *dare not*: addressed to himself or to the reader: 'do not dare to accuse'.

62 A new year's sonnet. 1. *race*: course. 2. *compast*: circular. 11. *blend*: trouble.

63 1. *assay*: trials.

64 In this sonnet Spenser is concerned exclusively with the scents not the colours of the flowers, and in ignoring the latter produces occasionally ludicrous images. 5. *Gillyflowers*: wallflowers.

7. *Bellamoures*: no longer identifiable. 8. *newly spred*: newly opened. 12. *Jessemynes*: jasmine.

65 1. *misdeeme*: misjudge. 4. *earst*: formerly. 13. *brasen towre*: unlike Danae, whom Jupiter seduced in the form of a shower of gold, even though her father shut her in a brazen tower for protection.

66 5. *paragon*: excellence. 9. *gate*: got. 10. *sorted*: consorted. 14. *reflex*: reflection.

68 1. *on this day*: Easter day. 11. *all lyke deare*: all alike dearly.

69 4. *emprize*: undertakings. 13. *spoile*: spoils of war.

70 2. *cote-armour*: coat of arms. 9. *make*: mate. 12. *amearst*: punished.

71 1. *drawen work*: embroidery. 9. *above*: 1595 and Folio read 'about'. Emended de Selincourt and most modern editions.

72 10. *mantleth*: spreads its wings.

74 The three Elizabeths, his mother, the Queen and Elizabeth Boyle, his wife.

75 5. *assay*: attempt.

77 3. *juncats*: sweetmeats. 6. *unvalewd*: beyond valuation. 7. *Hercules*: the eleventh labour, to procure the golden apples of the Hesperides. 8. *Atalanta*: the golden apples which Hippomenes dropped in his race with her, thus enticing her to stop and pick them up, so that he won.

78 5. *synd*: signed.

79 1. *credit*: believe. 8. *ensew*: succeed, come afterwards.

80 As Renwick and others have pointed out, this sonnet proves that the first six books of *The Faerie Queene*, published in 1596, were completed by 1594. 7. *assoyle*: absolve, set free; hence, release, let forth. *that second worke*: presumably the second six books promised in the letter to Raleigh published with the 1590 edition of *The Faerie Queene*. 9. *mew*: retreat. 13. *low and meane*: a compliment to Queen Elizabeth but also, perhaps, a reference to the literary hierarchy, the sonnet being a lower 'kind' than the heroic poem.

81 6. *forth doth lay*: Elizabethan fashion allowed the breasts to be exposed. 10. *the gate*: her mouth. *dight*: furnished, arrayed. 14. *hart's*: a pun on Art (v. Nature).

82 4. *embased*: lowered. 5. *equall*: just. 7. *enchased*: set in gold.

83 This sonnet repeats 35 except for minor alterations of spelling, and line 6, 'seeing it': 35, 'having it'.

85 3. *Mavis*: thrush. 5. *skill*: understand. 7. *then*: than. 8. 'but not aspire to judge of her desert'.

86 2. *the Furies fell*: a cliché out of the popular Senecan drama. cf. Bottom's speech, 'Approach ye furies fell'. Certainly by the time of *MSND* and possibly even as early as 1594 this phrase had become a joke. 6. *hyre*: reward.

87 4. *protract*: tedious continuance. 6. *noyous*: vexatious. 7. *forlorne*: deprived.

88 9. *th'Idæa*: he glimpses the Platonic Idea by contemplating the actual image retained in memory.

89 1. *Culver*: dove. 3. *vow*: 1595 and 1609 Folio, 'vew'. Corrected in Folio 1611. 9. *hove*: remain. 12. *pleasauns*: pleasantness; but *sight*, *aspect*, suggest that the meaning of 'pleasance' as a pleasure garden is also there.

Epithalamion

Spenser married Elizabeth Boyle on 11 June 1594, probably in Christ Church, Cork. They had one son, Sylvanus. The bride was considerably (15–20 years) younger than her husband, well-connected, and she outlived him, marrying twice more.

1. *sisters*: the Muses. 22. *lusty hed*: cheerfulness. 26. *maske*: a pageant. 27. *Tead*: a torch. 30. *dight*: get ready. 32. *paynes and sorrowes past*: as related in *Amoretti*. 51. *discolored*: variously coloured. 56. *Mulla*: Spenser gave this name to the River Awbeg. 75. Tithonus was a mortal, abducted by Aurora, the dawn: he asked her to make him immortal, but forgot to ask to be made ageless. She tired of him as he aged. 87. *make*: mate. 98. *houres*: the Horae or Hours, three daughters of Zeus, associated with the seasons, hours of the day, and with order. 103. *handmayds*: the Graces; *Cyprian Queene*: Venus. 118. *lifull*: life-giving. 124. *boone*: request. 131. *Croud*: a Celtic antecedent of the fiddle. 140. *Hymen io Hymen*: Hymen, the God of Marriage, acclaimed with *io*, an interjection expressing joy: hurra! ho! 148. *portly*: stately. 149. *Phœbe*: the moon. 171–180. These lines draw on The Song of Songs (Chaps. 4–7) to describe the bride's physical beauty. 189. *red*: saw. 190. *Medusaes mazeful hed*: refers to the power of the Medusa's head to petrify. 217. *endlesse*: the middle word of the middle line of the poem looks forward to *endlesse* in l. 433. 234. *sad*: solemn. 266. *Barnaby the bright*: St Barnabus's day, 11 June, was the longest day in the Julian calender, which ran ten days before the Gregorian calendar (from 1582) until the latter was adopted in Britain (1752). 300. Hieatt notes that almanacs for 1594 gave 16¼ hours of daylight for 11 June, so *night* comes at 16¼ stanzas. 304. *Arras*: tapestry from Arras, France. 307. *Maia*: mother (her name means simply that) of Hermes by Zeus, a 'shy goddess' in the Homeric Hymn to Hermes. 310. The *Acidalian brooke* was associated with Venus. 316. *defray*: pay for. 329. *Tirynthian groome*: Hercules. 341. A *Pouke* is a hobgoblin, like Shakespeare's Robin Goodfellow. 376–80: *Cinthia*, the moon-goddess, *though now vnthought* ('it is not often brought to mind'), made love with Endimion, the *Latmian Shephard*. 388. *we*: the first person plural is used in the last

three refrains. 398. *Genius*, a male spirit presiding over generation. 405. *Hebe*: a daughter of Zeus. Her name means 'youthful beauty', and she had the power of rejuvenating Gods and men.

Henry Constable Diana (1592 text)

MODERN EDITIONS
The Poems of Henry Constable ed. Joan Grundy (1960) English Texts and Studies, Liverpool University Press.

Constable's *Diana. The praises of his Mistress in certaine sweete Sonnets* was first published in 1592. One of its sonnets, however, 'A calculation of the nativitye of the Ladie Riche's daughter borne upon friday in the yeare 1588' suggests an earlier beginning for the sequence, and that Constable was one of the first of the Elizabethan sonneteers, writing at a time when *Astrophel and Stella* was still circulating in manuscript, before the pirated edition of 1591. Constable himself, having been converted to Catholicism, went to the Continent in 1591 and stayed there until the accession of James I, so that his edition was published in his absence. It is a small volume, consisting of twenty-three sonnets, including an introductory one 'To his absent Diana', a concluding sonnet, and that on the birth of Lady Rich's daughter. In 1594 or thereabouts, there appeared another edition, *Diana or the excellent conceitful Sonnets of H.C. Augmented with divers Quatorzains of honorable and lerned personages*. This contains seventy-six sonnets, divided into eight decades, of which the last is incomplete; and this is the edition on which Sidney Lee and earlier editors based their texts, although there has always been uncertainty about which of the new sonnets were by Constable and which by the other 'honorable and lerned personages'. Joan Grundy's recent edition, however, goes back beyond the printed texts and relies primarily upon manuscript sources, especially the version of *Diana* included in MS. Dyce 44, commonly known as the Todd manuscript, which she argues very convincingly was probably arranged and supervised by Constable himself. This version is built around the mystical numbers 7 and 3, consisting of three parts, each part subdivided into three sections, each of which has seven sonnets. All the sonnets of 1592 appear in the Todd manuscript except the dedicatory sonnet 'To his absent Diana', which suggests that it is an authentic text and that Constable gave his approval to it by composing the dedication while he was in exile. Only twenty-seven of the sonnets in the 1594 edition are in the Todd MS. and most of these had already appeared in 1592. The authorship of the rest, apart from eight identified as by Sidney, remains uncertain.

There is not room in this edition for the full canon of Constable's love sonnets and I print therefore the text of 1592, excluding the sonnet on Lady Rich's daughter which does not properly belong to the sequence. The 1592 text has not been reprinted since its original appearance, and includes enough sonnets to give an adequate idea of Constable's quality. I have emended it in the light of Miss Grundy's text only on the occasions where 1592 is obviously inaccurate, and I have included the original version in the notes. The spelling and lay-out is retained, but the punctuation is emended where the sense demanded it.

The identity of Diana herself has never been established, although Constable addressed a number of sonnets to Lady Rich, Sidney's Stella; and the printer's dedication of 1592, *To the Gentlemen Readers*, describes the poet as one 'whose eies were acquainted with Beautie's Riches'. The second part of the Todd MS. *Diana*, is written to 'the generall honoure of this Ile, through the prayses of the heads thereof', and to 'celebrate the memory of particular ladies whoe the author most honoureth'. As well as three sonnets to Lady Rich, there are seven to the King and Queen of Scotland, later to succeed Elizabeth to the throne, two to Lady Arabella Stuart, also in the line of royal succession, and others to various noble ladies with whom he had dealings. It would seem that Constable's sonnets were more social and political than amatory in their motivation.

To his absent Diana: absent presumably because of Constable's exile in France. The dedication of the volume 'To the Gentlemen Readers' refers to 'these insuing Sonnets . . . by misfortune left as Orphans'.

1 14. *thyne eare* (Grundy). 1592/4, 'your eare'. *my voyce* (1592/4). Grundy, 'the voyce'.

2 1. *pretend*: intend. 4. 'causing your will to stoop to favour my wish'. 14. *thy hart* (Grundy). 1592/4, 'my hart', which is clearly a misunderstanding of the argument of the sonnet.

3 4. *Comets*: traditionally believed to be caused by hot and dry exhalations which rose from the earth to form the element of fire of which the highest layer of the terrestrial sphere was composed. This, when heated further by the friction from the rotating lunar sphere which surrounded and enclosed it, produced comets and shooting stars. *begin* (1592/4): 'are the cause of'. Grundy, 'become'.

4 2. *Thetis*: here confused with Tethys, goddess of the sea.

5 1–4. reference to Icarus.

6 13. *rewarded* (Grundy). 1592/4, 'revenged'.

7 1. *helplesse* (Grundy). 1592/4, 'hopelesse'. 2. *my love to slaie* (Grundy). 1592/4, 'my hope to slaie'.

8 2. *dumbe wonder*: i.e. my joy would be beyond expression.

9 5. *pyle*: the pointed metal head of an arrow or lance. 6. *the sight . . . levell*: the sight by which you take aim.

12   2. *descrie*: observe and cry out against.
13   4. *partiall*: biased.
14   7. *pinde*: starved.
15   1–3. 'my love in itself produces much sorrow, my despair more . . .
my folly most of all'. 4. *this last griefe*: i.e. the grief produced by my
folly in loving one I am sure to miss. 5. *All paines if you commaund
it, joy* (Grundy). 1592/4, 'All paines if you commaund, it joy': i.e.
'All pains will prove pleasures if you command it, and it is wisdom
to seek pleasure.'
18   10. *tame* (Grundy). 1592/4, 'tane'.
19   13. *But hurle out love thou canst not* (Grundy). 1592/4, 'But hurle
not love: thou canst not'.
20   5. *Saint Frances had the like*: i.e. the marks of Christ's wounds
which he found on his body after his vision of the cross.
Last sonnet 9. *but not* (Grundy). 1592/4, 'and not'. 14. *be*
(Grundy). 1592/4, 'is'.

Barnabe Barnes Parthenophil and Parthenophe. Sonnettes, Madrigals, Elegies and Odes (1593)

MODERN EDITIONS
Parthenophil and Parthenophe: A Critical Edition ed. Victor
A. Doyno (Southern Illinois University Press, 1971).

Barnes's work, probably published in 1593, is of considerable size. It
consists of three parts, the first comprising more than a hundred fourteen-
and fifteen-line sonnets, interspersed with madrigals in the manner of the
songs in *Astrophel and Stella*; the second, a series of love elegies; and the
last, a collection of odes, canzoni, a sonnet and a final sestine. The whole
sequence is strung along the story of Parthenophil, the lover, wooing in
vain and driven to distraction by the mixture of coquetry and coldness on
the part of Parthenophe, until in the end he resorts to magical charms in
the manner of Theocritus's Idyll and gains his desire. The consummation
is described in the last sestine with considerable dramatic power and
understanding, and the Petrarchan sequence ends in a very Ovidean
manner.

The only part of the work relevant to this volume is the first section,
which is an orthodox Petrarchan sonnet cycle. Barnes is one of the most
lively, varied and 'conceited' of the minor Elizabethan sonneteers. His
verse ranges from the extravagance of the 'Zodiac' sonnets (36–7) to the
sweet pastoral nostalgia of his best-known sonnet, 'Ah sweet content'
(66), and he has a line of witty audacious sexuality which is all his own.
Although some of the individual sonnets have dramatic quality, there is
no overall dramatic development as in *Astrophel and Stella*, for example,

and nothing is lost by separating particular sonnets from their context. No firm identity has been established for Parthenophe, and Victor Doyno has pointed out that both of the title names derive from the Greek root meaning 'virgin'. Only one original copy of the text is extant, that in the British Museum. I have retained the original spelling and format but modernised the punctuation where necessary.

36   These are two of the twelve sonnets which Barnes wrote around the
and signs of the zodiac. He charts the fortunes of his 'unbridled
37   Phaeton', his 'worlde's bright fierie sunne', by which he means his passionate and ambitious heart, as it takes its course through the zodiac of love; and he describes with great ingenuity both his own sufferings and the various moods of his mistress in terms of the predominant sign.

36   Leo, July/August. 8. *they* (Doyno). 1593, 'the'. 10. *rac'd*: tore. 14. *manne's woe*: Doyno points out the traditional play upon this and 'woman'.

37   Virgo, August/September. 7. *Delian goddesse*: Diana, the virgin Goddess. 8. *with honest colour*: in the name of Diana, she could hide her real inclinations under a pose of virginity, which set up a conflict between his love and his desire. 14. *infortunate*: unsuccessful.

60   3. *'bove starres do mount*: raise to poetic immortality. 5. *valure*: valour. 7. *Godfrey*: Godfrey of Bouillon, hero of Tasso's *Jerusalem Delivered*. 11. *one captaine blinde*: Cupid. 12. *did nothing boote*: nothing availed to resist his power.

63   1–4. reference to the most frequently quoted of Jupiter's metamorphoses. 4. *coelestiall*: celestial. 8–9. a play on vain and vein. 14. For critical reactions to this very un-Petrarchan wish, see Doyno's notes to the sonnet.

84   3. *The golden number*: the number of the year in terms of the nineteen-year cycle which the moon takes to return to the same apparent position in relation to the sun. 4. *in carde*: in the chart.

Giles Fletcher the Elder Licia or Poemes of Love (1593)

MODERN EDITIONS
The English Works of Giles Fletcher the Elder ed. Lloyd E. Berry (University of Wisconsin Press, 1964).

The dedicatory epistle 'To the worthie, kinde, wise, and vertuous Ladie, the Ladie Mollineux . . .' is dated 1593, the probable year of publication; and internal evidence suggests that the sonnets were written after 1591. The full description of the work on the title page, 'In honour of the admirable and singular vertues of his Lady, to the imitation of the best Latin Poets, and others' is an indication of how Fletcher saw his own work. His dedication to Lady Mollineux presents it very much as a literary exercise, beginning with a general defence of love as a passion, and going on to justify the writing of love poetry on the best humanist grounds: 'Peruse but the writings of former times, and you shall see not onely others in other countryes, as Italie, and France, men of learning and great partes to have written Poems and Sonnets of Love; but even amongst us, men of best nobilitie, and chiefest families, to be the greatest Schollers and most renowned in this kind.' The writing of verse is a proper leisure occupation for a gentleman and a scholar, both of which Fletcher could claim to be – in his younger days he had been Fellow of Kings and Public Orator. He makes it refreshingly clear that to write love poetry one need not be in love – 'I am so liberall to graunt thus much, a man may write of love, and not bee in love, as well as of husbandrie, and not goe to the plough'.

I include a selection of *Licia* in this volume because it may be said to embody the norm of sonnet sequences. It makes no claim to be original and avoids all that is extravagant or outlandish: it rings the changes on the traditional sonnet *topoi* with graceful competence and considerable lyric charm: above all, it is always under control, always clear. It provides an excellent demonstration of how a poet of limited ability and ambition may be helped by a strong convention.

17 14. *immortall.* 1593, 'immotall'.
27 4. *pearlike*: i.e. pearl-like. 5. *resolved*: changed into vapour.
41 Charon's job was to conduct the souls of the dead in his boat over
and Styx and Acheron to the underworld. Fletcher's conceit is based,
42 like many others in his sequence, on the poetry of Renaissance
   Latinists (see Berry, Explanatory Notes to *Licia*).
41 2. *wafftage*: conveyance across water. 3. *rend*: split.
42 3. *let*: obstruct.

Thomas Lodge Phillis: Honoured with Pastorall Sonnets, Elegies and amorous delights (1593)

MODERN EDITIONS
The Complete Works of Thomas Lodge, 4 volumes, Hunterian Club 1883. Vol. ii. (reprinted Johnson Reprint Coy 1966).

This sequence, published in 1593, is an example of the fashion for pastoral sonnets established by the poems in Sidney's *Old Arcadia*. Lodge's verse, however, has a colour and a sensuous use of mythology which owes something to the University Wits, Marlowe, Peele and Greene.

(Anon) Zepheria (1594)

Nothing is known of the author of *Zepheria*, but the book was printed in London in 1594, and the strongly legal flavour of so many of the conceits suggests that it was written by a young Inns of Court man for an audience of fellow lawyers. The author apologises in his Poem for his 'artless pen' and his 'home-spun Verse', but this conventional disclaimer need not be taken too seriously: of all the Elizabethan sonnet sequences, this is the most extravagantly rhetorical, the most ostentatiously 'artificial'. There is little dramatic development in the series, though if one can penetrate the tangle of legal metaphors in sonnets 21 and 37, for example, it would seem that the lovers are under parental pressure to separate and are doing their best to resist it. The general impression, however, is of a poet whose main objects were to display his rhetorical virtuosity, to show his mastery over language by inventing new words or putting old ones to new uses, and to make 'in' jokes for the entertainment of his colleagues. Yet the poet has remarkable skill in handling extended double meanings and making legal puns, and some of the sonnets have vitality and real if very idiosyncratic charm. *Zepheria*, however, was notorious in its own day, and is the only sonnet cycle to be mentioned specifically by name in Davies's *Gullinge Sonnets*. It is to be found in Sidney Lee's *Elizabethan Sonnets*, vol. ii.

8 2. *devining*: rendering divine. 5. *Leda's lovely twins*: Castor and Pollux, begotten by Jupiter in the guise of a swan. 7. *esperance*: hope. 8. *ripe*: probably a pun: Latin, *ripa*, a shore.

17 1. *habiliment*: proper attire. 2. *depaint*: painting or description. 4. *acquaint*: accustomed, appropriate. 5. *The golden seeling*: presumably her golden hair. 6. *architure*: architecture. 8. *depure*: make pure. 13. *limn'd*: painted.

20 2. *breviat*: a lawyer's brief, a summary.

21 6. *indentures*: deeds of contract, originally executed in duplicate with the edges correspondingly indented for the purpose of identification. 9. *advertize*: call attention to the matter. 11. *counterpane*: connected with counter-pawn, counter-point, i.e. counterpart. Also a pun on counter-pane in its modern sense of a bed-cover. 14. *duresse*: illegal constraint.

37 2. *proces*: the formal commencement of an action at law. 3. *Supersedeas*: writ commanding the stay of legal proceedings. 5. *to a partie*: to become an accessory in an action at law. 6. *Disperpling*: dispersing. 8. *dispence*: relaxation of the law. 14. *premunire*: a legal summons.

38 2. *neare*: never. 4. *accomptants*: accountants. *crackt*: gone bankrupt. 5. *irrotulat*: entered in the roll. 6. *list*: care. 9. *of assise*: normally assessed. 13. *foyaltie*: allegiance.

Richard Barnfield Certaine Sonnets. From Cynthia. With Certaine Sonnets, and the Legend of Cassandra (1595)

MODERN EDITIONS
The Complete Poems/Richard Barnfield. ed. George Klawitter (Susquehanna University Press, 1990).

Barnfield published *Cynthia. With Certaine Sonnets* (1595) between *The Affectionate Shepheard* (1594) and *The Encomium of Lady Pecunia* (1598). There is a fourth attributed work. Like many of the sonneteers, Barnfield's short sequence of sonnets appeared when the poet was a young man (his dates are 1574–1627). They are chiefly remarkable for his attempt to assimilate the gambits and stances of the genre to his own homosexuality, the desire he had handled pastorally in the sub-Marlovian enticements of *The Affectionate Shepheard*. As Barnfield's sonnets depend so much on what the heterosexual sonneteers were producing (though his mythological and other classical references are necessarily more individual), they compare interestingly with them, and contrast with the independence of Shakespeare's 'Young Man' sonnets. The convention of the poet's unreciprocated love for a chaste and cruel beauty keeps Barnfield's sequence clear of real difficulties: he can only dream of fulfilment (6, 8, 16). Ganymede assumes heterosexual love to be the cause of Daphnis's woe in 11 l. 9. The annotations here give some signposts to sonnets with comparable conceits in the other sequences. To do Barnfield full justice, his most successful sonnet, 'If Musique and sweet Poetrie agree' has also been included, from the *Poems in divers humors* section of *The Encomium of Lady Pecunia*, which after its appearance in *The Passionate Pilgrim* (1599) was wistfully assigned to Shakespeare by early scholars.

  2 Compare *Astrophel and Stella* 52. 6. *faire*: fairness, beauty. Could be a misprint in 1595 text for 'haire'. 9. *I*: Aye. 14. *lists*: combat (from the term for the boundary of a place of tournament).

  3 3. *Academicks*: followers of Plato, from his Athenian 'academia'. 5. *Perrepatetickes*: followers of Aristotle, from his school, the Peripatos.

  4 Compare *Delia* 28. 2. *Ganymede*, used by Barnfield as the poetic name for his beloved here and in *The Affectionate Shepheard*, from the beautiful youth abducted from Mount Ida by Jupiter in the form of an eagle, subsequently cupbearer to the gods.

5 A post-Homeric story: Achilles wounded Telephus, son of Hercules, with his spear. An oracle told Telephus that Achilles alone could heal him. By offering to lead the Greeks to Troy, Telephus secured Achilles's help. Achilles scraped rust from his spear, from this grew the milfoil or common yarrow (*Achillea millifolium*). This healed the wound. For a range of classical and Elizabethan references, see annotations on *Henry VI Part II*, V i 100–1 in the Arden text.

6 The erotic arousal of a dream is a common topic, e.g. Linche, *Diella*, 24 (in *Lee*). 4. *Daphnis*: Barnfield's pastoral name for himself, here and in *The Affectionate Shepheard*. A quintessential pastoral name, but in one classical tradition, Daphnis was the male lover of Mercury.

7 Compare *Astrophel and Stella* 103. The sonnet expresses fear of a female rival (*Thetis*, generic name for a water nymph, from the mother of Achilles). Among the boys loved by *Apollo* were *Hyacinthus* and *Cyparissus*, who was also beloved by *Silvanus*.

8 Compare Barnes 63 or Lodge 34 for sonnets of erotic self-transformation.

9 *Ganymede* is fashioned by *Venus* from snow and the blood of the chaste *Diana*. 13. *Paphos* is used synonymously for Cyprus, the island sacred to Venus.

12 3. *him whom lovely Laeda lost*: possibly her son, Castor. 4. *Ecchoes love*: Narcissus.

13 Compare in *Lee* similar sonnets by Watson (29), Barnes (89), Percy (15), Smith (22). Barnes's Ode 2 also begins, 'Speak, Echo! tell'.

15 13. *Molorchus* was a shepherd. In return for his hospitality, Hercules killed the lion that had killed his son. Apparently associated with the constellation Leo, in which the brightest star, Regulus, might serve as a morning star in late August and early September, an evening star in late February, early March.

16 13. *Ixion* tried to seduce Hera, wife of Jupiter, but was sent a cloud in her shape by the god. For his presumption, he was bound to a wheel of fire in hell. For other allusions, see Daniel, 16, 49.

18 The sonnet has a bizarre combination of allusions. 1, 2. See Plutarch's Life of Agesilaus, king of Sparta. The 11th section details his love for the Persian boy, Megabates 'a very handsome youth, to whom Agesilaus was passionately attached . . . although whenever the boy was present, he summoned up all his determination and struggled to master his passion', section 25 the love of his son Archidamus for Cleonymus, 'a handsome young boy', the successive Spartan kings being the 'two great Kings' of l. 5. 10. *fil-beard*: the filbert, the nut of the cultivated hazel. 12. Barnfield's recollection of Virgil, *Eclogue* III, where *Damoetas* is *Aegon's man*, but it is his rival in a singing match, Menalcas, who loves the boy Amyntas, and woos him with gifts.

19   1. The sense reads directly on from 18. Barnes's sonnet 51 (in *Lee*)
      plays the vowels/consonants game exhaustively.
20   8. *these lines*: in the Ode which follows the sonnets, Barnfield
      announces in a perfunctory way that though he thought he loved
      Ganymede, he now loves a 'Lasse' whose beauty surpasses his 'As
      Phoebus doth the smallest starre' (notice the male exemplar of
      beauty). Barnfield did subsequently marry and have a son.
      9,10. Pastoral names adopted by Spenser (Colin Clout) and
      Drayton (Rowland).

To his Friend Maister R. L. In Praise of Musique and Poetrie

R. L.: the initials have been used to identify him with Richard Linche,
author of *Diella* (1596). 5. *Dowland*: composer and lutenist, called
'the English Orpheus'. 7. *Spenser*: Barnfield claimed, rightly, to have
produced with his *Cynthia*, 'the first imitation of the verse of that
excellent Poet, Maister *Spencer*, in his *Fayrie Queene*'. 14. *One
Knight*: unidentified, though Sir George Carey, governor of the Isle of
Wight, patron of Dowland and lover of Emilia Lanier, has been
suggested as a candidate.

Sir Robert Sidney (c. 1596)

MODERN EDITIONS
The Poems of Robert Sidney ed. P. J. Croft (Oxford, Clarendon
Press 1984).
The Poems of Robert Sidney: A plain text ed. Katherine
Duncan-Jones, *English* Vol XXX Number 136 (1981).

Sir Robert Sidney's untitled sequence of sonnets, songs and pastorals is
preserved in an autograph manuscript, now British Library MS. Add
58435. P. J. Croft identified the author in 1973, and subsequently edited
the poems. Robert (1563–1626), knighted 1586, created Earl of Leicester
1618) was a younger brother of Philip (b. 1554) and Mary (b. 1561)
Sidney. He married a Welsh heiress, Barbara Gamage, in 1584. They had
eleven children, the eldest being Mary (b. 1587) who married Sir Robert
Wroth in 1604.
    The author's copy of the poems, in which the poet is still making
revisions, perhaps prior to transcribing a presentation copy, is on paper
which shares a watermark with letters Sir Robert was sending in
October–December 1596. The sixth song deals transparently with his
separation from his wife: he was governor of the garrison town of
Flushing, while Barbara remained largely in England.

A soldier, present at the battle of Zutphen and at the deathbed of his brother, wounded in battle himself, governor of a town where he had to fear surprise attack by the Spanish as well as ejection by the resentful Dutch, a courtier whose personal ambitions were thwarted by a posting from which he recurrently begged leave of absence, a man whose opponents at Court encouraged the Queen to consider him 'too young, and too amorous to be conversant with and amongst the ladies', Robert Sidney had ample reason to use in his sonnets images of agony, frustration and desire. An attempt has been made to identify the lady of the sequence, 'Lysa' (later revised to Charys), 'my life's Queen', with Elizabeth Carey (Hilton Kelliher and K. Duncan-Jones *British Library Journal* 1 1975), but she can also be understood as an enabling fiction, allowing Sidney to articulate the helplessness of a courtier kept from the centre of power, the impatience of an aristocratic soldier confined to garrison duties in an ill-supplied, poorly fortified and unhealthy town, as well as the more obvious frustrations of a husband living apart from his wife.

Robert Sidney apparently tried to live in Flushing with as much of the Wilton House culture as he could manage: cultivating a garden, and producing a sequence in the mode of his elder brother's *Astrophel and Stella* and Fulke Greville's *Caelica*. The manuscript has a dedication, 'For the Countess of Pembroke'. The poems he wrote would in their turn bequeath images to his daughter, Lady Mary Wroth.

This selection of twelve of Robert Sidney's thirty-five sonnets modernises the spelling.

1. Sonnets about eyes early in a sequence register their power to fascinate. See *Astrophel and Stella* 7, *Amoretti* 7.

6 12. *Repulses*: revision in MS. of 'Refusals', perhaps to anticipate the extended figure in 7.

7 14. *dear*: costly defeat, also a foiled attempt on what was dear.

9 In this sonnet, one quarter way into the sequence, the lady is addressed directly for the first time. cf. *Astrophel and Stella* 30. The poet recalls former loves, which have made him like seasoned kindling (l. 13); the present love will consume him.

17 The sonnet uses two forms of futile endeavour (the alchemist's search for the philosopher's stone, and a traveller's quest for a land of rest) for love, where avoiding disaster leads into it. 12. *leese*: lose. Croft (Appendix C) notes Lady Mary Wroth borrowing from this sonnet.

23 3. *If*: Duncan-Jones reads 'Of', the poet feeling the same as sea travellers who prayed for land now wrecked on the shore. But the sense seems to read, he would complain against absence *If* such a situation didn't (l. 5) *paint out*: (= provide an image of) his life (Duncan-Jones here suggests 'pant'). Croft (Appendix C) notes Lady Mary Wroth borrowing from this sonnet.

26 In 1586, the surgeons did not amputate Philip Sidney's shattered leg. 10. *Dearer*: Duncan-Jones's emendation. Croft reads 'Nearer'. The MS. is smudged. 14. *cankers*: Croft modernises 'Cancres' in the MS. to 'cancers'. Sidney originally wrote 'vultures', an instance of the poet excising a classical illusion.

27 2. *lazar-like*: numbness is an early diagnostic sign of leprosy, in the disease's full phase, lepers 'unable to feel pain or heat or cold will suffer wounds that go unfelt and unnoticed' S. Brody, *The Disease of the Soul* (Cornell, 1974), p. 30. 5–6. *a sure/Standing*: hunting terminology, a place from which the hunter cannot miss (*O.E.D.* 'standing' *vbl sb 4c*). 8. *like did assure*: he told himself that the love returned for his would be as trustworthy.

31 Sidney does not capitalise 'time' in this or sonnet 35. The syntax of the sonnet requires a single sentence: Forsaken woods... Gardens... Meadows... *Say all*...

35 The final sonnet in the numbered part of Sidney's sequence. See Drayton 17. Croft suggests the shared opening phrase in this and Daniel's 23rd sonnet in the 1601 *Delia* could be the result of writing to a set theme for Mary Sidney at Wilton House.

B. *Griffin Gent* Fidessa, more chaste then kinde (1596)

Fidessa, dedicated to the gentlemen of the Inns of Court, was published in 1596. It is a relatively late cycle which has absorbed the more obvious and fashionable mannerisms of its time and borrows extensively from its English predecessors. It is nevertheless a competent sequence and a good example of the run-of-the-mill sonneteering against which the originality of the greater writers should be assessed. There is no modern edition, but it is included in vol. ii of Sidney Lee's *Elizabethan Sonnets* (1904).

13 This sonnet runs through the whole gamut of 'lover' comparisons, as Donne does in *The Canonization*, but without the ironic self-consciousness and the dramatic dimension which transform them in Donne's poem. 3. *the foolish boy*: Phaethon, who borrowed the chariot of the sun and could not control it.

15 Borrowed directly from Daniel, *Delia*, sonnet 49.

16 The figure of rhetoric around which this sonnet is built is called (by Puttenham) Clymax or the marching figure in his *Arte of English Poesie*. It is parodied in number 3 of Davies's *Gullinge Sonnets*.

William Smith Chloris or the Complaint of the passionate despised shepheard (1596)

Chloris, published in 1596, is another pastoral sequence, whose debt to previous cycles in English is unusually obvious. This sequence is in vol. ii of Sidney Lee's *Elizabethan Sonnets*.

18 1–4. cf. Sidney, *Astrophel and Stella*, 3, 6, etc.

20 A sonnet heavily indebted to the pastoral eclogues of the *Old Arcadia*.
26 cf. Daniel, *Delia*, 36, 37.

Sir John Davies Gullinge Sonnets

MODERN EDITIONS
The Complete Poems of Sir John Davies ed. Grosart (1876). Vol. ii.
The Poems of Sir John Davies ed. Robert Krueger (Oxford, 1975).

These sonnet parodies were not printed until Grosart discovered them in manuscript form in Chetham's library, Manchester. He published them in 1873 in *The Dr Farmer Chetham MS* Part I (Chetham Society vol. 89), and subsequently in his edition of Davies's poems three years later. The sonnets were probably written round 1594 since they attack *Zepheria* by name, and they thus anticipate the main onslaught on the sonnet from Hall and Marston by several years. Davies was himself an Inns of Court man, and his sonnets were written for the kind of sophisticated audience he would find there.

Dedicatory sonnet. 3. *Antick*: jester. 4. *fond*: foolish. *lewde gulleries*: illiterate shams. 7. *whiskinge*: light, superficial. 13. *formall*: capable of making only the conventional judgement. 14. *begg him for*: set him down as.

1 5. *But for*: but because. 7. *gracious*: emended Krueger. MS., 'gracous'.
2 8. *Which doe* (MS.). Krueger, 'Which does'.
3 See Griffin, *Fidessa*, sonnet 16 and note for 'Clymax or the Marcher'. 14. *weare*: i.e. were.
5 Sidney started the fashion in England for this kind of 'Correlative verse', mainly as an exercise in verbal skill. The most elaborate example is Philoclea's sonnet in Book III of the *Old Arcadia*.
6 8. *pointes*: laces joining the doublet and hose through 'Iletholes'. 12. *pantofels*: slippers. There is no logical affinity in this extended metaphor between Love's garments and the qualities they represent. See, as a contrast, *Astrophel and Stella*, 49.
7–9 Three sonnets parodying the legal conceits of Barnabe Barnes and the anonymous author of *Zepheria*.
8 9. *repleave*: bail out. 11. *Shreife*: sheriff. MS., 'Sheife', emended Krueger. 12. *esloynde*: removed out of the jurisdiction of. 14. *with-ername*: in an action of replevin, the reprisal of other goods in lieu of those taken and esloynde, (*O.E.D.*). Grosart emended 'in wit her name'.

9 2. *in warde*: The crown was the legal guardian of all minors, unmarried female orphans and idiots who held their land in return for military service which they could not render. In practice, wardship was often farmed out to individuals who were entitled to the revenues of the estate, dowries, etc. 4. *intreate*: treat.

Lady Mary Wroth Pamphilia to Amphilanthus (1621)

MODERN EDITIONS
The Poems of Lady Mary Wroth ed. Josephine Roberts (Louisiana State U. P., 1983).
Pamphilia to Amphilanthus ed. Gary F. Waller (Salzburg, 1977).

Among the poems Lady Mary Wroth (1587?–1653?) appended to her prose romance, *The Countesse of Mountgomeries Urania* (1621) was this regular Petrarchan sonnet sequence of 48 sonnets, arranged in 8 groups of 6 sonnets, the sets separated by 7 songs. The unified sequence is signed with Lady Wroth's chosen pen-name after the 48th sonnet, and the remainder of the collection, 35 sonnets and 12 songs, is more miscellaneous, and lacks the formal grouping of the main sequence. It is the first sequence of Petrarchan sonnets written by an Englishwoman.

Because she was a Sidney, an aristocrat brought up to the high artistic accomplishments expected in the Wilton House coterie, and because she was left a young widow, with large debts, and had the amorist William Herbert, Earl of Pembroke, as her lover, Lady Wroth was artistically able and personally impelled to produce such a sequence. But still her achievement in being an imaginative writer at all is remarkable, for there were inevitably those who willed her to follow rather 'the rare and pious example of your vertuous and learned Aunt (the Countess of Pembroke), who translated so many godlie bookes'. But Lady Mary appropriated the sonnet sequence, formerly in English a genre only exploited by male writers, for herself.

Her sonnets come late in the tradition. Some may date before 1613, most were probably written in the second decade of the 17th century. They may be seen as part of the neo-Elizabethanism which has been noted as a cultural feature of the second decade of James's reign, marked by such revivals as John Ward's Madrigals (1613), a reversion to old styles in the portrait miniature, a revival of History plays as a theatrical genre, and a latently oppositional stance to the Court of James.

The title of the sequence, *Pamphilia to Amphilanthus*, in part retires the poems behind the protective bulk of her prose romance, which nevertheless identifies her with Pamphilia, the 'all-loving', and, more discreetly, Amphilanthus, the 'lover of two', with her lover William

Herbert, her cousin, by whom she had two children. He was married (from 1604), and was in Clarendon's opinion, 'immoderately given to women'. Lady Wroth, widowed herself in 1614, seems to have made a personal cult of constancy and came to terms with the behaviour of her lover by considering it as typical of all men.

As Lady Wroth was a writer who, when not absorbed in the 'melancholy abstraction' (as Gary Waller puts it) of her poetry, intricately worked her family, friends and acquaintances into the *Urania*, it may be significant that there is one figure from the Sidney myth apparently missing from her fictionalised re-creation of its personnel and concerns. This was Penelope Rich, 'Stella', godmother of her brother, and fellow dancer with her in *The Masque of Blackness*, whose re-marriage in 1605 brought to a head the scandal of her liaison with Charles Blount, and who was notorious beyond her death (1607). The resemblance of Lady Wroth's position to Penelope Rich's, as children were born to the extra-marital relationships of both women, perhaps explains the absence of a place for her in Wroth's *roman à clef*. Wroth, with her cult of constancy, a moralist, will not identify with the story of Stella. In her own relationship with a man who was a talented amateur poet, Wroth was in effect faced with the challenge: become 'Astrophel' before becoming someone else's 'Stella'; make herself as the poetry reader's latest Sidney before she became gossip's latest Penelope Rich. She seems to have quite successfully avoided scandal, though it could have been debts rather than discretion which kept her from the Court; music, poetry and drama was dedicated to her, her poetry was praised. It is typical that Ben Jonson, who eulogised Lady Wroth in dedicating *The Alchemist* to her, and who 'exscribed' her sonnets, considered her 'unworthily maried on a Jealous husband'.

Understandably, Lady Wroth was steeped in the literary output of the Wilton House coterie, the poetry of her uncle, that of her father, and had also the enabling example of her aunt. Fulke Greville's more disillusioned poetry was probably also an influence. The less-remarked influence on her poetry is that of the verse her talent as musician exposed her to, the lyrics of John Dowland's *Ayres*. Lady Wroth's poetry repeatedly has echoes of the highly expressive, highly emotive verse Dowland wrote or chose to set (see notes to sonnets 19 and 37). Lady Wroth's poems can give the impression that there was another expressive medium haunting the writer's mind, the song to the lute. The literary idiom chosen is one in which metaphor and verbal decoration have been pared back. But while Dowland could successfully set lingering verses which are expressive within their narrow emotional range, Lady Mary's poems repeat too often their plangencies of night, darkness, and uttermosts of grief.

The sonnet was not a form Lady Wroth seems to have thought she handled particularly well, careful though she was in her alternations of Italian and English forms. Sonnet 39 is conventional enough self-deprecation, but the remarks of Pamphilia: 'I seldome make any but Sonnets, and they are not so sweet in rehearsing as others that come more roundly off' (*Urania* 3 392) are accurate as self-assessment. Her lyric pieces probably came more easily to her (for example, **Song 4**); in sonnets she struggles with the form, and can when pressed emerge as an unscrupulous rhymer, capable of reckless inversion of sense to get her rhymes. What we must always remember is how difficult it was, how little her culture could allow direct expression of a woman's desire, being unable to countenance the notion that a woman could woo or solicit her beloved. Equally, the genre in which she was writing might have facilitated some poems about eyes, but thereafter left her quite high and dry when it came to blazoning the beloved's beauty or praising *his* activities.

The pared-back means, the concentration upon the self and general absence of the beloved will often recollect to the reader of Renaissance poetry the poetry of Wyatt, rather than suggest the 'cantabile' (to borrow Auden's choice word) of the Elizabethan sonneteers. And this, for our taste, is not a bad resemblance to have, and the psychological focus, the troubled quality, the *insistence* of these sonnets should find them readers, readers perhaps who have had too much of the mellifluous school as typified by Daniel. And to repeat the point already made, through thick and thin, the project is remarkable, and we should attend carefully.

I have chosen the 1621 text as my copy text, because it is important that the sequence be seen as publicly printed poetry (and so doubly daring in the author), for spelling which is somewhat more modern than the Folger manuscript, and because it evidently represents a later stage of arrangement and revision than the MS. (in which, for example, sonnet 4 does not appear). Readings from the manuscript have nevertheless been adopted where 1621 is obviously corrupt. Punctuation is editorial, but tries to respect the main features of Lady Wroth's punctuation.

As Lady Wroth's sense is not always immediately clear, I have attempted some paraphrases, as well as annotation of vocabulary and allusions. In these notes, *F/Roberts* is the Folger MS. text, as edited by *Roberts*, *Waller* is Gary Waller's 1977 edition, and 1621 the first printing in *Urania*. *Lewalski* is Barbara K. Lewalski, *Writing Women in Jacobean England* (1993).

Note on Sonnet Forms:
Lady Wroth alternated between Italian (ends with two tercets) and English (ends with a couplet) forms of the sonnet in this sequence. Sonnets 1–6 (first group) are Italian, sonnets 7–12 (2nd group) English, 13–18 (3rd) Italian, 19–24 (4th) English, 25–30 (5th) Italian, 31–36 (6th) English, 37–42 (7th) Italian. The last group is mixed. Sonnets 22 and 41 do not fit this scheme, and may have been transposed. When not using ABBA-ABBA for her octave, Lady Wroth uses ABAB-BABA. Sonnets 16, 20, 32, 39 and 45 contain minor oddities, as noted below.

Title: Appears in 1621 as *Pamphilia, to Amphilanthus*.

1 The dream vision of Venus and Cupid is compared by *Roberts* to the opening of Petrarch's *Trionfe d'Amore*; *Lewalski* (p. 252) contrasts the donation of a flaming heart to the poet-speaker with Dante's first sonnet, where the poet's flaming heart is offered to Beatrice. 2. *hyre*: lift. 11. *shut*: shoot.

2 The typical gambit of an early sonnet about the beloved's eyes, conventionally compared to stars. But these are the eyes of the man, nor do they, as *Lewalski* (p. 253) notes, initiate love, already aflame in the lover's heart. 3. *oft*: this ed. 'of' 1621, F/*Roberts*.

3 Second quatrain: Love, lodged in Amphilanthus's breast, is asked to set in motion pity for the flames which burn in hers, and so exile his inconstant thoughts, *or* thoughts of love which diminish ('waste') and are not in the constant. 9–11. 'My spirit is so distressed, as, pale and famished, I cry for mercy'. 12–14. Love is to think of the responsibilities of his rule. 14. *lye*: depend, rely.

4 7. woes take the place of pride. 9. the Dantean idea of the misery of recollecting former happiness.

5 7. For the Renaissance notion that the eyes emitted sightlines, see Spenser's Corflambo, *Faerie Queene* IV viii 39, or Donne, 'The Extasie', 7–8. 9. *wunn*: from F/*Roberts*, 'none' 1621, 'eyes having won a pleasing sight'. 14. 'show how much you dislike rejection, and how much you joy in reciprocation'.

6 Perhaps the most salient example, in its submissiveness, of a gender-reversed Petrarchanism. 3. *haplesse me*: recurs in Song 1, sonnets 9, 37, 47. 4. *And byding make*: and make their stay. The sorrows are given by him, and (either) to bring more sorrow on her is superfluous, such further sorrows are *lost*, (or) her loss comes from the sorrows he causes her.

Song 1 restates sonnet 6 in pastoral terms, and gives a statement via pastoral about the inception and purposed readership of the sequence.

7 1. *hand*: upper hand, victory. 3. *band*: bonds, also forces. 10. *will*: there is a latent pun on William (Herbert). 14. Either 'I love, but not blindly' or the personified Love is told she doesn't obey him blindly.

8 2. Either her false surmise about his, or his failure of belief in her constancy. 3. *bought*: used for the rhyme, but a subdued metaphor of expensive purchase. 5. The effect of his unkindness within her heart. 7. *unknowne*: incommunicable, also unexperienced before. 14. *allay*: diminish.

9 7–8. pleasures show their opposite sides to her. 9. *bereav'd*: snatched away. 10. *hand*: upper hand. 12. *since despised*: contraction of 'since I am despised'. The social transaction underlying the sonnet is of the parentally negotiated marriage; *Despaire* governing

her, and marrying her to *Sorrow*.

10 6. Content rises in the traveller like souls ascending heavenwards. 8. In this sonnet of renewed hope, new pleasures make her as content as in the *first borne bliss* of her love. The sonnet is about the joy of ceasing to be suspicious – the indefiniteness of what the traveller *sought* (l.1) corresponds to her mentally exhausting *wrong conceit*, which didn't know what it was looking for.

11 3. Oppressed in love by disdain, she fears that she will never more feel love's favour. 5. *stay*: cease. 8. *last*: ed., 'least' in *F/Roberts* and 1621.

12 12. *and all of woes esteeme*: Lady Wroth can use 'esteeme' loosely when she needs a rhyme (cf. 40). Perhaps 'all Night's attributes elevate woe', or 'are held in esteem by woe'. Compare *Astrophel and Stella* 89.

13 13. *desert*: a lover's due or reward, which, here, a sight of him would be. 14. The chameleon was reputed to live on air, see *Hamlet* III ii 92–4.

14 Second quatrain: 'before I submit to Love, Love must first lose his arrows, acquire self-knowledge' (etc.); mixed with an impossibility topos; 'only when spring hates sweet flowers will I' (etc.). The sonnet is strongly influenced by *Astrophel and Stella* 47.

15 6. 'resembles my soul and heart together'. 10. *as of*: 'as if through'. The sonnet is influenced by *Astrophel and Stella* 31, compare *sober pace* and the 'sad steps' of Sidney's moon.

16 Reverses the usual invocations of sleep, contrast Daniel 49, Philip Sidney 39. 11. *My that while*: for that time. The octave of this sonnet rhymes AAAA-AAAA.

17 3. *and mine*: 'and it to be a disgrace to me'. 6. *joyings*: enjoying's, enjoyment's.

18 8. *alight*: set foot on, discover. 9–11. about jealous rage, which she can see feed upon the errors which are bred by 'Shame, doubt, and feare', yet is bold in its mistaken opinion. 14. *spill*: destroy, mutually destruct.

19 First quatrain: a general indebtedness to the lyrics set by John Dowland may be felt: compare 'Lachrimae' or 'Mourn, day is with darkness fled' in the *Second Book of Songs* (1600), or 'In darkness let me dwell' from *A Musicall Banquet* (1610). 4. *controule*: hold back. 6. *distrest*: deprived, with a latent pun, dis-tressed.

20 10. *Desart*: empty place. 13–14. The couplet repeats rhyme words from the octave.

21 3. *no times delay*: no length of time since actually seeing him. 12. 'Just as his image gives her pleasure'.

22 The sonnet uses 16th-century ideas of beauty, when women avoided the scorching *favours* of the sun, to preserve their *whitenesse*. Thus the sense of the second quatrain is: 'better to be simply black than

white not through beauty but through being full of grief'. Lady
Mary danced in the *Masque of Blackness* at Court on 6 Jan 1605,
of which a witness said 'Instead of Vizzards, their Faces, & Armes
up to the Elbows, were painted black, which was Disguise
sufficient . . . but . . . you cannot imagine a more ugly Sight, then a
Troop of lean-cheek'd Moors'. 10. *chose*: chosen.

23 6. *day-like night*: the benighted activities of the world. Sonnet 38
repeats the sentiments.

24 3–4. age and experience delivers wisdom free from fear and
personal bias. 8. *young faults*: faults of my youth. 9. *fear'd my
Love*: distrusted who I loved, or was distrustful in loving. 13. *In
time shun this*: while you have time.

25 8. *that lost*: that being lost. 11. The line re-uses the terms of l. 4: the
loss suffered by those who fell in love through the agency of
Pamphilia's eyes was no *gaine* to her.

26 1. *will*: determined course or testament, with perhaps a latent pun
on 'William'. 4. *blest*: best 1621. 8. *though heartlesse my life spill*:
though being without a heart will end my life. For the exchange of
hearts topos, see Sidney, 'My true love hath my heart and I have his'
in Ringler (ed.), *The Poems*.

27 4. *Trophees*: rewards of hope *or* examples of betrayal. 7. *hands
free*: generous hands. 9. *slight*: sleight, deception. The figure of a
town captured by treason passes into one from alchemy – hope
'ruined' her, and must be 'tried', and might prove 'true' (gold).

28 12–14. the lines negotiate with Grief, to lay every weight on her, but
not bring her grief from those she loves.

29 8. *sorrowes faster ty'de*: more strongly attached sorrows.
12–14. These obscurely phrased lines might mean disdain is a poor
spark compared to the fires suffered by true lovers undergoing
absence, or, if disdain is equated with an absence of love, the last line
could be read as a maxim, 'Those whose fires of love are arrested by
disdain burn in love less brightly than true lovers'.

30 14. *so*: in this extreme fashion.
Song 5 5–6. *a pleasure not to move*: a delight in not changing.
11. *least*: in the least.

32 The octave uses the same rhyme words for its quatrains. 7–8. *retire/
Was for Despaire*: 'retire' means retiring, reluctance to come
forward, to allow despair and harm to arrive instead. 11. *masters*:
i.e. the beekeeper's.

33 1. *guard*: keep you from. 3. *some say*: as some say. 4. love should
not be expected to be happy. 6. *question hard*: dispute or difficult
distinction. 8. *unbar'd*: lacking restriction. As Love can guide
the heart, in this sense Love isn't blind. 14. *or be borne without
fire*: be born lacking passion, (or) procreate without passion
(16th-century physiology considered it necessary for a woman to

have an orgasm to conceive).

34 The sonnet is radically ambiguous, between 'Guard your secret' and 'Be true to your constancy'. The mention of *your best Love* in l. 10 encourages the sub-sense of the sonnet as talking down a secondary love-impulse. 1. *cast*: shape, but also throw. 2. *betray*: reveal, or 'be false to'. 5. *Catch*: notice, or capture. 7. *them*: the watching eyes or your desires. 10. 'those that tried to find your hurt (*or* "probe your wound") for insincere purposes'.

35 4. First quatrain: the figure is of miscarriage or abortion. The proverb in l. 4 stems from Ovid, *Metamorphoses* 3, 466, 'Inopem me copia fecit'. Narcissus speaks: 'The thing I seeke is in my selfe, my plentie makes me poore' (Golding trans.) See 17 l.13, 39 l.9. 13–14. *the pride/Of our desires*: the phrase is repeated from 34.

36 5–6. 'whatever Joy her heart has felt, she was still tortured (etc.)'. 11–12. In the narrative of *Urania*, Pamphilia confides her love only to Urania (The Countess of Pembroke) and Amphilanthus, though her secrecy causes her pain.

37 Night is the subject of sonnets 1, 4, 12, 15, 18, 19. Dowland's songs about night perhaps account for this frequency. For the opening, compare Dowland's 'Welcome, black night'.

38 4. *a biding crave*: ask to stay. 9. 'The heart is judged to be the conscious part as far as joy is concerned'. 14. 'was born only to be miserable'.

39 Second quatrain: her 'wit sick' poetry is worthless to her, even as it is first drawing breath (or being sung). The lines might also mean that such poetry is as the breath of life to 'pleasant wits'. The sonnet, about her own 'crossed' or afflicted lines, rhymes anomalously ABAB ABBA, perhaps to enact her impatience.

40 The sonnet continues the thought of 39. 2. *fond*: foolish. 3. *swearings gloze*: to swear deceiving oaths. 6. *those chosen blowes*: in Lady Wroth's predominantly painful view of love, amatory success is here only the preferred form of pain. But also a hard-sought rhyme. 8. *doth not him beseeme*: are not worthy of him (i.e. conquests by mere looks). 13. *desert*: merit. The sonnet resembles *Astrophel and Stella* 54; the rueful ending is also Sidneian.

41 12. *th'eith*: the height, 'th'earth' (1621). 13. *gives*: give (1621), *love-rulde eyes*: love-rould eye (1621).

42 The sonnet recollects the first and second ayres of Dowland's First Booke (1597), 'Unquiet thoughts' providing the 'pensive heart' and 'Who ever thinks or hopes of love for love' (a lyric by Fulke Greville) being echoed in lines 5 and 10.

43 11–12: All lights should be extinguished so that the (unspecified) black deed has an excess of darkness.

44 13–14. 'The sweet spring should never dry up, and my days and unhappiness never be separated.'

45 In the *Urania*, the character Antissia, antetype to Pamphilia, behaves madly. The B rhymes recur in the last tercet.

46 10. *flame*: paine (1621). 13. *as shee*: i.e. the well.

47 With its talk of *a wretched gaine*, this sonnet approaches being a palinodic closure to the sequence.

48 As in sonnets 7 and 26, *will* (l. 14) may involve a pun on William Herbert.

Mark Alexander Boyd (1563–1601)

Boyd was a Scottish writer noted mainly for his Latin poems. This sonnet, the only one he is known to have written, was printed c. 1590.

2. *Owrhailit*: carried away. 5–6. *blin'* ... *bairn*: blind Cupid. 7. *wyf*: Venus rising from the sea. 8. *lichter*: lighter. *dauphin*: dolphin. 10. *teils*: tills. *sawis*: sows.

SUGGESTIONS FOR FURTHER READING

Background studies

Durling, Robert M., (trans.) *Petrarch's Lyric Poems* (Cambridge, Mass. 1976) gives a text and translation.

Fuller, John, *The Sonnet* (The Critical Idiom, Methuen 1972).

Krailsheimer, A. J., (ed.), *The Continental Renaissance 1500–1600* (Pelican Guides to European Literature 1971).

Minta, Stephen, *Petrarch and Petrarchism: The English and French Traditions* (Manchester U. P. 1980).

The Elizabethan sonnet in general

PRIMARY TEXTS

Lee, S. (ed.), *Elizabethan Sonnets* 2 vols. (Westminster 1904).

BOOK-LENGTH STUDIES

Lever, J. W., *The Elizabethan Love Sonnet* (2nd ed. 1968).

Roche, Thomas, *Petrarch and the English Sonnet Sequences* (AMS Press, 1989).

IMPORTANT ARTICLES/DISCUSSIONS

Alteri, Charles, 'Rhetoric, Rhetoricity, and the sonnet as performance', *Tennessee Studies in Literature*, 25 (1980).

Ewbank, Inga-Stina, 'Sincerity and the Sonnet', *Essays and Studies*, 34 (1981).

Fowler, A., *Triumphal Forms: Structural Patterns in Elizabethan Poetry* (Cambridge U. P., 1970).

Fumerton, Patricia, 'Secret Arts: Elizabethan Miniatures and Sonnets', *Representations*, 15 (1986).

Lewis, C. S., *English Literature in the Sixteenth Century* (Oxford, 1954).

Marotti, Arthur F., '"Love is not Love": Elizabethan Sonnet Sequences and the Social Order' *ELH* 49 (1982).

Neely, Carol T., 'The Structure of English Renaissance Sonnet Sequences' *ELH* 45 (1978).

Nelson, Lowry, 'The Matter of Rime: Sonnets of Sidney, Daniel, and Shakespeare' in Mack, Maynard (ed.), Lord, George deForest (ed.), *Poetic Traditions of the English Renaissance* (Yale U. P., 1982).

Warkentin, Germaine, '"Love's Sweetest Part, Variety": Petrarch and the

Curious Frame of the Renaissance Sonnet Sequences' *Renaissance and Reformation* 11 (1975).

Wilson, Scott, 'Racked on the Tyrant's Bed: The Politics of Pleasure and Pain and the Elizabethan Sonnet Sequences' *Textual Practice* 3 (1989).

Individual authors

Barnabe Barnes

Doyno, Victor A. (ed.), *Parthenophil and Parthenope, 1593* (1971).

Richard Barnfield

Klawitter, George (ed.), *Complete Poems* (Susquehanna U. P. 1990)

Morris, Harry, *Richard Barnfield, Colin's Child* (Florida State University, 1963).

Bray, Alan, *Homosexuality in Renaissance England* (London, Gay Man's Press, 1982).

Smith, Bruce R., *Homosexual Desire in Shakespeare's England: A Cultural Poetics* (Univ. of Chicago Press 1991).

Henry Constable

Grundy, Joan, (ed.), *The Poems of Henry Constable* (Liverpool U. P. 1960).

Samuel Daniel

Rees, Joan, *Samuel Daniel* (Liverpool, 1964).

Sir Philip Sidney

Ringler, W. A. (ed.), *The Poems* (Oxford, Clarendon Press, 1962).

Duncan-Jones, Katherine, *Sir Philip Sidney, Courtier Poet* (Yale U. P. 1991). (Important chapter on *Astrophel and Stella*.)

Waller, Gary F. (ed.), Moore, Michael D. (ed.), *Sir Philip Sidney and the Interpretation of Renaissance Culture* (Croom Helm, 1984). Collection includes essays on *Astrophel and Stella* by Marion Campbell ('Unending Desire: Sidney's Re-Invention of Petrarchan Form'); Charles S. Levy ('Sidneian Indirection: The Ethical Irony of *Astrophel and Stella*); Jacqueline T. Miller, ('What words may say: the limits of Language in *Astrophel and Stella*'); Gary Waller ('The Rewriting of Petrarch').

Duncan-Jones, Katherine, 'Sidney, Stella, and Lady Rich' in Van Dorsten, Jan (ed.), Baker-Smith, D. (ed.), Kinney, Arthur F. (ed.), *Sir Philip Sidney: 1586 and the Creation of a Legend* (Leiden, 1986).

Ferry, Anne, *The Inward Language* (Chicago U. P. 1983).

Fienberg, Nora, 'The Emergence of Stella in *Astrophel and Stella*' (*Studies in English Literature* 25 1985).

Hulse, Clark, 'Stella's Wit: Penelope Rich as Reader of Sidney's Sonnets' in Ferguson, M. (ed.), Quilligan, M. (ed.), Stimpson, C. (ed.), Vickers, N. (ed.), *Rewriting the Renaissance: The Discourse of Sexual Difference in Early Modern Europe* (Chicago U. P. 1986).

Jones, Ann R. and Stallybrass, P., 'The Politics of Astrophel and Stella' (*SEL* 24 1984).

MacLeod, Christine, 'Stella Speaks: The Petrarchan Convention Revisited' (*Critical Survey* 3 1991).

Miller, Paul A., 'Sidney, Petrarch, and Ovid: Or, Imitation as Subversion' (*ELH* 58 1991).

Montgomery, Robert L., 'The Poetics of Astrophel' in Allen, M. (ed.), Baker-Smith, D. (ed.), Sullivan, M. (ed.) *Sir Philip Sidney's Achievements* (NY AMS 1990).

Roche, Thomas, 'Astrophel and Stella: A Radical Reading' in Kay, Dennis (ed.) *Sir Philip Sidney: An Anthology of Modern Criticism* (Oxford, 1987).

Sinfield, Alan, 'Sidney and Astrophel' *Studies in English Literature* 20 (1980).

Sir Robert Sidney

The Poems of Robert Sidney ed. P. J. Croft (Oxford, 1984). Reviewed H. R. Woudhuysen, *TLS* 26 Oct 1984.

The Poems of Sir Robert Sidney: A plain text ed. Katherine Duncan-Jones, *English* XXX number 136 (1981).

Hay, Millicent V., *The Life of Robert Sidney, Earl of Leicester (1563–1626)* (Folger Shakespeare Lib., 1984).

Waller, Gary, *English Poetry of the 16th Century* (Longman, 1986), pp. 163–171.

William Smith

The Poems ed. Lawrence A. Sasek (Louisiana State U. P. 1970).

Spenser

Gibbs, Donna, *Spenser's Amoretti: A Critical Study* (Scholar Press, 1990).

Johnson, William C., *Spenser's Amoretti: Analogies of Love* (Bucknell U. P. 1990).

Dasenbrock, Reed W., 'The Petrarchan Context of Spenser's Amoretti' *PMLA* 100 (1985).

Turner, Myron, 'The Imagery of Spenser's Amoretti' *Neophilologus* 72 (1988).

Villeponteaux, Mary A., ' "With her own will beguiled": The Captive Lady In Spenser's Amoretti' *Explorations in Renaissance Culture* 14 (1988).

Warkentin, G., entry on Amoretti and Epithalamion in *The Spenser Encyclopaedia*, ed. A. Kent Hieatt *et al.* Univ. of Toronto Press (1990).

Lady Mary Wroth

Kathryn Sutherland at the University of Manchester is co-ordinating a teaching and Learning Technology Programme on Women Writers of the 16th and 17th centuries.

Roberts, Josephine (ed.), *The Poems of Lady Mary Wroth* (Baton Rouge: Louisiana State U. P., 1983).

Paulissen, May Nelson, *The Love Sonnets of Lady Mary Wroth: A Critical Introduction* (Elizabethan and Renaissance Studies, Salzburg, 1982).

Beilin, Elaine V., 'The Onely Perfect Vertue': Constancy in Mary Wroth's *Pamphilia to Amphilanthus Spenser Studies* 2 (1981).

Hannay, Margaret P., 'Mary Sidney, Mary Wroth' in Wilson, Katharina M. (ed.), *Women Writers of the Renaissance and Reformation* (Athens, Univ. of Georgia Press, 1987).

Lewalski, Barbara Kiefer, *Writing Women in Jacobean England* (Harvard U. P. 1993).

MacArthur, Janet, 'A Sydney, Though Unnamed: Lady Mary Wroth and her Poetical Progenitors' *English Studies in Canada* 15 (1989).

Miller, Naomi A., 'Rewriting Lyric Fictions: The Role of the Lady in Lady Mary Wroth's *Pamphilia to Amphilanthus*' in Haselkorn, Anne M. (ed.), Travitsky, Betty S. (ed.), *The Renaissance Englishwoman in Print* (Amherst: Univ. of Massachusetts Press, 1990).

Quilligan, Maureen, 'The Constant Subject: Instability and Female Authority in Wroth's Urania Poems' in Harvey, Elizabeth D. (ed.), Maus, Katherine E. (ed.), *Soliciting Interpretation* (Chicago U. P. 1990).

Waller, Gary F., 'Struggling into Discourse: The Emergence of Renaissance Women's Writing' in Hannay, Margaret P. (ed.), *Silent but for the Word* (Kent State U. P., 1985).

INDEX OF FIRST LINES

POETRY
IN EVERYMAN

Amorous Rites: Elizabethan Erotic Verse
edited by Sandra Clark
Erotic and often comic poems dealing with myths of transformation and erotic interaction between humans and gods
£4.99

Selected Poems
JOHN KEATS
An excellent selection of the poetry of one of the principal figures of the Romantic movement
£6.99

Poems and Prose
CHRISTINA ROSSETTI
A new collection of her writings, poetry and prose, marking the centenary of her death
£5.99

Poems and Prose
P. B. SHELLEY
The essential Shelley in one volume
£5.99

Silver Poets of the Sixteenth Century
edited by Douglas Brooks-Davies
An exciting and comprehensive collection
£6.99

Complete English Poems
JOHN DONNE
The father of metaphysical verse in this highly-acclaimed collection
£6.99

Complete English Poems, Of Education, Areopagitica
JOHN MILTON
An excellent introduction to Milton's poetry and prose
£6.99

Women Romantic Poets 1780–1830: An Anthology
edited by Jennifer Breen
Hidden talent from the Romantic era rediscovered
£5.99

Selected Poems
D. H. LAWRENCE
An authoritative selection spanning the whole of Lawrence's literary career
£4.99

The Poems
W. B. YEATS
Ireland's greatest lyric poet surveyed in this ground-breaking edition
£7.99

All books are available from your local bookshop or direct from:
Littlehampton Book Services Cash Sales, 14 Eldon Way, Lineside Estate, Littlehampton, West Sussex BN17 7HE (*prices are subject to change*)

To order any of the books, please enclose a cheque (in sterling) made payable to *Littlehampton Book Services*, or phone your order through with credit card details (Access, Visa or Mastercard) on 01903 721596 (24 hour answering service) stating card number and expiry date. (*Please add £1.25 for package and postage to the total of your order.*)

In the USA, for further information and a complete catalogue call 1-800-526-2778

DRAMA
IN EVERYMAN

The Oresteia
AESCHYLUS
*New translation of one of the
greatest Greek dramatic trilogies
which analyses the plays in
performance*
£5.99

**Everyman and Medieval
Miracle Plays**
edited by A. C. Cawley
*A selection of the most popular
medieval plays*
£4.99

Complete Plays and Poems
CHRISTOPHER MARLOWE
*The complete works of this great
Elizabethan in one volume*
£5.99

Restoration Plays
edited by Robert Lawrence
*Five comedies and two tragedies
representing the best of the
Restoration stage*
£7.99

**Female Playwrights of the
Restoration: Five Comedies**
edited by Paddy Lyons
*Rediscovered literary treasures
in a unique selection*
£5.99

**Plays, Prose Writings
and Poems**
OSCAR WILDE
*The full force of Wilde's wit
in one volume*
£4.99

**A Dolls House/The Lady from
the Sea/The Wild Duck**
HENRIK IBSEN
introduced by Fay Weldon
*A popular selection of Ibsen's
major plays*
£4.99

**The Beggar's Opera and
Other Eighteenth-Century Plays**
JOHN GAY et. al.
Including Goldsmith's She Stoops
To Conquer *and Sheridan's* The
School for Scandal, *this is a volume
which reflects the full scope of the
period's theatre*
£6.99

**Female Playwrights of the
Nineteenth Century**
edited by Adrienne Scullion
*The full range of female nineteenth-
century dramatic development*
£6.99

All books are available from your local bookshop or direct from:
Littlehampton Book Services Cash Sales, 14 Eldon Way, Lineside Estate,
Littlehampton, West Sussex BN17 7HE (*prices are subject to change*)

To order any of the books, please enclose a cheque (in sterling) made payable to
Littlehampton Book Services, or phone your order through with credit card details (Access,
Visa or Mastercard) on 01903 721596 (24 hour answering service) stating card number
and expiry date. (*Please add £1.25 for package and postage to the total of your order.*)

In the USA, for further information and a complete catalogue call 1-800-526-2778